THE CHILDHOOD EMOTIONAL PATTERN

Other Books by Leon J. Saul:

Emotional Maturity (1947), Third Edition 1971

Bases of Human Behavior (1951), Greenwood Press 1972

The Hostile Mind (1956)

Technic and Practice of Psychoanalysis (1958)

Fidelity and Infidelity (1967)

Dependence in Man, with H. Parens (1971)

Psychodynamically Based Psychotherapy (1972)

The Psychodynamics of Hostility (1976)

THE CHILDHOOD EMOTIONAL PATTERN

The Key to Personality, Its Disorders and Therapy

Leon J. Saul, M.D.

VAN NOSTRAND REINHOLD COMPANY

NEW YORK   CINCINNATI   ATLANTA   DALLAS   SAN FRANCISCO

LONDON   TORONTO   MELBOURNE

Van Nostrand Reinhold Company Regional Offices:
New York   Cincinnati   Atlanta   Dallas   San Francisco

Van Nostrand Reinhold Company International Offices:
London   Toronto   Melbourne

Library of Congress Catalog Card Number: 76-54858
ISBN 0-442-27360-6

Manufactured in the United States of America

Published by Van Nostrand Reinhold Company
450 West 33rd Street, New York. N.Y. 10001

Published simultaneously in Canada by Van Nostrand Reinhold Ltd.

15 14 13 12 11 10 9 8 7 6 5 4 3 2 1

Library of Congress Cataloging in Publication Data

Saul, Leon Joseph, 1901–
    The childhood emotional pattern.

    Includes bibliographies.
    1. Psychoanalysis—Cases, clinical reports, statis-
tics. 2. Child psychology. I. Title. [DNLM: 1. Emotions—In infancy and childhood. 2. Affective disturbances—In infancy and childhood. WS350 S256c]
RC506.S27   618.9′28′917   76-54858
ISBN 0-442-27360-3

To my colleagues and friends

"Raising a child is an awesome responsibility."
Anna Meigs Haiman

But it can be done well:

"Dear Dad:

"Seventy-five years living in the world is something deserving of special congratulations. But what can a daughter give her father in commemoration of such a significant birthday and in honor of such a significant life? I can think of no object at all that would serve as an adequate symbol of the feelings evoked by such a milestone (and they just don't make milestones like they used to). Besides, I now know first hand, as a mom, that the real gifts exchanged between parent and offspring are quite intangible, often undefinable and always unreturnable.

"So let me just say that I feel a boundless appreciation for the stars, or whatever other accident, that put you and me together in the world as father and daughter. What great fortune for me that there is you, that you are who you are and that I chanced to be put together by the likes of you and Mom! The truths, the wisdom, the gentle guidance by which you raised me will remain to serve all the generations born to those who've been lucky enough to know you directly over your many years.

"I remember that in my adolescence I was often impatient with your constant love and caring, that I often overlooked its worth. Nonetheless, I absorbed the best of it. Your personality has become a powerful force in my daily living and in my relationships with my own children. As I see it, my life and my goals, as a person and as a mother, are a tribute to you and your life. I only hope you can see clearly enough the magnitude of your contribution that I may use my love and appreciation for you as a birthday present. There is no way I could ever repay, even in part, the jillions of kindnesses and comforts you have given and continue to give. But please see in my *wanting to* the shining gift of your own accomplishment. Thank you, Father. *HAPPY 75th BIRTHDAY!*

Love,
Cathy"

PREFACE

Sydenham came to the rescue of the Hippocratic principles and again turned his attention to the sick man; he regarded his individual symptoms not as distinct entities and insisted on observing his reactions as a whole.

Alvis E. Greer, Evolution of Medicine,
Journal of the American Medical Association *148(2): 103–105*

The development of psychosomatic medicine has signified increasing interest in emotional factors in many diseases, and in making the art of medicine more of a science. This means trusting less to the natural psychological capacity of the individual physician, with its wide variations from one to another, and seeking some dependable knowledge of the patient's emotional life and some systematic methods for obtaining this. It is here that an understanding of childhood emotional patterns and how to discern them has a potential contribution for the physician who sees the results of these patterns in his adult patients; such patterns would be especially useful to the pediatrician, who, if he is aware of them, can view them in *statu nascendi* and who, as friend, guide, and counselor to the family may be in a position to influence these patterns favorably and thereby prevent future psychopathology, with all its anguish to the child and its parents. Intuition is an unequally distributed gift and cannot really be taught. But the origins, nature, and effects of childhood emotional patterns is something that can be taught and learned systematically, giving the physician a psychological instrument for understanding his patients as human beings.

Therefore, although this book is addressed to analytic psychotherapists, it should prove of value to all physicians, especially pediatricians concerned with preventing emotional ills, and internists and others interested in psychosomatic conditions, and all physicians who wish to give the art of understanding human personality a more scientific base.

What can be deduced for childrearing from everything that is known of the origins and lifelong effects of childhood emotional patterns? Primarily this: good childrearing is not *techniques* but is in large part emotional, a matter of the *feelings* or absence of feelings toward the child in those who are responsible for him and close to him. It is a matter of loving the child, and this love is not simply demonstrations of affection or physical expression of it; expressions can be overdone to the permanent detriment of the child. True love is an interest in the other person for his or her own sake, without expectation of reward. It means a true interest in what is best for the child, its welfare, and its physical and emotional development. It means respecting its individuality and identifying with its needs and feelings, including its self-respect. It means trying to understand it emotionally, being on its side, being available to it emotionally. If well-meaning parents turn the child over to an emotionally cold nurse who has little or none of these feelings, the nurse may do everything correctly, yet the lack of love can damage the child for life. The essence is good feelings for the child and not the learning of techniques, valuable as these may be if used in a setting of love, respect, and sympathetic emotional understanding.

The adult in command can train the helpless child, give it orders, and enforce these by his superior strength. But what the adult cannot control is the child's tendency to identify with the adult, to imitate him and behave like him. This dilemma is succinctly expressed in the old aphorism "Do as I say, but not as I do." That is impossible for the child. We all relate to another person in two main ways: one is as an object, to be dependent upon, to vent anger on, to enjoy sexually, to exploit as a slave, and so on. The other way is to identify with, to introject, to imitate, to model oneself upon another, and this way is mostly unconscious. We can imitate consciously, but identification and introjection in the child are mostly or all unconscious. If you use force on the child, he will identify with it and tend to treat others in like manner. He may come to hate you and to fight off an identification with you, but the tendency toward force is still there. This is the essence of the basic problem of getting a better world. We can only achieve it by raising children to be better people. But how can we get infantile, hostile, neurotic parents to rear their children to become mature, responsible, independent adults? At least a thorough understanding of the nature of childhood patterns clarifies the problem and the task, although it also reveals its difficulty.

The central point of this book, the specific relationships of childhood emotional patterns to those of adult life, although long implicit and surely used by all analysts in their practice, has not to my knowledge appeared before in the literature as an explicit, definite, detailed formulation. Therefore, this book may seem to be open to the criticism of belaboring what is already known. But in the author's experience in teaching and referring patients, there is an urgent need for bringing this knowledge into much sharper focus to make it more effective.* When goal-consciously used as described herein, it is remarkable how efficacious it can be.

The central continuing core of the author's experience has been private practice. This has drawn from the middle class of society, with a few patients from the lower and a few from the upper socioeconomic levels. Therefore the question may be raised of whether the findings are generally applicable or are narrowly limited by social class. Probably not the latter. The formulations in this book deal with traumatic influences during childhood that cause lasting results in emotional disorders for life. These are universal for all human beings the world over, regardless of race, creed, color, or socioeconomic status. In fact, higher animals other than man also reflect this truth; experienced ethologists, veterinarians, or animal trainers can usually tell quickly by its present behavior how a particular animal was treated in the past, especially during early life.

Generally, scientific papers present factual data to support their points. In psychoanalysis, however, professional articles have mostly taken the form of essays. This is probably because of the voluminous nature of the raw data (all the patients' utterances); and because of Freud's own literary bent, talent, and convincing style; and because most of the early analysts came to this field from the humanities and not from the sciences. This tradition of the essay form has advantages and disadvantages that we need not list here. This author came to psychoanalysis via chemistry, physics, and neurophysiology, and tries to present adequate data to support the points of the book. Many analysts seem in their thinking to follow authors who write with authority and attract father or mother transferences. But this author's goal is to have his points accepted only because proven by *observable*

---

*For currently developing ideas in psychoanalysis see the survey: *Modern Psychoanalysis*, ed. by J. Marmor, New York: Basic Books, 1968.

fact. Therefore, ample verbatim or near-verbatim clinical reports are included so that the reader can draw conclusions of his own, whether they differ from the author's or not.

Evidence for childrearing in other times and places appears in the *History of Childhood Quarterly.* For the effects of early life experience on animals in nature there are excellent field studies by ethologists such as Jane Goodall-van Lawick (*In the Shadow of Man*).

This leads to a potentially important use of childhood patterns in other behavioral sciences. Anthropology, for example, has need for a clinical technique to reach the internal motivations of personality as distinct from the immediate reactions to external situations (e.g., see Robert A. LeVine's *Culture, Behavior and Personality*, Aldine Press, 1973). The determination of childhood patterns and the formulation of dynamic diagnoses seems readily adaptable for providing such a research instrument for anthropology and the other psychological and behavioral sciences.

To understand the childhood emotional pattern as this term is used herein, it is necessary first to be fully acquainted with the major emotional forces in the mind. These motivations and reactions are described and discussed in the author's *Emotional Maturity* (3rd edition, 1971). They include the persisting or regressive primary dependence of the baby upon its mother or substitute, and the progressive thrust toward independence; the libidinal side of this in the child's needs to receive love versus the maturing capacity to *give* responsible love; inferiority feelings, usually from failures in maturing, and egoism, competitiveness, and drives for power; formation and force of conscience, and training and standards; the fight-flight reaction, with the consequences of the fight in hostility, violence, guilt, and anxiety and of the flight in all forms of regression and shame; the sex urge as a drive and as a pathway of expression; and the grasp of reality in all of these.

Once one is thoroughly familiar with these basic motivations and reactions, it is necessary, for an understanding of the personality and its problems, to become equally aware of their interactions in each individual. For just as relatively few features of eyes, nose, and mouth combine in different ways to make the distinctive, recognizable faces of our billions of human beings, so these relatively few basic motivations and reactions combine in an infinite number of emotional patterns to constitute the cores of the whole vast range of personalities with their individual characteristics and disorders, from St. Francis to Hitler. Therefore, one must know intimately the emotional forces and reactions and also their commonest interrelations.

The author will try to demonstrate this in every example in sufficient detail to establish the point, except in listing the strengths of the personalities, where these are accepted and used as a healthy base to work from therapeutically and the reasons for these strengths are not given in detail, but left for the reader to analyze. Usually the sources of the strengths are not difficult to find if one examines what good, positive feelings for others—as objects or by identifications—existed in the childhood pattern.

LEON J. SAUL

ACKNOWLEDGMENTS

My thanks to my friends and colleagues: Dr. Silas Warner, who read the manuscript, made valuable comments, and co-authored Chapter 21; Dr. Donald Kent, who contributed much time and thought, and co-authored Chapter 22; Dr. Peter Bennett, Dr. Stanley Yantis, and Linda (Mrs. John) Conboy who generously contributed some of the material; and Virginia Briscoe who took time from her overloaded days to make valuable critical suggestions.

As always, my wife gave unfailing support, love, friendship, and understanding throughout the process of thinking through, writing, revising, and editing.

Susan Bender, my peerless secretary, did all the typing and secretarial work on the manuscript and made many excellent editorial suggestions. Acting as my personal "bosun," she shouldered such responsibilities as driving me to and from appointments with Dr. P. Robb McDonald, friend and preeminent eye surgeon, whom I wish to thank publicly for his indispensable care and help over the years. Profound thanks also to Dr. Henry Kimmel and Dr. John Sayen for keeping me healthy and active. June Strickland, librarian of the Institute of the Pennsylvania Hospital, was invaluable in providing references. Thanks to Helen Ross and others of the Chicago Institute for Psychoanalysis for sending me my patient files from which are drawn the clinical illustrations of Section II.

Certain portions of the book are modifications of previously published articles and are used here with the kind permission of the *Psychoanalytic Quarterly*, *Psychosomatic Medicine*, and the *International Journal of Psychoanalytic Psychotherapy*.

CONTENTS

THE CHILDHOOD EMOTIONAL PATTERN

SECTION I:
THEORETICAL

He impaired his vision by holding the object too close. He might see, perhaps, one or two points with unusual clearness, but in so doing, he necessarily lost sight of the matter as a whole. There is such a thing as being too profound. Truth is not always in a well . . . by undue profundity we perplex and enfeeble thought.

Edgar Allen Poe,
The Murders in the Rue Morgue

1

EARLY EMOTIONAL INTERACTION

As a whole, theory and psychodynamic knowledge which became more and more precise, lost intimate contact with each other . . . (our) theory has been prematurely developed into a consistent system, and has tended to become dogmatic and rigid. The same is true of our therapeutic technique. Our teaching of theory and therapy, therefore, must be less didactic and more critical.

Franz Alexander,
The Scope of Psychoanalysis

Not long after World War II, a friendly colleague and I were chatting. He was about to begin a teaching conference and invited me to sit in. He said a very interesting case would be presented. I think he said it was a young man whose problems stemmed from rejection by his father and overprotection by his mother. He spoke of the young man with sensitive observation and keen insight, and I accepted his invitation to sit in with pleasurable interest. But once the conference got under way, the interesting young man and his parents were so far lost in a sea of symbols and libidinal levels that I wondered if the discussion were about a real human being.

It may well be that the baby is "polymorphous perverse," with mouth and anus as special erotic zones, which become dominated by the genital. Freud's libido theory is important in pointing out to us how much of our mental and emotional life is basically physical. But also, difficulties in oral, anal, or genital erotism or in the character traits Freud related to these imply problems with whomever was responsible for the child's feeding and toilet training and sexual manifestations. This means certain emotional patterns of interaction of the baby or small child with those who rear it and are close to it, patterns that may develop from excessive permissiveness or restrictiveness, or any other abuses of omission or commission.

Of course, I had often seen the oedipus complex in patients—but it was most frank in a young man whose mother had been openly seductive sexually. The boy had rushed out on a dance floor when he was only three years of age to separate Father from Mother. He had Mother to himself during the war and resented the return of his father after four years in the army. Was the oedipus complex of equal importance in every one, and in those whose mothers were not as physically seductive, and if so, why did some successfully "pass" the oedipal stage (Freud, 1924) while others did not? Clinical observations seem to show that the intensity of the oedipus complex and its degree of resolution vary with the personalities and behavior of the parents, e.g., the physical seductiveness of the mother, the strength or weakness or absence of the father, the presence or absence of sisters and brothers, the sleeping arrangements, and so on. Thus, the oedipus complex is one of the emotional patterns of childhood, and the details of its form are highly individual, varying from person to person with all the circumstances of the individual's life from 0–6.

I had observed castration fear most clearly in a man whose father had emphatically threatened to "cut it off" if he ever again found the boy in sex play with the little girl next door. As late as his *Outline of Psychoanalysis*, Freud wrote as though it were a universal experience for a boy's mother to threaten to have his father cut off his penis. The effects of this threat, Freud wrote, depend upon "quantitative relations" (1940, p. 183).*

Also, in practice, penis envy is sometimes clearly evident and sometimes not. One girl made an artificial penis for herself, through which,

---

*In his *Outline of Psychoanalysis*, Freud says:

> The boy's mother understands quite well that his sexual excitement refers to her. Sooner or later she thinks to herself that it is wrong to allow this state of things to continue. She believes she is acting rightly in forbidding him to manipulate his genitals . . . at last his mother adopts the severest measures: she threatens to take away from him the thing he is defying her with. As a rule, in order to make the threat more terrifying and more credible, she delegates its carrying out to the boy's father, saying that she will tell him and that he will cut the penis off. . . . The effects of the threat of castration are many and incalculable; they affect the whole of a boy's relations with his father and mother and subsequently with men and women in general . . . his sexual life often remains permanently under the weight of the prohibition.

Note that in the last sentence, Freud says *often* (author's italics). The actual threat of castration is itself an external factor, and there are other variable factors to account for the "often." Thus here again we see that a certain emotional pattern is formed in the child by his instinctual sexuality interacting with his mother and father and *their responses* to his sexuality.

This was what I had seen in the Navy for four years—trauma acting upon specific emotional vulnerabilities in the personalities of the men who suffered from different degrees of "combat fatigue." The important task in helping them was to understand their personality makeups with their strengths and vulnerabilities, and how the trauma impinged on the vulnerabilities (Saul, 1971).

with the aid of a funnel, she could urinate. But here, too, it was the "quantitative relations"; her brother was openly and grossly preferred to her because he was a boy. And before his birth, from the time she was a tiny tot, her parents raised her as a boy, emphasizing in the little girl boxing, wrestling, and other "manly sports." Here the penis envy was an intelligible reaction to how she was treated during childhood, a reaction to the feeling that only as a male could she be accepted and loved. But is it a universal psycho-biological trait of women? Do all women who enjoy being women simply repress their penis envy?

In these patients, whatever innate tendencies might exist because of erotic zones, or oedipus or castration complexes, or penis envy, they did not of themselves alone form the patient's personality and direct his life, but were minimized or exaggerated by his interactions with the persons important for him during earliest childhood. This interplay of feelings was called by Freud "psychodynamics" (1923), an excellent term, analogous to thermodynamics and electrodynamics, conveying the concept of an interplay of forces, in this case, of emotional forces. It may well turn out that of all the contributions of Freud and psychoanalysis, the major one will be the birth of a science of psychodynamics. It would be a logical sequel to the discovery of the dynamic unconscious and the methods of reaching it through free association, the life history, and the great discovery of the interpretation of dreams (Freud, 1900).

Whatever Freud was or is criticized for, rational or irrational, whatever therapies arise, the essence of his work is a solid permanent contribution to psychological science—namely, the discovery of the "dynamic unconscious," the fact that in every human being there is an interplay of motivational forces and reactions, of which he or she is not completely aware, that is more or less unconscious. Columbus may have been a poor navigator, mistaken in what he had discovered, and a failure as an administrator, but the fact is that he *did* sail on where others had not, and did discover a new continent. He *did* it, he *went there*. So did Freud. He discovered the dynamic unconscious and went there. He went there mostly by free associations and the royal road of the interpretation of dreams, and showed others how to go also. The efficacy of his therapy is of little relevance to the scientific discovery of the dynamic unconscious. It may be years or decades before this scientific knowledge is developed into a more effective therapy. Meanwhile, regardless of effectiveness, duration, and cost, the therapy has the great advantage of being rational and causal, based upon a method of *understanding* those emotional forces and reactions in each person which "make him tick," which form his personality and cause his sufferings and symptoms. It is this discovery that is the great advance. Its applications are another matter. It is analogous to the great discovery by Faraday of current electricity, the innumerable applications of which are still being invented and developed.

If one concentrates upon the interplay of emotional forces, he continues to learn in the office and clinic from every patient, and in his entertainment from every drama and every biography he may read, and from his every interaction in living. Then there is little danger of premature crystallizations of theories which are remote from psychic reality, or from what Freud called "the ever green fields of observation."

After some decades of observing patients and of reading contributions by colleagues, it seems to me that the true analyst is one who, regardless of training, searches for that emotional interplay in the patient which produces his symptoms and strengths and weaknesses. What he is looking for we shall shortly try to formulate in a few sentences.

References

Freud, S. (1900): The interpretation of dreams, *S.E.* 4, p. 231.*

_____ (1923): The descriptive and the dynamic unconscious, *S.E.* 19.

_____ (1924): The dissolution of the oedipus complex, *S.E.* 19, p. 173.

_____ (1940): Outline of psychoanalysis, *S.E.* 23, p. 183.

Saul, L. (1971): *Emotional Maturity*, Third Edition. Philadelphia: Lippincott, p. 207.

*All references to the works of Freud in this book are to the Standard Edition, Hogarth Press, London, and will be denoted simply by "*S.E.*"

2
SOME COMPONENTS OF EMOTIONAL PATTERNS

Before attempting a condensed formulation, we must consider some necessary components of it.

One of these is the fight-flight reaction, which appears in almost all psychic manifestations—dreams, symptoms, and everyday living.

Walter Cannon (1929), in *Bodily Changes in Pain, Hunger, Fear and Rage*, reported experiments with animals and humans (e.g., students before big football games or critical examinations) that demonstrated unmistakably that under stress the body's physiology is stimulated to an emergency mobilization for effort that may take the form either of flight or fight. Cannon studied *emergency* mobilization, but the implication is unavoidable that such arousal to flight or fight is a general *biological mechanism of adaption*—to the effort of relieving the stress by fleeing from or destroying its cause. The "neurotic"—in Freud's broad use of the term as "emotional disorder"—is under inner stress and therefore more or less chronically mobilized against an unknown cause, leading to efforts at flight, mostly by tendencies to regression, and to fight, as hostility, anger, or destructiveness, usually more or less repressed. Both the flight and the fight are usually more or less expressed and defended against psychologically in different ways and degrees in different personalities. Sociologically, the flight is evident in widespread alcoholism, drug abuse, and cultish passive withdrawal; and the fight is evident in the prevalence of crime, cruelty, and violence. When repressed, both fight and flight are still observable clinically by the analyst as part of symptom formation, and they appear in most dreams.

It seems to me that analysts have not fully appreciated the value and power of the concept of the fight-flight reaction as an adaptive mechanism, in simplifying analytic theory and as an aid in therapy. It provides a single physiologically established basis for two of the most common and powerful forces seen in every patient, namely hostility (or, if one prefers, "hostile aggression") and regression. Although probably unacquainted with Cannon's work, Freud touched on this in the *Outline of Psychoanalysis* (1940), concerning the origin of neuroses in early childhood:

> The helpless ego fends off these problems by attempts at flight (by repressions) which turn out later to be ineffective and which involve permanent hindrances to further development.

Freud does not mention the fight, i.e., the hostility or aggression; he never made a detailed clinical study of this, but he discusses it in the Schreber case (1911), *Beyond the Pleasure Principle* (1920), and *Civilization and Its Discontents* (1930). In his *Outline of Psychoanalysis* he summarizes his conclusions, in terms of the death instinct (1940, p. 148).

Freud continues to describe how the groundwork for neurosis is laid (1940, p. 183):

> We can speak with a fair degree of certainty about the part played by the period of life. It seems that neuroses are only acquired during early childhood (up to the age of six), even though their symptoms may not make their appearance until much later . . . in every case the subsequent neurotic illness has this prelude in childhood as its point of departure . . . we can easily account for this preference for the first period of childhood. Neuroses are, as we know, disorders of the ego; and it is not to be wondered at that the ego, while it is weak, immature and incapable of resistance, should fail in dealing with problems which it could later manage with the utmost ease.

This period can be called, in shorthand, "0 to 6," i.e., that childhood period ranging from conception to the age of about six or seven years. This includes the period from conception to birth (which is advisable because of the increasing observations upon the effects of prenatal physical and perhaps emotional influences). As a rough guide we can look for the sources of psychosis and other more serious disorders during 0–2 or 0–3, and of the neuroses and milder disturbances from 0–6.

Details are of great importance. We would all like to achieve the goal formulated by Anne Freud (1937) in our clinical understanding of every patient:

> At the present time we should probably define the task of analysis as follows: to acquire the fullest possible knowledge of all the three institutions of which we believe the psychic personality to be constituted and to learn what are their relations to the ego, to explore its contents, its boundaries and its functions and to trace the influences in the outside world, the id and the super-ego by which it has been shaped and, in relation to the id, to give an account of the instincts, i.e. of the id-contents, and to follow them through the transformations which they undergo.

But whatever his perception of details and minutiae, above all the analyst *must* know the *main features*—knowing these *main features* is the indispensible imperative. The analyst must understand his patient, i.e., the essentials of the dynamics which are causing his or her problems. It is important to know the sources and dynamics of the patient's health and strengths (including "conflict-free areas"; Hartman, 1964); but the analyst's primary task is to correct the psychopathology, and therefore he must be certain to understand the pathological dynamics even if not *all* of the dynamics: in short, the pathodynamic parts of the childhood patterns of emotional interrelations, i.e., what proved traumatic. By "dynamics" (psychodynamics) we mean of course the "interplay of emotional forces," which reach a dynamic balance. And by childhood we mean that period previously mentioned and defined by Freud as "0–6."

The analyst must know how *intensively* and *extensively* the childhood pathology affects the adult mind, from narrow manifestations such as single symptoms to more generalized and more widely spread effects, as in personality disorders.

Another concept which has stood up over the years in the author's experience, and in relation to discussions in the literature (e.g., Hartmann, 1964) is that of "mental health." Freud is said to have defined it practically as "the ability to work and love." I think a psychodynamic formulation that includes the basic elements can be reduced to the bare essentials of (1) *adequate maturity* and (2) *adequate adjustment*. This represents the fundamental concepts and includes the details of development and of adaptation (Saul, 1971, p. 347). Of course, we are always speaking only of the physiologically healthy individual without intellectual or physical impairment in what has come to be called "the average expectable environment" (Hartmann, 1964).

As Freud repeatedly pointed out, there is no sharp demarcation between neurosis, psychosis, and mental health; it is mostly a quantitative matter. Emotional maturity provides a degree of satisfaction and comfort within oneself and usually means a relative degree of satisfaction and comfort in one's environment. Adequate adjustment is not only possible but commonly observed in practice, in patients who complain not at all of their life situation or style, but only of inner emotional symptoms, e.g., a young matron who is happy with her husband, children, friends, income, and life style but comes for help because of anxiety in the form of a sense of impending catastrophe (see p. 223). Emotional maturity, like all else in the emotional life, is quantitative. As an ideal, it can be approached but probably never fully realized. The author has devoted a book to an analytic concept of it (Saul, 1971). In brief, emotional maturity consists in achievement of relative *development out of* the child's dependence upon its parents *to* relative independence (Parens and Saul, 1971): i.e., separation-individuation (Mahler, 1965). It is development out of the child's intense need *for* love to the ability to *give* love, out of extreme narcissism and competitiveness to object interest and a paternal or maternal and fraternal or sisterly identification, to live and let live; it is relative harmony with one's superego and (the result of this development) relative freedom from domination by repressed childhood emotional patterns—all of this yielding a relatively accurate sense of reality and the flexibility to feel, think, and act in accordance with reality and without undue frustrations and without undue hostility and regressive trends from a too-strong fight-flight reaction.

References

Cannon, W. (1929): *Bodily Changes in Pain, Hunger, Fear and Rage.* New York: Appleton.

Freud, A. (1937): *The Ego and The Mechanisms of Defence.* London: Hogarth, pp. 4–5.

Freud, S. (1911): Psychoanalytic notes on an autobiographical account of a case of paranoia (dementia paranoides), Part II, *S.E.* 12.

———— (1920): Beyond the pleasure principle, Parts I–VII, *S.E.* 18.

———— (1930): Civilization and its discontents, Part VI, *S.E.* 30, p. 117.

———— (1940): Outline of psychoanalysis, *S.E.* 23.

Hartmann, H. (1964): Psychoanalysis and the concept of health, in: *Essays on Ego Psychology*. New York: International Universities Press.

Mahler, M. (1965): On the significance of the normal separation-individuation phase, in: *Drives, Affects, Behavior*, Vol. 2, ed. M. Schur. New York: International Universities Press, pp. 161–169.

Parens, H., and Saul, L. (1971): *Dependence in Man*. New York: International Universities Press.

Saul, L. (1971): *Emotional Maturity*, Third Edition. Philadelphia: Lippincott.

3
FORMATION OF
CHILDHOOD PATTERNS

That emotional patterns which continue for life are shaped in the earliest, most formative years, has long been known in folk wisdom and by philosophers, novelists, and poets, e.g.: "Give me the child until he is seven and you may have him for the rest of his life"; "As the twig is bent, so is the tree inclined"; "The apple falls not far from the tree"; "The hand that rocks the cradle rules the world."*

The effort of the scientist, besides the exploration of the unknown by the accumulation of endless detail, is to reduce the principles that underlie the mass of data to the simplest possible formulations. Freud's concepts of dynamics, of early patterns toward parents which are transferred to others in adult life, and of the importance of the first six years, can be combined with his descriptions of neurosis as conflict and defense, in such a way as to condense all of these concepts into a single brief formulation of the essential dynamics of neurosis and of much psychogenic psychosis. This provides a formulation for each patient which the analyst seeks to understand and to use as the basis of his treatment.

*Glass, J. (1974): *Reflections on a Mountain Summer.* New York: Knopf, p. 291, contains "Scrub," a poem by Edna St. Vincent Millay:

> If I grow bitterly,
> Like a gnarled and stunted tree,
> Bearing harshly of my youth
> Puckered fruit that sears the mouth;
> If I make of my drawn boughs
> An inhospitable house,
> Out of which I never pry
> Towards the water and the sky,
> Under which I stand and hide
> And hear the day go by outside;
> It is that a wind too strong
> Bent my back when I was young,
> It is that I fear the rain
> Lest it blister me again.

Freud's formulation of the idea of childhood *patterns*, if not the term itself, is implicit in his libido theory as indicated in Chapter 1, and appears as early as Freud's relationship with Breuer, for example, when Freud pointed out that Anna O's throwing her arms around Breuer was only the transference to Breuer of an early emotional pattern (1925). The childhood pattern or nuclear emotional constellation (Saul, 1971, pp. 186–189) as we shall use it means that pattern of emotional interplay between the child and those most important for it, especially from ages about 0 to 6. "Emotional pattern" is a good term because it includes both oedipal and pre-oedipal, and it covers both Freud's emphasis on the ego's difficulty in handling the instincts and the emphasis of other analysts on the effects of environment in causing neurotic problems. For faulty environment in childhood intensifies instinctual forces that the then weak ego cannot handle without pathology, or the nucleus of pathology that will emerge later. Needless to say, the pattern is not a rigid structure but a dynamic balance of emotional forces in a certain equilibrium. For example, a girl rejected as a child by her mother goes through life *feeling rejected* and angry about this no matter how devoted her husband, children, and friends may be. Or a man bullied by an older, bigger, stronger brother or by his mother or father forms a pattern of fear and hatred of authority that continues for life. Thus rejection, deprivation, overprotection, seduction, guilt, and shame-producing mental treatment or physical threats or abuse or any combination of these and other mistreatments, by omission or commission, especially before age six, form neurotic patterns of interaction of emotional forces that the child's weak ego cannot comprehend, verbalize, resolve, or outgrow, and which persist to some extent and degree for life. This concept of persisting childhood patterns was interestingly illustrated by Freud with a personal example, viz. Freud had a nephew, John, a year older than himself, about whom he wrote that:

> Until the end of my third year we had been inseparable. We loved each other and fought with each other, and this childhood relationship . . . had a determining influence on all my subsequent relations with contemporaries.

And further, Freud indicated that this relationship

> . . . had become the source of all my friendships and all my hatreds. All my friends have in a certain sense been reincarna-

tions of this first figure . . . my emotional life has always insisted that I should have an intimate friend and a hated enemy. I have always been able to provide myself afresh with both, and it has not infrequently happened that the ideal situation of childhood has been so completely reproduced that friend and enemy have come together in a single individual. . . . (1900).

It seems true that from conception the growing organism interacts with its environment, in ways we shall discuss in more detail in Chapter 4. From birth the child, with its innate instinctual urges and responses, interacts with those responsible for it and close to it. This interaction shapes a pattern which is usually relatively settled in its fundamentals by the age of about six or seven and is specific for each individual. This specificity is because no two persons are born with identical temperaments, motilities (Fries and Woolf, 1971), intelligence, and other attributes, nor acted upon by the same emotional and physical forces and conditions from conception to age about six ("0 to 6"). This childhood pattern of interacting with others formed in earliest life continues in its essentials basically unchanged for all the rest of each person's life; it affects the person's adult behavior, either facilitating the development to maturity if favorable, or hindering it or warping it if unfavorable. This pattern, if it contains elements of distorted human relationships, constitutes a nucleus of psychopathology. For example, the unloved child tends to continue to feel unloved and angry about it; the dominated child continues either intimidated or hostile to authorities. That is, the patterns toward the most significant persons of childhood are transferred to other individuals in the course of one's life. Psychoanalysis endeavors (1) to study these childhood patterns, which generally are mostly unconscious, and (2) to use its understanding of them therapeutically in those parts of the patterns which are producing symptoms, that is, to influence the causes of the symptoms at their source (Saul, 1972).

References

Freud, S. (1900): The interpretation of dreams, *S.E.* 4.

_____ (1925): Joseph Breuer, *S.E.* 19, p. 280.

Fries, M., and Woolf, P. (1971): The influence of constitutional complex on developmental phases, in *Separation-Individuation*, ed. J. McDevitt and C. Settlege. New York: International Universities Press.

Saul, L. (1971): *Emotional Maturity*, Third Edition. Philadelphia: Lippincott.

_____ (1972): *Psychodynamically Based Psychotherapy*. New York: Science House.

4
FORMULATION OF A
THERAPEUTIC ATTITUDE

We are justified then in attempting a formulation of the essentials which is as concise as possible, namely, one in which the analyst views his patients with the following attitude and questions:

What are the main features of the pathodynamic childhood pattern, and (1) in what ways and (2) how intensively and extensively do these affect the total personality in its feeling, thinking, and behavior, in life, and in the transference; and in these dynamics, what is the status of the fight-flight reaction, the hostilities and the tendencies to dependence and regression; and just how does the pattern cause the patient's symptoms and suffering?

Clinical data will be presented in Section II. This formulation is advanced as one that the author has found consistently useful for orientation, understanding, and therapy. It can be used in stocktaking sessions in long analyses; certain selected patients employ it to good effect by using it as a guide in formulating their own dynamics in a therapeutically effective way. Of course, this is an intellectual formulation, but its insights can be of considerable help in working through to emotional realization. Needless to say, analyst and patient must ever be alert to these pathodynamic childhood patterns as they are seen in free associations and dreams, in childhood material, in the transference, and in life.

Childhood patterns sometimes are relatively flexible in the adult, as when during childhood one has had good relations not only with parents but with others such as grandparents, aunts and uncles, and siblings. Then one has the basis for a whole variety of patterns of good relationships throughout adult life. Sometimes, however, these early patterns are very rigidly set and live the adult's life for him in a fixed, almost reflex, fashion. One of the major goals of psychoanalytic therapy is to *help free the person from this inexorable automaticity of his unconscious childhood patterns.* The first step (but only the first step) toward accomplishing this is insight, making these unconscious patterns conscious. And this is because the ego [the higher faculties of (1) perception, including consciousness and sense of reality; (2) integration, including memory and reason; and (3) the executive functions, including decision and responsibility] can now deal consciously with what was a hidden, unconscious "neurotic," *automatic* response pattern of childhood, and which now, by analysis, has been transformed into a conscious problem. The unconscious dynamics of the neurosis have been made into a conscious problem which the person can comprehend and work on resolving by practice in living.

A man was too dependent and submissive but did not realize it. He was only aware of the resulting sense of inferiority which enraged him and produced anxiety and over-ambition and difficulties with people. After learning the source he set about reducing his dependence and submissiveness and gradually outgrew these childhood patterns toward his parents. The insight turns the unconscious neurotic pattern into a conscious problem. The *first* step is for the patient to *understand* his own dynamics, to see his emotional problem so that he can bring all his reason and determination to bear on resolving it and outgrowing it by practice in living.

Now this raises the important question of psychic determinism. To some extent, the patient has been released from the tyranny of the automaticity of his unconscious childhood pattern. As Freud put it, "Where id was, there now is ego."

Does this mean emancipation from determinism and causality in the mental and emotional life? By no means. Rather, it seems that they can now operate in a wider, more variable, more complex way. It implies an increase in capacity to learn, in adaptability, and in a range of choices and options in his decisions and behavior. There are more and wider choices in human relations in the large and small decisions and tasks, at home and in the workaday world. The possible responses to external and internal circumstances are now increased in kind and number. There is an increase in adaptability and also in the capacity to change not only one's attitudes but also one's circumstances. To change one's environment requires a strong sense of reality and capacity for imagination, responsibility, and willpower. The problem of "will" has received relatively little attention in the psychoanalytic literature, while that of responsibility for tasks has been almost totally neglected.

It seems to me that it can be accepted as an established fact, confirmed by the clinical observation of every patient seen by an analyst, that there exists in everyone a pattern of emotional interaction, and such patterns may encourage the development to maturity or may be more or less neurotic, i.e., pathological, blocking the development by fixations.

But precisely how these early patterns are formed and persist for life has not, so far as I know, been thoroughly explored. Freud discussed it in *The Ego and The Id* (1923), and some analysis of it appears in Therese Benedek's "Parenthood as a Developmental Phase" (1959), where, in speaking of the child, she writes:

> . . . The introjection of the "object" of the drive along with the sensations, affects, related to the gratification or to the frustration of the drive, are basic to continuity of interpersonal communication. As the continuity of object relationship is maintained, the memories of object relations plus drive experience become stored as object representations and self-representations and become the nuclei of organization in the mental apparatus . . . introjection and identifications are terms which refer to processes by which memory traces of drive-motivated interpersonal relationship are stored during the entire course of life.

Whatever the details of the process of forming the pattern, the fundamental seems relatively simple and can be expressed in terms of conditioning, learning, or psychoanalytic structural theory. The essential is the formation of healthy "images." For example, a child is the first-born, much wanted, much loved, and highly valued; he grows up with an image of people loving and adoring him and takes over into his own mind (introjects and is conditioned to) this view of himself. Freud mentioned this in discussing how the self-confidence given Goethe by his mother's love contributed to his success. By way of contrast, a girl who was the sixth and last child was quite neglected, treated without interest or attention; as she grew up, she continued to feel unwanted, an outsider, of no value or importance to anyone. She had developed that kind of imago; the authority of her childhood formed that basic part of her superego. Another child had a secure, loving home until her father died. She then fixed her longings entirely

on her mother, who—having to earn a living and seeking to remarry—
now rejected the child, who continued to long and to hope but who
also built up a hidden, repressed rage at her mother for the neglect.
This pattern continued into her married life.

In other words, the child adapts somehow to the treatment ac-
corded it by those emotionally important for it and continues usually
unconsciously in the same pattern. If mother is always loving, that
is what the child learns to expect, is conditioned to, is the imago he
forms. That seems to be the essential; the remaining problems, however important, are ones of detail, e.g., the connections with drives
and memories and the processes of object relations and of
identification.

References

Benedek, T. (1959): Parenthood as a developmental phase, *J. Am. Psychoanal. Assn.*
   7(3): 389–417.
Freud, S. (1923): The ego and the id, *S.E.* 19.

5
ON THE FORMATION AND TRANSMISSION OF CHILDHOOD PATTERNS
"Dynamics Are Destiny"

Every baby is born with certain potentials. Which of these are inherited and which reflect experiences in the womb in reaction to the mother's nutrition, activities, emotional state, and other conditions during the pregnancy is usually not clear. But certainly marked differences are obvious to a mere glance around any hospital nursery. The newborn are of all shapes and sizes and degrees of motility and responsiveness. But their congenital capacities and potentials are only a part of what will determine the sort of adults they will become. The other part is what they are born *into*—what sort of physical and emotional setting they will grow up in through the next weeks, months, and years of their lives, especially the first six years, which are the most formative. For on these tiny, immature organisms will impinge many powerful forces: the physical conditions of the home; its economic and emotional security; whether or not there are brothers and sisters, and whether this baby is the first, last, or somewhere in between; and especially the personalities of the parents, whether they are loving, understanding, and supportive or neglectful, rejecting, and even physically abusive (Horney, 1937; Alexander, 1940, 1961). The prevalence of abuse within families has been confirmed statistically in a study which reveals that some form of physical violence between family members is almost universal (Straus et al., 1976). Women and children are generally the victims. Other statistics show that:

- As many as ten million cases of child abuse occur in the United States each year.

- From 30 to 35 percent of all murders involve one family member killing another.
- Between 20 and 40 percent of most divorces involve physical abuse.
- In one urban study, about 50 percent of all assaults involved husbands and wives.
- Another study reported that 62 percent of high school seniors admitted violence in the home.
- Between 84 and 87 percent of parents use physical punishment at some point in a child's life.

We no longer live in the wilds of nature with our instincts as guides. We live in societies, cultures, civilizations: and this living in a community requires a degree of control of instinct (Freud, 1927). A baby not only requires love, security, and understanding, but will have to be socialized, to learn to live in an organized community, be it a small primitive tribe or a huge, highly complex industrial nation.

This socialization in our country is always very difficult for many reasons; among them are the nature of the child and the personalities of the parents and their relations in the marriage. The child has *physical* needs which are not easy to meet, such as proper feeding during infancy and cleanliness, especially regarding excretions. The process of toilet training requires timing, sensitivity, judgment, and patience. Then there is need of proper conditions for shelter, clothing, and sleep; and *watchfulness* that the child does not injure himself, and does not become seriously ill. Besides all these physical needs there are the emotional requirements, for love, affection, security, a sense of importance. In addition, all this (which constitutes a full-time job) must be provided to a growing, changing being so that there is no sharp end-point, and the parental concern and effort must extend through adolescence when new problems, like those of sex, independence, and responsibility peak. There is never a complete end for parental effort, but there is at least a relative decrease after 20 years or more when the child reaches maturity and achieves sufficient independence and responsibility to take care of itself.

Everything the parent needs to do for the child, from conception onward, lacks sharp definition; it cannot be just stated and learned intellectually and applied in a set way, which is what every parent wants in order to simplify the enormous task of childrearing. Unfortunately, it is not possible; the best diet and guidance for a baby's first year are not correct for the second or third year. The child constantly changes. All that can be stated basically is that parents must have great sympathy, sensitivity, and respect for their child, together with constant alertness and infinite patience with the child's incessant demands. Few tasks require more energy and self-control than the loving care of a small child.

Other major difficulties lie within the parents themselves. The mother becomes exhausted by the unremitting demands of the child and finds herself irritable and wanting to get away from the home for relief and distraction. The father is fatigued by his job as breadwinner, loses his tolerance for the noisy demands of the child, and snaps at both wife and child. Some children, from birth, are so winning that their responsiveness is a soul-satisfying reward; others are tense and not cuddly.

It increases perspective to consider childrearing of animals in the wild, and even the rearing of animals within the artificial confines of domestication. The animal young and its mother are dominated by instinct, are almost all id, with minimal ego and superego; i.e., judgment, choices, and decisions enter but little, nor are social standards and ideals involved. This does not mean that the young of animals in the wild do not also need to adapt to their societies. Adaptation is clearly described by Jane Goodall-van Lawick in her observation of chimpanzees (1971). (Other scientists studying orangutans and gorillas in their natural habitat are Birute Galdikas-Brindamour and her husband Rod, and zoologist Dian Fossey.) Yet this adaptation of young animals in the wild is accomplished with smooth naturalness, and nowhere have I yet read of animal young who were the victims of their parents' fight-flight reactions, or of the parental sadism seen in battered babies (Richette, 1969; Steele, 1970; Chase, 1976).* It *is* true, though, that some animal fathers are so remote from the process of childrearing that the young must be protected from them by the mother—but still this protection is not to control the father's hostility, but only his need for food.

Human young are so much more complex compared to animal young, and they make so many more demands for so much longer—often 25 years or more—upon their parents. The parents have so many interests besides their children, and so many struggles in finding their

---

*See extensive references on the battered child at the end of this chapter.

ways in our complex society; and they are usually neurotic themselves because of their own upbringing and consequent childhood patterns.

An intermediate situation has been dealt with by Erik Erikson in his well-known *Childhood and Society* (1950). But I would like to mention here a beautiful book (Long Lance, 1928), which is autobiographical and not scientific, by an extraordinary man, Chief Buffalo Child Long Lance. In it he describes his own childhood growing up as a Blackfoot Indian when this tribe and several others inhabited the northern plains. Boys grew up to be great athletes, successful hunters, and fighters. There were no other choices of career except for the rare youth who became a medicine man. Girls grew up to be wives and mothers and do the domestic jobs. There were no complex choices of career for them either; girls could not become braves and boys were threatened with being brought up as girls if they showed a lack of courage, bravery, and fortitude. The children slept in the teepee with their parents, and the whole (sub)tribe was their family. Crime was not tolerated, nor was lying. Any dishonor reflected on the entire tribe. How different that is from the situation of the young man of today who, for example, wants to be a writer but knows that he cannot make a reliable living as such and is therefore suffering his way through engineering school, his frustrations meanwhile generating serious tensions with his young, beautiful, talented wife. How different from the situation of a young man who settles for a career in business, but whose immediate superior has him spending time at three-hour lunches, with endless cigarettes and martinis, until the young man feels his health being undermined and changes to another company which is no better, with all this tension affecting both his loyal patient wife and young family.

The central point is this: complex human young, mostly the offspring of fatigued, neurotic parents who are struggling in a complex industrial society, interact with their parents and others close to them (the nuclear family) and are subsequently conditioned in certain ways during their most formative periods, from birth to about age six or seven; they form an emotional pattern of reaction to those persons most important for them from 0–6. This pattern, once formed, persists in its essentials for the rest of the child's life, although often hidden from view. As Freud said: the child we once were lives on in all of us. And this child is the key to the personality. The pattern of our 0–6 is our destiny, the basis of nobility in some and of all manner of psychopathology in others—psychosomatic problems, neurosis, psychosis, perversions, addictions, and criminality, expressed as individual hostility or expressed collectively in violence which is frankly criminal or rationalized as political, devoted to some worthy cause.

No longer can we see society as a great bulk of normal healthy personalities, with a few deviants suffering from emotional disorders. Instead, the great majority have pathological childhood patterns, which become manifest in internal suffering and overt or covert hostility to others. We may wonder no longer at all the man-made evils and suffering in the world, but rather at how it holds together as well as it does.

The young, with their pathological childhood patterns, grow up physically to the age of mating and marriage. The disordered patterns emerge, sooner or later, toward each other, as they inevitably must between any persons who are close enough to interact emotionally. That is why marriage is a difficult adjustment, even at best, as is evident at all levels and segments of society. Small wonder when so many men and women have such disordered childhood patterns that, joined together, they suffer from disordered marriages and parenting. The pathology and problems of the marriage inevitably affect the children born into it, assuring disordered patterns in the children that continue for the rest of *their* lives and are in turn transmitted to the following generation. Mankind's greatest problem is how to interrupt this chain of transmission of pathological childhood patterns, for it is this which makes our neuroses, psychoses, addictions, perversions, crime and wars, and every daily manifestation of the worldwide hostility and cruelty of man to man.

To make a good, harmonious, happy marriage, to provide a proper setting to rear emotionally healthy children, both parents need childhood patterns of good, harmonious, happy feelings. Otherwise, they must hope that the pattern of the one who is somewhat disturbed will mesh and fit into the pattern of the partner, but this is risky. For example, a girl who had been rejected in childhood but not excessively so, married a man who also had been somewhat rejected by his mother but had been adored by an aunt and given much love and confidence by his father. In the marriage he was able to repeat toward his wife the identification with aunt and father and give her enough warmth and support to keep her childhood needs under control. If she had been more deeply rejected in childhood she probably would have followed the common pattern of feeling rejected in her marriage, regardless of how much warmth and support her husband gave her. Another example is the man who had been somewhat dominated by his mother. His wife recognized his dependence on her and submissiveness to her, but her own dynamics enabled her in part to satisfy these needs, while in part forcing him out of them. Early in the marriage she told him sharply, "I am not your mother, and do not intend to be!" They were close enough to complement each other's dynamics for this to be a stable marriage.

If you want to be reasonably sure of a happy marriage, you must yourself have a pattern of good relations from 0–6. How can an individual find out if his own pattern is a good one? The most direct way is to visit a professional who is trained and experienced in psychodynamics and can find this out in one to three interviews—a psychoanalyst, dynamic psychiatrist, psychodynamically trained psychologist or social worker. If this is not feasible, you might be able to find out something yourself through independent reading (Saul, 1971).

It is fair to let your intended marriage partner know the results of your investigation into your 0–6, and he or she should give you the same information before marriage. This may require some tact and may not be possible to do all at one time. But each partner should know his or her own childhood patterns and dynamics; for, we have said, inevitably in a marriage these patterns develop toward each other. A girl takes a huge chance if she marries a man who has had bad relations with his mother from 0–6, or if he lacks a stable father to identify with, a father who loved his wife and son. The same holds for a man who wants a stable, loving wife. She must have the emotional pattern for this, and it is formed basically from 0–6.

References

Alexander, F. (1940): Psychoanalysis revised, *Psychoanal. Quart.* 9: 137–165.
———— (1961): *Scope of Psychoanalysis.* New York: Basic Books, pp. 407–409, 424–439.
Chase, N. (1976): *A Child is Being Beaten.* New York: Jason Aronson, Inc.
Erikson, E. (1950): *Childhood and Society.* New York: W. W. Norton.
Freud, S. (1927): Civilization and its discontents, *S.E.* 21.
Goodall, J. (1971): *In The Shadow of Man.* Boston: Houghton-Mifflin.
Horney, K. (1937): *The Neurotic Personality of Our Time.* New York: W. W. Norton.
Long Lance (1928): *Long Lance.* New York: Farrar & Rinehart.

Richette, L. (1969): *Throwaway Children*. Philadelphia: Lippincott.
Saul, L. (1971): *Emotional Maturity*, Third Edition. Philadelphia: Lippincott.
Steele, B. (1970): Working with abusive parents from a psychiatric point of view, DHEW Publ. No. OHD 75-70.
Straus, M., Gelles, R., and Steinmetz, S. (1976): Violence in the family: An assessment of knowledge and research needs, a speech given at a meeting of the American Association for the Advancement of Science, Boston, January 1976.

*   *   *   *   *

For further information on the battered child, see "Selected References on the Abused and Battered Child" from the National Institute of Mental Health, and also the following references:

Elmer, E. (1967): *Children in Jeopardy: A Study of Abused Minors and Their Families*, with the research assistance of B. Girdany, T. McHenry, and J. Reinhard. Pittsburgh: University of Pittsburgh Press.
Elmer, E., and Gregg, C. (1968): Developmental characteristics of abused children, *Annual Progress in Child Psychiatry*, pp. 555–567.
Fleming, G. (1967): Cruelty to children, *British Medical Journal*, May 13.
Green, A. (1968): Self-destructive behavior in physically abused schizophrenic children, *AMA Arch. General Psychiatry* 19(2): 171–179.
Greengard, J. (1967): The abused child: a second look after state legislation, *Medical Science*, May.
Gladstone, R. (1971): Violence begins at home: the parent's center project for the study and prevention of child abuse, *J. Am. Acad. Child Psychiatry* 10(2): 336–350.
Guttmacher, A. (1967): Unwanted pregnancy: a challenge to mental health, *Mental Hygiene* 51(4): 512–516.
Helfer, R. (1968): *The Battered Child*. Chicago: University of Chicago Press.
Holter, J., and Friedman, S. (1968): Principles of management in child abuse cases, *Am. J. Orthopsychiatry* 38(1): 127–136.
Johnson, B., and Morse, H. (1968): Injured children and their parents, *Children* 15(4): 147–152.
Kliman, G. (1968): *Psychological Emergencies of Childhood*. New York: Grune, p. 154.
Kunstadter, R. (1967): The battered child and the celiac syndrome, *Illinois Medical Journal*, September.
Laury, G., and Meerloo, J. (1967): Mental cruelty and child abuse, *Psychiatric Quart. Supplement* 41(2): 203–254.
Havens, L. (1972): Youth, violence and the nature of family life, *Psychiatric Annals* 2(2): 19–29.
Martin, H. (1970): Antecedents of burns and scalds in children, *British J. Med. Psychology* 43(1): 39–47.
———— (1970): Parents' and children's reactions to burns and scalds in children, *British J. Med. Psychology* 43(2): 183–192.

Myers, S. (1967): The child slayer: a 25-year survey of homicides involving preadolescent victims, *AMA Arch. General Psychiatry* 17(2): 211–213.

Oliver, J., and Taylor, A. (1971): Five generations of ill-treated children in one family pedigree, *Brit. J. Psychiatry* 119: 473–480.

Ostow, M. (1970): Parents' hostility to their children, *Israel Ann. Psychiat. and Related Disc.* 8(1): 3–21.

Rascovsky, A. and M. (1969): On filicide and its meaning in the genesis of acting out and psychopathic behavior in oedipus, *Psychoanal. Quart.* 38(2): 345–346.

Rheingold, J. (1967): *The Mother, Anxiety, and Death: the Catastrophic Death Complex.* Boston: Little, Brown.

Silver, L. (1969): Does violence breed violence? Contributions from a study of the child abuse syndrome: brief communications, *Am. J. Psychiatry* 126(3): 404–407.

Silver, L., et al. (1971): Agency action and interaction in cases of child abuse, *Social Casework* 52(3): 164–171.

Silver, L., et al. (1969): Child abuse syndrome: the 'gray areas' in establishing a diagnosis, *Pediatrics* 44(4): 594–600.

Steele, B. (1968): Parental abuse of infants and small children, a study of the effect of early infantile experience on adult parenting behavior, *Bulletin Phila. Assn. Psychoanal.* 18(4): 209–213.

Terr, L. (1968): The battered child rebrutalized: ten cases of medical-legal confusion, *Am. J. Psychiatry* 124: 1432–1439.

Wasserman, S. (1967): The abused parent of the abused child, *Children* 14(5): 175–179, Sept.–Oct.

Zalba, S. (1966): The abused child, *Social Work* 11(4): 3–16.

_____ (1967): The abused child: a typology for classification and treatment, *Social Work* 12(1): 70–79.

_____ (1971): Battered children, *Trans Action* 8(9)(10): 58–61.

6
FINDING THE CHILDHOOD
EMOTIONAL PATTERN

When to Find the Pattern

Years ago in the days of strict psychoanalytic orthodoxy, while discussing with me the matter of understanding the patient, a colleague said, "Maybe after about 150 hours you have some idea." This seems incorrect on many points: if the analyst does not understand a great deal about his patient, how can he recommend treatment? How does he know psychoanalysis is not contraindicated? And how does he know what he expects it to accomplish? The idea that if a person free associates on the analyst's couch a certain number of days a week for a long enough time, some great liberation of the spirit will occur is semi-mystical and unscientific.

The analyst must try to understand his patient in the very first interview. In fact, the first few interviews must be focused upon diagnosis, upon understanding the patient's main dynamics and particularly his pathodynamics that are producing his complaints and symptoms. If this is not accomplished in the first interview or so, a golden opportunity is lost. So important is this that ample time should be allowed for the first interview, preferably two hours. The opportunity of these first interviews is golden because they provide a more objective setting for observation before a flow of free associations that must be read at a lower level of consciousness, and before patient and analyst are involved more deeply in transference and countertransference feelings and all the effects of these upon their thinking and perceptions.

Thus the conclusion to which we are led by clinical experience with many patients and by reason is that the best interest of the patient and the proper procedure for analysis require that the patient's main dynamics (and especially his *patho*dynamics) be discerned and formulated in the first session or at most in the first few sessions, which are thus primarily diagnostic, not descriptive diagnosis by symptoms but at least a first approximation of the central psycho-dynamics—a "dynamic diagnosis."

Obviously this does not mean that the analyst and the patient do not continue to pursue assiduously all the dynamics as the analysis proceeds: but this further continuing study and expansion of knowl-edge of the dynamics is usually much less difficult and more orderly if at least a skeleton of the dynamics can be clearly discerned in the first hour or so, to provide a framework to build upon, however much it must be altered with time and analytic work. Clearly the analyst must not become so enamored of the dynamics he sees in the first diagnostic hours that he cannot continuously change his understanding of them with increasing material, study, and insight. But this is enormously less a danger than wallowing unguided for 150 analytic hours with no clear idea of the central dynamics.

How to Find the Pattern

1. A good opener is to start by letting the patient talk spontane-ously. Usually the more freely he pours out his story the better, but we do not want him to start free associating until we know what is neces-sary to discern his main dynamics. He may have told his chief com-plaints, but we want to be sure to get them clearly and sharply and also something of their history, their onsets and course and surroundings, and possibly the precipitating circumstances. I saw a young woman who had vaginal bleeding and seemed to be terrified that she had cancer. She denied this fear but told me she could not eat, vomited on the least provocation, and could not sleep even with medication, and her bowels did not move with laxatives and enemas. She was a heroic counterphobic, but the paralysis of her physiology hinted at her panic.

2. Apart from the symptoms we must also learn the pattern of the patient's current emotional life, his major libidinal investments in persons, job, interests, including his "life style," and a typical 24-hour day. Not infrequently, this repeats rather closely his childhood patterns, perhaps with spouse substituted for parent.

3. Then it may be necessary to tell the patient gently that we must interrupt him for a little in order to ask him some questions about the emotional background of his childhood.

History-taking is perhaps more an art than a science, but in our particular experience it is best to go from the general to the specific.

Therefore we usually ask first the general question: "What do you consider to have been the major emotional feature or features of your life from birth to the age of about six or seven? Most people do not remember this period well, but do you have any general feeling for how it was?" Such a question is meant to be as little "leading" as possible so that we can note what the patient himself selects as important. However, we can never or rarely ever let him go off very far on tangents, because at this point we must elicit systematically his early emotional relationships. Therefore, the next question is the more specific one: "Who was the most important person or persons for you, emotionally, from birth until age about six?" Then if need be we ask not only about the family group but about each and every individual member of it, i.e., mother, father, each sibling, other members of the household such as aunts, uncles, grandparents, nurses or other helpers, and even pets.

This exploration of the childhood pattern from 0–6 usually gives a good idea of the central dynamics and is worth going into in considerable detail; the picture it gives can then be checked against other details, and having even a rough idea of this picture usually saves much time later.

It leads naturally into asking the patient for his *earliest memories*, making clear that we are not asking for his regular, continuous memories but for those little, often uncertain scraps and fragments that usually go far back to age about three or even two, or sometimes even earlier. These first memories bring us into an area that requires analytic skill in interpreting the unconscious.

It leads naturally into inquiring about *dreams*, especially recurrent ones, of childhood and through to the present.

If the pattern of 0–6 is well fitted and supported by the earliest memories and the dreams and seems to explain pretty well the patient's current life pattern and symptoms, then we can be reasonably confident we are somewhere on target even if not in the bull's eye in this preliminary formulation of this patient's central dynamics. At least, we have an illuminating formulation that can be modified in the course of therapy, and one that tells us what our goals in therapy should be. We are now working in the light of *understanding the patient* and not blindly plowing behind him trying to understand his associations without a perspective upon his essential dynamics, which is like a surgeon operating without a clear picture of the pathology and what his intervention is meant to accomplish.

During this search for the patient's central dynamics, the analyst has heard the patient describe his loves, hates, fears, ambitions, frustrations, and the like in ordinary language. Everyday English, developed by Chaucer and so amazingly advanced by Shakespeare (somewhat corrupted but also refined by slang) is admirably suited to the expression of every shade of feeling with clarity and accuracy, and is generally more precise than the broad, technical terms of psychoanalysis, such as "narcissism," "oedipal," and so on. Therefore, it is well for the analyst to shun these technical terms in understanding and talking with his patients. The patient usually will be speaking of his own "emotional forces," a term which seems logical and useful, for it signifies feelings and emotions, but also implies quite correctly that they are forces—the results of the forces of instinct (as sex), of motivation (as ambition or guilt), or of reaction (as anger or flight, expressing the flight-fight reaction). It does this without having to get into broad or narrow definitions of instinct, motivation, or reaction.

In general, it is conducive to clarity of concept to avoid thinking of the emotional forces in all their interactions in complexes, e.g., "oedipus complex" or "castration complex," but to try to dissect out each emotional force individually and then see it in all the interrelations with other emotional forces in the complex. For example, the drive to responsible independence and the regressive pull to dependence are two centrally important emotional forces. The regressive trend to be dependent and usually also passive very commonly creates feelings of inferiority and shame at being weak and childish, and these feelings make anger and sometimes exaggerated overcompensation drives to be strong and independent. These forces, in turn, often interact with needs for love, which lead into still other connections with other emotional forces. Therefore, the analyst must be thoroughly familiar with each emotional force and with its most frequent connections, but always able to keep the basic individual forces separate and in perspective (Saul, 1971, Chap. 25).

The ease or difficulty and the success or failure in discerning the childhood dynamic pattern in each patient depends upon the analyst's knowledge and familiarity with dynamics and upon his skill (closely related to this familiarity) in taking this sort of history (Saul, 1972, Chap. 5). But of course the success or failure also depends upon the patient's dynamics themselves, including most obviously the resistances. But whatever is learned is invaluable for seeing the goals of the therapy and for foreseeing the transference and resistances, so as best to be able to deal with them when they emerge as powerful forces in the analytic treatment. It is certainly true for the analyst that knowledge is power and to be forewarned is to be forearmed. It is always important for the patient as well as the analyst to have some idea of the prognosis, of how long and difficult treatment is apt to be, and what sort of result can be anticipated. If an analysis is not progressing well therapeutically, a careful, thorough, goal-conscious review of the 0–6 childhood patterns provides an instrument for investigating why it is not.

Summaries of each patient's 0–6 emotional pattern usually, with a little study by the analyst, reveal the essentials of their dynamics in a form which can be reduced to a brief formulation in a few phrases, on a card. It can then be discussed carefully in detail with the patient; if analyst and patient agree as to its accuracy, each can keep a copy—the analyst for his record and the patient for ready reference as he uses the insights of his therapeutic experience in his living, and while he continues to expand his consciousness of his own motivations and reactions, which of course derive so largely from his childhood emotional pattern and are usually mostly unconscious. This formulation thus provides a "dynamic diagnosis," which can be of help therapeutically as he lives his life and increases his insights, making his unconscious more and more conscious.

Personally, I have not always felt satisfied with the dynamic diagnoses that I have formulated (see Section II, "Clinical Observations"). These were first attempts, and they can be done better. But I am convinced of their effectiveness in clarifying the dynamics and aiding treatment, and also of their potency in most patients. If other analysts try them, they will of course develop their own procedures, which will no doubt become more accurate and effective. To make them requires study and work by the analyst outside the treatment session. But I think the patient has a right to this.

References

Saul, L. (1971): *Emotional Maturity*. Philadelphia: Lippincott, Chap. 25.
———— (1972): *Psychodynamically Based Psychotherapy*. New York: Science House, Chap. 5.

7
A VERBATIM INTERVIEW WITH ELSIE DEVILLE

The following patient was interviewed by the author in the presence of residents, as a teaching experience. Elsie DeVille was a patient in the hospital clinic, highly attractive and quite willing—even eager—to have the interview. Although our time was limited to only one hour, the technique of interviewing follows the basic method outlined in the previous chapter. Its value lies in the fact that it is *verbatim*. For although during an interview the analyst can jot down, in his own shorthand, an accurate account of what the patient is saying, it is obviously very difficult to concentrate on one's choice of words to the patient and write at the same time. A recording releases the analyst from this pressure and provides an *exact* account. This session with Elsie was done with a conference microphone on a dictating machine of the day; while not fully audible it does provide at least a fragmentary verbatim sample.

In this interview I tried to establish rapport on a simple, realistic basis by discussing the patient's main interests and profession, progressing as smoothly and imperceptibly as possible to the main questions about her 0–6. Time did run out before I could elicit Elsie's main dynamics as sharply as I wished, and I was not able to distill them into a clear dynamic diagnosis.

* * * * *

Introduction by the presenting physician, Dr. Dalton:

My patient is forty-three years old, divorced about six years ago; she entered therapy a little over a year ago, was severely depressed and was referred to the clinic by Dr. McDermott. At the time she started treatment in the clinic there was a very stormy series of outbursts which got progressively worse during the first months of therapy, during which time she was unable to work, she couldn't sleep, she was prone to hysterical crying spells. The content of her thoughts at that time was that she was too old for any kind of meaningful relationships, that she was no longer attractive, that the relationship she had been involved in for the last five years wasn't working out and she felt unable to either get out of it or get the guy to meet her needs—so she was in a fury about this. At the same time she was implacably angry with me; somehow I felt I couldn't meet any of her demands which were either to tell her to stop working altogether, to go find another relationship, and when I wouldn't tell her directly what to do, she would get very angry with me.

At one point, she became suicidal and had to be dealt with by me very strongly. I became angry with her at one point. Her history included hypo-manic periods—intense activity—and other periods when she was quite low and depressed, and no apparent clear-cut reason for some of these mood swings. She began cooling down, lost her hysterical spells, and in the ensuing year—in about ten months—she began to gain some insight into her relationship with her parents, which seems to be at the root of much of her problem.

Some brief family history:

Her mother is an Italian immigrant who is a very hard-working, perfectionistic woman, moralistic and demanding, rigid. She gives love conditionally; if you are good, you get love, if you are not good she withholds it. The father is a passive, weak individual who was so vague and distant that Elsie didn't even know what kind of work he did, even though he was in the same job for forty years. Her childhood was a difficult experience. They were poor.

She was engaged to a man whom she loved very much, but somehow that didn't work out; he couldn't meet her economic demands, which entailed no longer being poor. She really wanted an image of love and beauty to somehow counteract this past, so she got involved with a black Haitian, a flamboyant man, whom she married on the image of this very flamboyant wheeler-dealer, had two children by him, but the marriage was terrible from day one practically. She felt like a slave, and after twelve years of a miserable marriage got a divorce.

I don't want to go into too much detail . . . her problem, as I have said, was her depression, her inability to get into a good relationship now, and just feeling that she was "over the hill," that there was nothing more for her, a feeling that she couldn't get out of these destructive attitudes and relationships.

* * * * *

COMMENTS BY DR. SAUL: In practice, I usually allow two hours for an interview of this kind, but because we are limited to one hour today I believe I will begin by asking a little about her present life and present dissatisfactions and then get back into the point Dr. Dalton made, that her childhood had something to do with it. And then, of course, there is the question of why she has done so well in such a short time.

ANALYST: I am not going to be guided by what Dr. Dalton has told me; that is, let's just start in by my asking you about today. I understand you teach music?

PATIENT: Yes.

A: High school?

P: Yes.

A: And how do you teach that . . . do you have assignments, do you have instruments, or how is that done?

P: Well, in a comprehensive high school, which I'm in, they have all instrumental, vocal programs, theory, general music classes, piano classes . . . .

A: And you teach all this?

P: Yes, I have.

A: Do you teach harmony and various instruments?

P: Yes.

A: And piano . . . ?

P: Piano primarily.

A: Piano primarily . . . is that commercial or classical?

P: Well, reading music, that's a primary skill, and then they can transfer to any instrument, really. So we do read . . . jazz, of course isn't written out at all, it's improvisational, so they do read classical music, mostly serious music.

A: So it's really more learning music than it is sight reading . . . I mean, they don't have to sight read?

P: Well, they do in theory classes, which is the attempt to get them to read at sight.

A: Do you like teaching music?

P: I love it!

A: Is that your love, is that for you?

P: Yes, it is.

A: You know, there is an old saying, "Blessed be he who has found his work. . . ." The other half of it is, "Let him ask no other blessedness. . . ."

P: I enjoy the students, it's not so much the music, but it really is the kind of feeling I have when I am working with students in the classroom.

A: Maybe it's both.

P: I love music, yes, but I think primarily it's working with the youngsters.

A: So you have no complaints about your profession, it's a great success?

P: Yes.

A: What is your day like, then; what time do you get up and when do you have to get to the school?

P: Eight twenty-five; it's a very short day, we have no lunch period. We work straight through, and we are finished at one twenty-five, but I rarely leave before three: I always see students after school.

A: You have a good healthy blood sugar, I gather!

P: I feel fine; it's after school I think when I begin to make the switch to what's happening, to how I'm feeling personally.

A: Would you tell us a few words about that?

P: It always seemed that when I was in school I felt my whole self, and when I would leave I would begin to get the feeling that I have now, like I couldn't breathe, like I was immobile, that I couldn't handle what was happening on the outside to my life.

A: So the profession is great, but the big, bad world is not?

P: Or my world, at least.

A: Well, it's not that easy for anybody, Elsie, don't you agree? Who do you know that it's all that easy for, who handles it all that well?

P: I think some people probably *look* like they are handling it pretty well . . . you look like you're handling it very well.

A: But I have been at it a long, long time. Do you want to be a little more specific about why it is so difficult for you after you get out of school?

P: There are any number of things . . . let me start first with my son . . . I have a son and a daughter, and they are now pretty well grown up, but I feel totally responsible for them, a great deal of pressure; I am not married any longer, but when I was married I felt meaningless, even though I worked very hard. I was always there, fixing the meals, running the house, doing everything. I just didn't feel there was any meaning in it for me, I felt empty. It was like coming home and going to a hotel, strange. I felt like I wasn't connecting.

A: How old are your children now, then?

P: My son will be twenty shortly, and my daughter sixteen.

A: And where are they?

P: My son is at the University of Chicago and the girl is in tenth grade.

A: And your feeling of being disconnected . . . why do you think that was?

P: I didn't think that my husband at that time saw me or appreciated me, and from his behavior I felt used . . . totally used. With my children I was always so busy, had things to do at home, and now it seems that I never really talked to them, never really knew them.

A: Today?

P: No, in looking back it seemed that way; in retrospect, it seems like it was just work.

A: But how about today?

P: I feel a lot better; there are times when they want to talk to me, when they are coming to me . . . .

A: And that you like?

P: Oh, yes, that's a good feeling.

A: But I thought you said, when I asked you what troubled you, when you left the school at night, didn't you say your children?

P: Well, I started with my children . . . that was one thing. I just felt really guilty, first of all about the marriage, and especially guilty because I married a Haitian—it didn't work out. It was an interracial marriage and all of a sudden I just felt very guilty about putting them in that situation.

A: Your children?

P: Yes. And I used to just look out for everything . . . I had to do everything for them because I was so afraid that they wouldn't be successful, they wouldn't achieve . . . but in actuality . . . . Well, I would keep looking for neurotic things that they might do . . . .

A: Have you found any?

P: No; my son has a little twitch once and awhile, when he gets a little nervous, but he . . . it doesn't bother him as much as it bothers me. Every little thing, I think "Oh he's going to turn out to be . . . ." He is very bright; he has an "A" average in school; he is doing very well. But everything was exaggerated to me.

A: In your mind, you mean?

P: Yes.

A: So you were a little of an overprotective mother? Overanxious, anyway?

P: Overanxious, yes.

A: So you are bothered in life about your children, but that is more within yourself than any real trouble that they are in?

P: Yes.

A: They seem to be doing fine . . . .

P: Yes.

A: Well then, what else bothers you?

P: Myself . . . when I first came here last year I felt that no one really cared. There was never a person in my life that cared about me.

A: Is that reality? How far back does that feeling go? You said "never in your life," but your life starts nine months before you are born. I will settle for starting at birth . . . .

P: I just remember that my mother was always very busy . . . we were poor. I don't remember ever really talking to either of my parents; I don't remember any conversation, any experiences, I just remember seeing my mother ironing, for example. . . . I remember looking at them but never having any other kind of communication.

A: Now were you raised with brothers and sisters?

P: Yes, I have an older sister, 16 months older, in California.

A: Has she been having any kind of emotional problems?

P: Well, she is married for the third time, but she seems to bounce around like a ball; she never seems to get down—she seems to be very flexible.

A: Well, after all, she's in California where three times isn't so often to be remarried! Let me put this last question in a different form: What do you consider the main feature or features of your life below seven years old?

P: The main feature was a routine . . . a schedule every day the same, and Sunday I went to church.

A: And what was your routine every day?

P: Just eating breakfast, and even that I don't remember . . . I remember sitting there, but I don't remember any words. When I was an adult I used to say, "Can't you *say* something?" Everybody would go "Ummm." It was just a routine—we would get up, my

clothes were always washed and ironed and in the closet, everything was neat, I would go to school . . . I *loved* school. I would
walk home and practice the piano, that was it. We had no parties,
I can't remember people coming in; we didn't have a telephone, a
radio or anything like that. It was just a very routine existence.

A: Was that in Chicago?

P: Yes. When I was three I went to Europe for three years.

A: But you think what you have been describing . . . . I know you don't
remember from birth to three, or I think you don't . . . but do you
think what you have been describing might have been true for those
very early years?

P: Yes, I feel almost certain that it must have been that way.

A: Now the gist of that would be disconnection, lack of emotional
relationship? You say routine, but as you describe the routine it
sounds as though you are complaining about it because there was a
lack of closeness. Am I wrong about that?

P: Now I guess I am saying all that, but as I look back, I always used
to say that I had a wonderful childhood. I don't ever remember
being worried or anything . . . it just seems to be a right kind of
childhood.

A: Was it secure?

P: If I had to say how I felt then, I would have to say, "No, I didn't
feel secure." I don't know why, because I keep looking at this
proper situation where I did have parents who worked very hard
and I had meals cooked, and everything done for me, but I don't
think I felt secure . . . I felt insecure.

A: So the main feature was routine, but as far as your *feelings* go, what
did you feel?

P: I guess I felt . . . I remember playing the piano and I practiced and I
used to have visions of not being in that situation, visions of my
becoming a great musician, and that seemed to be my world, any
emotion seemed to be when I was practicing. I can remember at
night—I had a very small bedroom and there was this window that
looked out over factories, and I used to feel that someday I am not
going to have to look at this. I will be in a beautiful place with trees
and I'll have a handsome man that will love me very much. About
the only place this really came out in my life was when I was playing
the piano.

A: What kind of work did your father do?

P: He worked at a factory.

A: Did your mother work?

P: She worked in a laundry for 20 years without missing a day. That's my mother!

A: Is she still living?

P: Yes, both of them are.

A: Healthy?

P: Yes; my father has a heart condition; my mother just goes on, there's no end.

A: Goes on with what—the routine?

P: Oh, yes, she has the worst routine that I know. She still works very, very hard.

A: She has adapted to her routine?

P: Yes, I think that is happiness for her, being able to work and take care of my father.

A: How young were you when you started playing the piano?

P: I was very young . . . I think about five or six.

A: And the trip to Europe, did that change anything? What part of Europe was it?

P: Northern Italy near Trento.

A: Did that change anything? How long were you there?

P: Three years, so my first language was Italian. And when I came here I spoke nothing but Italian. It didn't change anything. However, with the war I can remember feeling torn all the time, because we lived in an Irish neighborhood and we were one of the few Italians there. My mother had four brothers, two of whom were in the Italian army, and two in the American army. And I was feeling torn all the time because everyone was against the Germans and Italians, of course . . . hate, hate, hate. So of course I grew up . . . I don't remember specific situations but I just grew up not understanding . . . my mother's brothers in the Italian army were killed, and I remember her crying and it never made any sense to me, the whole thing; I have the feeling now that I had then: this is stupid, why are you hating?

A: You could still say that to the world today, couldn't you?

P: Yes, yes . . . .

A: It was like the Civil War, brothers fighting on both sides. But our time is so short, there are things I want to cover to get to the main issues with you. Let me go back to that birth to age six again, and put the question a different way: Whom do you consider the main persons in your life, emotionally speaking, from birth to age six or seven?

P: My mother.

A: Do you want to go into some detail about that? She was the main person in your life during those years. Now what was that relationship with her, emotionally speaking?

P: It was a very dependent kind of thing. It was as though, if she disappeared, the world would crumble, there would be no more routine, I wouldn't be able to go to school, I wouldn't be able to do anything because my mother was always there and always had everything ready. She made things possible.

A: Now your father, what was your relationship with him? Rather, let me restate that: Your mother was of first importance; who was of second importance?

P: That's difficult, because I don't know my father.

A: Don't let me suggest anything to you; take the time to think.

P: I think it was my mother's brother, one of the two that were here, because they lived with us. I related to him more.

A: More than to your father?

P: Oh, yes, more than to father. My father . . . there is just nothing there, one way or the other. You are talking about *feelings*—I don't remember any feelings toward him.

A: Well let's go back to your mother. I got things a little out of order there. What was the emotional relationship to your mother? I asked you about the most important person in your early life and the details, and as I understood it, the most important part about mother was that she made the routine, so if mother wasn't there the routine would collapse and there would be no world. But is it part of the same question, or could I ask, what is your *emotional* relationship to mother? You have described her as a housekeeper, who ran things, but what was the emotional feeling? How did she feel about you and you feel about her?

P: I have to make the assumption, the way I am feeling now . . . she *was* a housekeeper and she always was taking care of us physically. It's funny, but I can remember a tub in the sink—I don't know how old I was—but I remember taking a bath or getting washed off or something. . . . That was it; I don't remember holding, or anything aside from just having breakfast and so forth.

A: And do you remember your feeling toward her, anything at all?

P: I used to sometimes feel like crying; I used to feel that she was so wonderful, how come she had to work so hard, take on all those burdens. I felt sad that she didn't have a big house, and I sort of resented my father a little bit for not making that possible.

A: And so you are saying that you sort of identified with your mother and felt sorry for her but had some resentment of your father because he didn't give her more.

P: Yes, he didn't make the world better for us.

A: As you think back now, do you believe that those were fairly constant feelings?

P: Up until recently, yes. Now I feel very differently.

A: All right, how do you feel now?

P: If I have resentment, it is more toward my mother. I was resentful because I felt that she should just let it drop, this whole business of breathing for everybody; you know, just let us *be*, let us *grow*. And then when she responded in trying to be the kind of person that I just described, then I felt love for her. I could see that she wanted very much for me to love her. She really needed that, she just couldn't put her arms around me. I talked to her a lot about her childhood. She raised four younger brothers . . . she was responsible for everything, a tremendous amount of work, in Italy . . . she remembers nothing but work and that's why she came to this country, because she was told she could not go on to school, she must work, so she left.

A: Was she in a town, a city?

P: A little tiny town, nestled in the mountains.

A: And she worked so hard as a sort of farm girl?

P: This is sort of interesting . . . her father left when they were very young in the war—I don't know what war that was—he was gone until she was six years old. She really didn't know her father, and her mother worked like she did. From what I could gather, her mother would always say, "Now do a good day's work." She used to clean the mayor's house. And she didn't have the time to come home . . . she would run into her house to see her mother when she was going to the marketplace on an errand for the mayor, to get the fruit. And I asked my mother, "Well, what did your mother say?" and she told me that her mother would ask her if she was doing a good job, if she were working hard . . . and she was only about ten or eleven years old. And then I began to understand my mother a little better, and the resentment sort of disappeared.

A: That makes it hard for me to understand you . . . because if you know your mother's background, you become so sympathetic with her that it becomes hard for me to find out whether, as a child, you were missing something or had resentment against your mother. As you got a little older, then, after six or seven, did things change?

P: Nothing changed.

A: Your relationship to your mother was the same?

P: Absolutely.

A: You said she ran the house and "did" for you, but I don't get the feeling . . . well, you even did say, she didn't hug you.

P: I don't ever remember her doing that . . . never remember being held, or any of that kind of closeness.

A: Do you think that it was a loss, did you miss something by not having that?

P: Oh yes, I think so, because now, when I talk to her, that's what I want. And I've told her this . . . it sounds simple, but that's really what I wanted I think. She still can't do it; I went over to her and put my arms around her, but I really wanted her arms around me.

A: Do you think that was a strong feeling during childhood?

P: I don't remember thinking about it in childhood, but I feel it was really important. It makes me feel good now, so I feel it would have made me feel even better then.

A: But when I asked you about it before, you got sympathetic with your mother and said you wished that your father had given her more. You were sorry that she had such a hard life. But whatever the reason, whether she had a hard life, or her mother couldn't give love to her . . . I am struggling with whether it is correct or not to say that you missed something, in demonstration of affection.

P: Yes.

A: Now is there anything else that you think was not right in relation to your mother?

P: I think that because she was always perfect in my mind, always doing everything perfectly, I sort of felt if I were not perfect myself, I wouldn't get her love; she wouldn't love me unless I followed the same sort of routine she did and did exactly the same sort of thing, going to church, being kind to everyone, all those things. I felt if I weren't that way then she wouldn't love me.

A: Okay, very good. That is, very clearly expressed. You say she imparted a high level of behavior, not verbally, but by example?

P: By example . . . I don't remember verbal things, but I just remember seeing her and the whole image in my mind is of her being a very Christian, right person.

A: Were they Catholic?

P: My father was a Catholic, and I don't think it made too much difference to him. My mother was a practicing Protestant.

A: What denomination was that?

P: Lutheran.

A: Was she pretty strict about that?

P: Well, we just went to church; I don't remember her ever saying we *had* to go, but this was our life, we just went . . . until I went to . . . graduated high school. And then my life changed. I went to Northwestern, I began to talk to other students, and then my life was broader, but up till then you went to church every Sunday and you just sort of did it I guess . . . I never questioned it.

A: Now let me ask you about your mother's brother. What was the relationship with him like in childhood? He was the second most important person for you emotionally.

P: The reason that I say that is because, he would go up to his room and play his harmonica, and I loved him because of that, because it was something he was doing that no one else did in the house. No one else would think of doing something like that. He seemed freer, somehow, a free spirit. And my mother treated him as the younger brother, she took care of him, she took care of everyone. But I liked him very much because of that . . . he would go up to his room after dinner and play that harmonica and I somehow felt closer to him.

[Lapse while record was being changed.]

P: I guess I was angry about that; I was angry at being poor. I guess I blamed my father. I resented not being in a superior position in life. I resented just the situation.

A: Do you think you resented your mother, that you were angry at her?

P: No, I don't remember it, I don't remember resenting my mother, at least until now when there's a lot of resentment.

A: And now why do you resent her? Why do you think now that you might have resented her then?

P: Because the important things . . . it's as though she is always work-ing and never *seeing* anything. She never seemingly feels any warmth, or is able to express it. She is always so busy taking care of us and her friends, and everyone adores my mother . . . they think she is a walking, living saint. But what I resent is that it is really like *ignoring* someone. It's like someone going through papers and they put their head up, off the cuff, but they are really not listening, their real interest is reading. That's the kind of feel-ing I have, but I don't like it. I want people to look at me once and awhile. When I told her I was sick, when I first came here what I wanted was not, "What can I do?" or panic—I just wanted *love*, I wanted her arms, I wanted her love. I looked at her and all of a sudden I saw that she loves me and her way of expressing that is always taking care of me . . . .

A: Do you think it would be too strong a word to say there was a certain amount of deprivation of love in your childhood?

P: No, I don't think that would be too strong.

A: Or maybe we should say, *some* deprivation. Do you feel pretty secure that that is the right definition?

P: Yes . . . a physical demonstration of love.

A: All right, some deprivation of a demonstration of love. And then, is there an element of strictness with herself as the model—you should work, you should go to church on Sunday, you should love everybody, you should have these high standards. Do you think it would be fair to say there was an element of somewhat over-strictness? Because you never branched out until you went to Northwestern? And you liked the uncle because he played the harmonica. Here I may be wrong but it sounds a little as though he were a freer spirit because he could go up and . . . .

P: Somehow he cut that dead routine, the sound of this harmonica.

A: How would we put that? Some overstrictness?

P: It wasn't that she enforced it as much as she was the overriding power, and it was her example, the only example I had. And it was like sort of I used to look out at the neighborhood—two weeks after we arrived in that neighborhood there was a picture in the newspaper, "The Cleanest Block On the South Side," and it had flowerboxes . . . so it was by example. It wasn't that she said, "You should go, you have to go" . . . .

A: So she didn't beat you into it?

P: No, I never was spanked. It was just that she was mother and you followed this example . . . she was overriding, a Valkyrie.

A: Now the question in my mind is, whether there was a certain resentment on your part toward your mother which was repressed because you loved her so much. With children who are sort of deprived, there is always a tendency to make mother into a goddess.

P: You hit the nail on the head, I think. Because I used to always say to myself, "She's so beautiful, she's so perfect, how could I possibly feel that anything is wrong with my mother?" That was the whole story. I am in my forties now, and I am just coming to realize that now . . . all my life I've said she is so perfect and so loving because her whole life has been one big sacrifice for her children and her husband . . . it never entered my mind, and it must have been very repressed, and I never could have come out and said like I say *now*, "Mom, really, will you stop bossing everyone?" And she likes it now . . . she seems to have adjusted to the change in me, but for years I could never say anything. I used to say to everyone, "I have the most wonderful mother in the world!" and I *do*, I really do. But I was never able to say along with that, "I don't like the way she sort of takes over and runs everything."

A: I know a couple of your dreams after consulting with Dr. Dalton, but we simply don't have time to go into them here, so I am going to try to put this all together. My question is whether there was this resentment toward your mother, very repressed, because you loved her so much and she loved you; she never abused you so that you could be mad at her if she spanked you or did something wrong. She was always very nice, very proper, very loving. Whether you resented her for those two reasons we did touch on: a lack of physical demonstration of affection for one and running things; a little too dominating, if that is the right word. It would have been different if she had let the house get a little dirty and taken her children in her arms. It may be your needs for love are intensified, so that today, at forty, your needs for love may be too strong because they were not that well satisfied at four. And there may be some resentment about that. And then the standard of strictness, imposed by the atmosphere of the family and the model your mother gave you caused some resentment because it wasn't as free as your uncle's. So maybe there was some resentment to your mother, but it had to be repressed. In her way she loved you, and in her way she took care of you, and in her way she was an angel, so you couldn't get mad at her. And now, have you tended to take out the anger on yourself? That's a difficult concept . . . it took me years in the field of dynamic psychiatry before I believed it even. I ask that because . . . are you familiar with the term "masochism"? Handling things in a way that makes oneself suffer?

P: Yes.

A: I don't want to overemphasize that because, you know, Winston Churchill said how hard it is to know our own self-interest. That's not all internal because the world is a very difficult and complicated place to find your way in. But I wonder if you repressed, because of these two main reasons, the resentment against your mother, because she was so good you could never take it out on her, and therefore tended to handle your life in a way that made you unhappy. For example, making an unhappy marriage. You have the looks, you are a teacher, you are an artist, you had all this going for you—why did you not find out until *after* marriage that it was not going to work? As I understood it, you found out almost instantly.

P: That's true. I think that it happened before I got married; the marriage wasn't the first indication.

A: Are we talking about doing something that was self-injurious?

P: Yes, that was a result of . . . I had fallen in love when I was nineteen, a first love, and I was physically close to the person, and when that didn't work out I felt like the worst person in the whole world. I think when I was in love it didn't seem evil, but when it was over, oh, boy, that's when I was immoral and a really rotten person.

A: This is a slightly different point: when you fell in love which involved the physical, that was going against your mother's standards, so then you felt guilty.

P: Yes . . . .

A: And then you punished yourself. And I wonder if your manic-depressive swings aren't very largely that, that you get so tired by being constricted by this early training and the work ethic and doing nothing but that, and when you break loose and throw off all this constriction, this thick layer of conscience you feel marvelous . . . .

P: Then when I am back at work I feel . . . .

A: When the guilt piles up, your conscience beats you down.

P: Right. And I think that's why I always felt so good in school. In contrast to my personal life . . . in school I feel right and good about myself and like a queen. I feel marvelous; it's like feeling powerful, not a horrible kind of power, but I feel wonderful, like I can just ride the waves and create and walk about. I love the kids and I love myself and I feel marvelous. And then, when I would come out of school all these things would gnaw away at me. I remember the year after I broke off my first love . . . it was just horrible, like being dead, I couldn't do anything, I couldn't listen to music, and I think I got married . . . .

A: On the rebound?

P: Yes, it was just so painful that I just couldn't live like that anymore.

A: I don't want to oversimplify it, but I think various of the themes, if we might talk in polyphonic terms, are in your motivations; and it is the masochism, the anger, turned on you, but of course the guilt from transgressing your mother's standards and the loss of love—it was your first love, you had it, and now you've lost it. So this really hit you in your emotional solar plexus and your point of least resistance—your emotional vulnerability. That's rough on everybody, but with your background it was particularly sensitive. I don't know if this adds anything new to what you have already been over with Dr. Dalton, but I'm sure he can help you with all of these things.

P: I feel good now, as though I've let out my whole life; I feel much better than when I came in.

A: That's great that you are able to do that. You know, insight alone doesn't cure everything, but that's the first step. If you are able to see what is going on, if you are conscious of it, then you are able to do something about it, like with your mother—you have talked these things over with her. If you don't know what's going on you are at its mercy. But we must stop now.

I am glad you have your music. You are not the first musician who has had troubles . . . you are in good company. You know, Beethoven was deaf and went through a suicidal phase, he was really depressed and couldn't hear—and music was his life. I don't know if you have ever read his letters, but he decided, "No, by God, I'm not going to let it get me down; I'm not only going to live and not commit suicide, but I'm going to go ahead with my music," and as a result he wrote his first symphony. He didn't write it until he was thirty years old. Best of luck to you, Elsie.

[This is, as I am sure you know, a "good ego." She has good powers of perceiving reality, of reason, and she has control of her behavior, her executive functions; in addition to this, there is a lot to work with. She has a musical talent, she loves what she does, and this is the kind of case one likes.]

*   *   *   *   *

When Dr. Dalton introduced me to the above patient, I was surprised. It would be no exaggeration to call Elsie beautiful. She was simply and tastefully dressed and well-groomed; her manner was pleasant. She smiled readily and seemed well poised, not only at the introduction but throughout the interview, and also seemed unaware of the 20 residents listening in attentive silence.

I wondered at the beginning of our interview what sort of dynamics would emerge from this poised, charming, attractive woman. Afterward, when some of them had been revealed, I wondered how many of the residents or indeed any observer would have been astute enough to perceive the complicated unconscious machinery behind this attractive part of Elsie's personality. Certainly I for one could not have envisioned what would emerge in our talk beforehand and what world of dark forces we would uncover. Elsie had good defenses to protect her, unlike those who seek to satisfy their internal frustrations by closeness to another person and then, when these frustrations intensify, vent their hostility on that other individual with rages and suicidal impulses.

8
A ROYAL ROAD TO THE CHILDHOOD PATTERN: THE FIRST TEN OR MORE DREAMS OF TREATMENT

A central problem in psychological work is how to make brief psychological diagnostic descriptions of patients. The formal diagnostic terms are mostly only descriptive and are not sufficiently specific for individual cases. To give a significant picture of each patient's psychopathology, the description must convey the main points of the psychological structure in psychodynamic and economic terms, as well as the status of the conflict and of the ego. This chapter is an effort in that direction.

The significance of the patient's first communications and early dreams in yielding insight into his psychology are well known (Freud, 1909). In endeavoring to make genetic psychodynamic formulations of cases from semiverbatim psychoanalytic records we have found the shortcut provided by the early hours and dreams to be a great time-saver (Saul, 1940). This experience has confirmed the generally accepted observation that the early current dreams of the analyses usually give the essence of the case. This has been demonstrated by following the later course of the analyses in many of these cases and also by a study of all the dreams in a number of others. Indeed, the most accurate and complete formulations are made by returning to the early dreams after a thorough study of the entire case and of all the dreams. But this is time-consuming, and as a shortcut the first 10 or 15 dreams alone usually yield a satisfactory formulation. These are usually more revelatory because they are not yet so much influenced by the transference and by interpretations and resistance material.

Adequate formulations cannot be made in all cases, but only in those in which the dreams are reasonably well understood. In a few instances no real structural formulation is possible because the resistances are so strong or the material is too chaotic and does not show sufficient structural organization. But they are the exception.

After the available data on the history and present situation are read, each of the first 10 current dreams, or more if necessary, is studied with its associations. After one understands the dream as thoroughly as possible, an effort is made to formulate the main tendencies seen in it. These are written down for each dream, and then all the dreams and notations of the main tendencies are reviewed for the central features that they have in common. The aim is to get a formulation from a sentence to a paragraph in length, of the main trends and their interrelationships that are seen to run through all of the dreams. Studies of the types of dreams in different psychological conditions have been made by other authors (Hitschmann, 1935).

Since there is a great deal of material in every dream, it has proved helpful to limit the scope of the formulations and to pay special attention to certain features. Each dream is studied as thoroughly as possible, but the interpretation is confined to those tendencies that are readily apparent in the manifest content in the light of the history, life situation, and associations. Very deep material or that which is only distantly alluded to in the manifest dream may not be included.

Secondly, a great deal is learned about the kinds and degrees of repression and about the status of the ego by paying special attention to the part played in the manifest dream by the dreamer himself in his own person.

A third important consideration is the status of the conflict situation, including the kind and degree of solution of the conflict as gratification and of the fight (hostility)–flight (regression) reaction, particularly as these appear in the manifest content of the dreams.

Formulations which include these points are usually adequate for general purposes of psychodynamic description and diagnosis. They are of course never complete, for there are unsolved problems in every case and every dream. For special studies additional formulations may be necessary in order to emphasize particular factors, for example, the balance between giving and getting.

* * * * *

To understand the basic dynamics of any case, including the main childhood pattern, more work may be required of the analyst than only "evenly hovering attention." There are at least two other procedures besides the analyzing of each hour that help the analyst in understanding his patient. The first is the review of the patient's major emotional pattern from 0–6, already discussed; the second is the one suggested here—a review of the early dreams of the therapy. The first involves sacrificing one or more regular analyzing sessions and taking rather detailed notes. The second requires keeping a record of the first 10 dreams and associations from the beginning of regular therapy. But this additional effort on the part of the analyst is well rewarded by increased understanding of the main dynamics of the patient, and by doing the regular therapy in the light of this understanding and thereby shortening the therapy and reaching its goals more securely.

The dreams which follow were collected for a different purpose, namely a study of hypertensive patients (Saul, 1940). This makes them all the more objective and useful as examples. The first patient, Maxwell Clark, was a forty-year-old successful businessman, with his own firm. In his childhood his mother had been sexually seductive, possessive, restricting, dominating, and controlling, using the patient for her social ambitions and grossly preferring him over the father. The patient's sister never broke away and remained a slave of the mother. The father was of a lower social level, somewhat crude, a rather heavy drinker, rebelling against his wife's domination mostly by drinking.

The patient's associations during the first seven sessions, which preceded the first dream (which occurred in the eighth hour), dealt almost entirely with the fear of being caught in forbidden sexual situations. A few of these were as follows (the first was an early memory): At the age of about five when he was in bed with his mother and younger sister, he reached toward them with sexual interest and then stopped because of fear. At the age of fourteen, he was nearly caught by his mother just as he wanted to touch the leg of a girl. Once when he went with a woman to a hotel, he was so afraid of the hotel clerk that he was unable to sign the register.

Further trends in the patient's psychology will be obvious from the early dreams. A typical situation recurs in almost every dream with certain omissions and alterations: The patient is with a woman in a direct or sublimated sexual situation, and fears, sometimes defies, another person, usually a man.

Although it has proven preferable to utilize at least ten dreams in making formulations, and ten were used in this case, in the interest of brevity six will be sufficient to demonstrate the point. I have tried to select a case in which the dynamics are relatively clear from the manifest content alone. Hence very few associations are given. No attempt is made to give a complete interpretation, but only to define the main trends.

*Dream 1**

(a) The patient is on the analytic couch. The analyst, on a chair next to him, is urging him on and straining with him like a football coach, saying "Out with it!" The patient does not resent this.

(b) The patient is in a box at the theatre with Miss C. Three or four men are in the box and are stealing glances down her evening dress at her breasts. The patient greatly resents this.

The associations reveal that the patient was having a clandestine affair with Miss C. and because of his anxieties was tortured with doubts as to whether or not to break it off. The transference meaning of dream (a) is that the patient wants encouragement from the analyst to help him confess what he is reluctant to reveal, and dream (b) shows this anger at the analyst's seeing what is revealed. Dream (a) shows further resistance against something, clearly sexual, being seen, and leads to the confession of the clandestine affair with Miss C., which is fraught with such anxieties as to cause the patient to be tortured with doubts about breaking it off.

The first part of the dream reveals a passive submissive wish toward a man and reluctance to confess (on the couch: urged by the analyst), which causes resentment which the patient denies. In the second part is seen the tendency to relinquish a heterosexual and oral attachment to a woman, and to a feminine identification. The patient reacts with resentment.

Dream 2 (nightmare)

The patient is in bed with Miss C., just to sleep, with no idea of intercourse. Mr. O., a puritanical businessman, calls the patient

---

*The numbering of the dreams denotes the chronological sequence of the dreams in the analysis.

and the patient tries to protect Miss C. from Mr. O.'s knowing that that it is she. He feels a terrible fear, tries to cry out and cannot.

The associations lead to a boss, a father figure whom the patient hated, feared, and defied.

This dream is perhaps the most characteristic one for this patient. In this dream he is caught in a forbidden sexual situation and feels intense fear; he is paralyzed and interrupted with a woman by a masochistic wish toward a father figure upon whom the patient projects his hostility, which reappears, as in the first dream, in the form of looking. The looking is directed toward the woman with whom the patient identifies. The transference reference is obvious—hiding the affair from the analyst, whom the patient expects to be puritanical, and censorious and punitive like his father and mother.

Dream 3

Some narrow-minded church-going people expect the patient to do something with a trout which is a girl, his wife and daughter. He is to prepare it for cooking but he drops it in the fire and then reproaches himself. He wonders if it tastes like trout, which is expensive. It is burned to ashes. Then there are books on radical sex literature and prostitution.

Again, the strict superego versus sex is evident. Also the emerging themes are submission and hostile protests against obligations. To the trout, he associates his wife's expensive tastes, and his intensely hostile wish to be rid of her and of his feeling of obligation toward her.

In this dream the patient rebels against submitting to his mother, represented by the church-goers who want him to do his duty toward his wife, whom in reality his mother selected for him. His rebellious anger is turned against his wife, whom he gets rid of with consequent guilt (and from whom in actuality he was divorced). He rebels against legitimate sexuality and wants the illicit.

Dream 6

The patient meets a brazen girl in the elevator of his exclusive men's club, into which no women are allowed. In this dream, the patient is again in a forbidden sexual situation.

He is inhibited in his feelings toward the girl by fear of the men and at the same time defies them by being with her. He says that he would like to be brazen but is afraid to, and reveals a degree of identification with the girl.

Dream 7

The patient hears Miss C. scream with pain. He asks if she has a good doctor and wants to go to her but his wife prevents it.

This is yet another repetition of the situation of being prevented by his mother from going with girls. It shows his hostility to the girl and, through his association of analyst with the doctor, shows his masochistic feminine identification with her. It also foreshadows what became overt in his associations and later dreams, that the patient turns toward the girl the hostility he feels against the analyst (originally toward his mother).

Dream 9

Miss C. is in the position of the analyst, behind the patient. He is her guest. She has little on and leans over the patient. The patient is happy.

To this dream the patient associates feeling depressed while walking with his girl and telling her not to be like his wife, whom the patient identifies with his mother, as the previous material has shown.

In this dream a beautiful girl is substituted for the analyst, thus seeking a solution to the conflict between superego and women and to his feminine identification. This type of dream is rare for this patient. Unlike the other dreams in which he is in an unsolved, anxiety-laden conflict situation, he here permits himself a little more satisfaction. But even this is alloyed, as the associations show.

In his dreams, as in life, the patient is paralyzed in the situation of being sexually agressive toward a woman (mother or sister figure) by fear of a man (father figure), from which he cannot escape. He is inactive, inhibited, or rejecting toward the woman, who is inactive, and he is inactive toward the man, who observes or threatens the patient or the woman or both. This manifest scene represents, in part, his sexual attraction to his seductive mother and his fear of his father; also his hostile rebellion against his mother's domination, which he transfers to men as well as women; his hostility to women, displaced from his mother to other women; and his competitiveness with men, displaced from his father. Also typical is the lack of a solution; he can neither (1) submit without feminine identification, hurt pride, and rage nor (2) rebel and find freedom (sexually and otherwise) without intolerable anxiety.

Thus a series of manifest dreams, early in treatment, even without associations, often provides a window to the patient's unconscious through which the analyst can see in dramatic form the central dynamics more simply and clearly than can be discerned in long hours of associations. Out of the maze of the patient's reactions in his life and in the transference, the dream very effectively and conveniently selects the essentials of the dynamics; in sleep the patient temporarily sheds most of his many reactions to the externals in his life that complicate his free associations.

The early dreams of another patient show a typical situation that is almost identical with the one just described (Alexander, 1959). Two dreams will illustrate this:

Dream 1

The patient is at a hotel with a girl. He avoids the public rooms where they might be seen and goes with her to a room where a man, apparently asleep, is lying on a couch.

To the girl he associates illicit sexual relations and to the man, industrial spies.

This dream thus shows the same conflict in a slightly different status from that shown by the first patient. He fears that the man will see him with the forbidden woman, and does nothing.

Dream 2

The patient is with his boss and a prominent woman. He secretly takes a drink. He thinks the lady prefers to be with him and they do succeed in getting rid of the boss, but the patient is afraid the boss has seen him drinking; so nothing happens.

This patient also is in a situation with a man and woman, and is inhibited sexually toward the woman by his fear of the man. The scoptophilia, primal scene references, and identification with the man and woman are also apparent. However, this patient got some satisfaction by drinking, which the early dreams reveal as chiefly a substitute for the sexual relation to the woman and as defiance of the father.

Dr. Roy Grinker, Sr., has kindly put at my disposal some dreams of a man with a nuclear conflict situation of similar content and status to that of the preceding two cases. The following dreams will illustrate this:

Dream 1

The patient goes to the house of a married woman and is going to have intercourse with her when something displeases him. He has difficulty in getting dressed. Her husband then walks in and then the patient's mother.

Dream 2

The patient is talking to a blonde girl who is small-breasted. He asks for a date and she leans over so that her breasts touch him. Sexually interested, he takes off his coat and vest, but then in the dining room he sees a group of men who are in authority over the patient and he becomes rooted to the spot.

Here again we see the patient paralyzed in the sexual situation by fear of a father figure. The oral component, in particular the detail of the breasts, is also similar to that in the preceding cases.

A young woman brought the following dreams early in her analysis:

Dream 1

Some girls are invited to dinner by an older man, but not the patient.

Oral competition with sisters for father—thwarted receptive.

Dream 2

A boy spits on the patient.

Masochistic receptive soiling.

Dream 3

A male teacher is present while the patient fights with another girl for a pencil but gives up.

Competition with sister for father—thwarted.

Dream 4

· The patient gets a bag which breaks and soils her.

Masochistic receptive soiling.

Dream 5

Patient sorts packages for someone.

Somewhat inhibited giving.

Formulation: receptive competition (with sisters for father) causes anal hostility (soiling), which through guilt results in (1) some over-compensatory rather inhibited giving and (2) turning of the hostility back against the patient (masochistically being soiled); and this masochistic soiling element, in receiving, causes severe inhibition of the receptive wishes.

* * * * *

This method of formulating cases is particularly useful when the patients themselves are not seen, but only the psychoanalytic case records are available for study. It is here that they prove an especially valuable shortcut, since the records are so voluminous that reading them is extremely time-consuming. In this brief chapter other formulations are not included.

One often sees a similar nuclear conflict, but in a somewhat different status. For example, a male patient frequently dreamed of being interrupted in a sexual situation. The interruption usually took place by a motherly woman, often carrying food, and the dream terminated in a rather satisfactory oral relationship to her. In other cases the nuclear conflict itself is different, such as that of the woman in the preceding example. One feature of the dreams of those cases reported above is the status of the hostility and sexuality, both of which are always aroused and are continually unsatisfied, although just on the verge of expression. This method is therefore a convenient one for comparing the nuclear conflict and its status in different psychosomatic and psychoneurotic conditions.

In sum:

1. By analyzing approximately the first 10 current dreams with their associations and reviewing them for common features in the conflict situation, role of the ego, and types of defense, and confining the interpretations to material that is readily apparent, it is possible in most cases to discern the main psychological features of the patient.

2. This method is therefore a convenient one for comparing the nuclear conflict and its status in different psychosomatic and psychoneurotic conditions.

References

Alexander, F. (1959): Psychoanalytic study of a case of essential hypertension, *Psychosomatic Medicine* 1(1):159.

Freud, S. (1909): Notes upon a case of obsessional neurosis, *S.E.* 10, p. 158.

Hitschmann, E. (1935): Beitrage zu einer Psychopathologie des Traumes, II. *Intl. Ztschr. f. Psa.*, XXI, p. 430.

Saul, L. (1940): Utilization of early current dreams in formulating psychoanalytic cases, *The Psychoanal. Quart.* 9:453–469.

9

OTHER DREAMS DURING TREATMENT

The formulation of the basic conflict situation from the dreams is of value not only for research purposes, but for the practical understanding and handling of many cases, especially those obscured by intense resistances. By reviewing the dreams for the main conflict situation that runs through them in all its variations, the central problem is brought into sharper focus, as are the patient's various methods of dealing with it, and the analyst gains a perspective which is otherwise difficult to achieve.

* * * * *

I. Cyril Mitchell is a brief example of the use of dreams in making a formulation:

He was beaten up regularly by a playmate who lived only a few doors away while Cyril was still a baby, from age two to three or four. This created an anxiety which drove him into an intensified dependence upon his mother. It resulted in a fixation, so that when he became a young adult and strove to make his way in the world, he had strong feelings of regression. Later on, he reported two dreams:

In the first dream, his young wife to whom he had been married only one year was divorcing him.

In the second, he was taken prisoner by the Mexican Army, but they were so inefficient that he managed to escape. He found refuge in a cave, but there was a dinosaur in the cave. Then he realized that he could talk to the dinosaur and it was a reasonable creature.

To the Mexican Army and being a prisoner he associated being in prison in the graduate school he was attending. The dinosaur he associated with the analyst, who was reasonable but also a threat. The threat, he said, was that if one becomes too dependent on anyone, then he is in their power. The cave reminded him of childhood and play and also of his mother, and of how at every possible opportunity he spent time at home with his mother. The gist of the dream was that he wanted to get rid of the responsibilities of adult life; he dreamt that he got rid of his marital responsibilities to his wife and also rid of his career responsibilities, going to school to be trained to be financially independent and self-supporting. He wanted to escape from both his marital and career responsibilities, to go back and be a small child cared for by mother. He was really in treatment with the analyst in order to help him make a goal of his life and be more independent; therefore, the analyst appeared as something threatening, although needless to say the analyst (myself) knew very well that it is better not to side with the patient's superego. The interpretation could not be avoided that to relinquish his wife and studies would be to ruin his life and court a nervous breakdown. Here again we see a patient's childhood pattern reflected in his dream, in this case split up into two dreams. We also see how the dreams confirm the childhood pattern. The hostility in the dream is evident; during this period, the patient expressed a lot of this anger by being mean, irritable, and sometimes cruel to both his mother and his wife. The reason for the hostility was that it was part of his fight-flight reaction. While he was tempted to relinquish his responsibilities toward wife and career, he was also in a rage at having to meet them (see the chapter on "Responsibility"), although so far he *was* meeting them in spite of his wishes for escape.

* * * * *

II. Years ago, Miss Q.'s dreams were recorded for a study on possible emotional factors in urticaria (Saul, 1941). The interviews at the time of Miss Q.'s attacks of urticaria often contained dreams. Therefore, we have a record of a patient which contains a series of dreams that can be reviewed today, not for their original purpose but to learn if they reveal any consistent pattern. They seem to, and it is a very different pattern from that of the foregoing patients. It provides a further example of what we are studying here: the existence in a patient's dreams, especially those early in the analysis, of a recognizable basic pattern formed in early childhood and varied only in its aspects and details. The following is excerpted from the original article:

Chief Complaints and Medical History

Miss Q., a pleasant, somewhat obese young woman in her middle twenties, with episodic severe, generalized urticaria especially about the face and eyes, gave a medical history which was not typical of a reaction to any commonly recognized specific allergen, nor was any clue discovered in an exhaustive allergic work-up by an allergist, including extensive skin tests, elimination diets, allergen-free room, eosinophile count, and so on.

On the other hand, she was upset emotionally. She suffered from migrainous headaches, dysmenorrhea, bulimic tendencies, feelings of incompetence, nightmares, and anxieties. She attributed all her current complaints to her "nervousness."

Life Experiences and Reactions to Them

Her mother divorced in order to marry the father when both were not yet 20. When the patient was one and a half her sister was born, and when she was two, her mother died, owing, it was rumored, to violence from the father. The father then married a divorcee and the children were placed in separate orphan homes when the patient was four. A year later, in 1917, he took them back in order to avoid the draft. He was always engaged in illicit or shady enterprises and served several prison terms. The patient was well treated by the stepmother until the age of six. Then the stepmother began to accuse her of things she had not done, for example, scratching the furniture, and would get the father to force a confession. This he did by cruel treatment with a sexual tinge. He stripped her and burned her with a poker, held her under water in the bathtub, forced her out into the cold scantily clad, and so on. This, she complained, was the only kind of attention she received from him. As soon as the children could help, they were put to doing charwork in the father's saloon and brothel. They knew abuse and drudgery, and the ostracism of the neighborhood and almost no pleasure. They longed for a good mother and a good father. Exposed to violence and promiscuous sexuality, they were forbidden all companionship with boys by the suspicious parents, who constantly accused them of sexual behavior and who threatened to shoot them and any boy they might be seen with. At the age of about eleven, the patient made three suicidal attempts.* At twelve, she succeeded in getting a job in a nearby city. With her first salary she bought ice

---

*At least one of these was serious. This was by cutting her arm and wrist necessitating five stitches. Previously she had attempted suicide by drinking hydrogen peroxide, and on another occasion by swallowing a bottle of black pills. At three, she fell through a trap door fracturing her leg, and still carries a scar of a gash on her leg which occurred when she fell while jumping at the age of ten.

cream and consumed all she could possibly eat. Through hard work she brought the sister to live with her and helped her through school. The patient did well at secretarial work and helped the sister until the latter's marriage at the age of 22. The patient was then even more miserably lonesome. She was befriended by a girl her own age, Miss N., who took her to live in her own poor and emotionally tense family. About this time the patient began going with a young man her own age upon whom she became dependent for male companionship, but who made no sexual advances, and who despite his abilities and his intentions of marriage, was perpetually unable to find a position which would have made the marriage possible.

The patient reacted against her early sordid, sensual environment by constant but only partially successful struggles to rise above it. She daydreamed of fair princes, love, and dancing at gay restaurants, and strove strenuously, but inhibitedly, to improve herself through night school, dramatics and discussion groups, and the like. But in her dreams she was often back in poverty, being attacked by a cruel man who clearly represented her father. She tried to break completely with her father, but could not. She was dependent on him emotionally, hated, feared, loved, and pitied him. Because of her masochistic dependence on him she was sexually repressed and frigid.

Throughout the analysis she had not a single frank, open sexual dream. Her sexual wishes appeared only in an extremely masochistic and never gratified form, such as being chased by a man with a gun or a big stick. The men were usually thinly disguised representatives of the father. Her extreme fear of sexuality was due to the severe repressiveness of her sexual training, to her concept, based on her early experience, of sexuality as something degraded, and to guilt from her own hostilities to her sister, stepmother and father. Moreover, during the analysis, she had not a single dream concerning impregnation.

The patient's Cinderella-like history reveals a childhood of drudgery and abuse in sordid surroundings, with no pleasure or escape except in daydreams of love and romance. Grown to womanhood, she retained these intense longings of her childhood, but was unable to satisfy them through a normal sexual life because of her fears.

She dreamed of a man with a high hat and a beard, very understanding and helpful, but who could never marry because his legs were paralyzed. And in life she became attached to such a man—one who gave her companionship and understanding and who made no sexual advances.

* * * * *

1. At the first interview on October 5, the patient spoke of how anxious she was for analysis, how she envied other children for having mothers, her expectation of marrying when her fiancé found a job, how inferior she felt about her education and her father's being a bootlegger, and how she hoped for help, having always helped others without thought of reward. The main theme was her thwarted wish for love and help.

2. A week later she came in with her upper lip swollen and reported that she found it to be so on awakening. During the night she had *dreamed:* "Father came to the office to say goodbye." She went on to say that she always feared doctors and was ashamed to tell them things. She then told of her father's marriage to the mother, his reputed violence to her, his cruelty toward the patient at the instigation of the accusing stepmother, to make the patient confess, and his sending her away to an orphanage. From the associations, the dream seems to indicate the patient's longing for her father, but also her wish for him to leave. She was reacting to the analyst with a pattern she had toward her father, as though the analysis was like the confession situations of childhood. She wanted the analyst's help and love but feared that, like her father, he would punish her and send her away. Again we see that her longings and expectations, in this case toward the analyst, were aroused but threatened with frustration.

3. Over a month later the patient reported that for the preceding weeks she had awakened almost every night sobbing, her pillow drenched with tears. This was always following a repetitive *dream* which recurred since early childhood—a long dream of which she could only remember the endings, that some object she had set her heart on slipped away through her fingers just as she was grasping it, leaving her terribly disappointed. Sometimes it was a figure in a white flowing robe. The object reminded her of her "wishes and ambitions, air castles which had not come true." She thought the figure was her mother, and that this repetitive dream reflected her childhood longing for the maternal affection that she had missed. Now, she said, she again felt that she was reaching for someone she could not get. She

then spoke of the intensity of her cravings for romance and their invariable disappointment. At adolescence she saw other girls go out on dates and parties, while the patient was not allowed to, even at sixteen, although she craved to. At fourteen she had a bad case of puppy love for a boy of sixteen, but when he talked to the patient, she ran away. At fourteen she yearned to be kissed by a boy she was in love with, but when he tried to she kicked and scratched, and thought that, if she did, she would be a bad girl and have a baby. Books and movies made her imagination run wild. Her unsatisfied wishes were overly strong, she said, because as a child she never got the affection she craved. It is clear that these internally frustrated sexual wishes were now directed toward the analyst, and that at their nucleus was her yearning for the love and affection of a good mother. She wished to satisfy these yearnings through a sexual relationship with a man, but was unable to because of her fears.

4. On January 7 she told that she awoke with hives from a *dream* that another girl's work was in a basket with the patient's and the patient could not tell which was which. The patient said she would help the girl, who was crying, but was so nervous that she was of no real help. In reality, she said, this girl was the new one at the office. She was motherless like the patient, then her father died, leaving her penniless, and now her boyfriend had died. The patient sympathized with her completely and tried unsuccessfully to get help for her from one of the women bosses. The patient became angered at this boss for her refusal of help. This dream is a reproach against the analyst for not helping the patient. In it she identifies herself with this other lonely, longing girl and takes the same compensatory protective attitude she had toward her sister. She demands consideration and help for the girl, and tries unsuccessfully to give her what the patient wants for herself. Her longing and frustration are self-evident from the dream and associations.

5. On January 18 she reported three *dreams:* The first was about a man who was shot. The second was about traveling. The third was her repetitive dream of reaching for something which slipped through her hand. Omitting further material, the dreams showed the patient's anger at her father, now at the analyst, because of her frustrated wishes and her feeling that because of her anger she would be sent away (traveling) and lose him entirely—the satisfaction slipping through her fingers.

6. On January 19 the patient *dreamed* that Miss A., the girl who

the preceding Christmas had invited her to visit her and her father in a neighboring town and whom the patient liked very much, repeated this invitation. The patient was very anxious to go but on the way to the station remembered an engagement with an elderly woman and at the very last minute did not go, and the girl was angry. Again last minute frustration.

7. The patient *dreamed* that she was married to a man who looked like her father. He slit her throat so she could not tell something, threw her down the stairs from the attic to get rid of her, and then ran away as the patient tried to yell. The patient thought that even though dead she would haunt him. At the end of the dream it flashed through the patient's mind that this was a punishment for something that she had never dared tell the analyst, namely, that in childhood she and the little girl next door experimented with each other sexually. We see here that she feared to confess her sexual impulses lest the analyst punish her and get rid of her as her father threatened to do.

8. The patient's fiancé actually got a position and urged her to marry him. But the position was a very poor and menial one, not at all in line with his ambitions, and in tragic contrast to the patient's dreams and expectations. She would even have to continue working. Urticarial swelling of the right eye occurred that evening and was followed by a *dream* in which she was to marry a young blonde man, not her fiancé, but in the end gave him up and was to marry the fiancé. Associating, she said the analyst was not blonde, and recalled that the preceding week she had *dreamed* directly that it was the analyst whom she was to marry. Now her marriage meant to her giving up her hopes of marrying the analyst and all the hopes that he had come to symbolize.

9. On January 17 she reported a *dream* in which her fiancé's mother brought her a wool suit in which to be married. The patient refused it and went to get the blue street dress she had decided upon for the occasion. But at the shop they did not have the dress and she was terribly disappointed. In associating, she said that she had given up the idea of having a white bridal costume, and felt that she must be satisfied with something practical. She did not like associating to blue because it made her afraid that she was really depressed about the prospect of her marriage, and went on to talk of a friend of hers who married a doctor—a wish of the patient's toward the analyst which now faced frustration.

10. On Friday, January 13, the patient had a long *nightmare* in which she was nearly attacked by a crowd while eating with her fiancé, and which ended with the patient's pinching the arm of a girl in a white satin dancer's costume who was looking longingly inside of a nightclub. The patient was very angry at her for trying to show that she was a goody-goody, when really she wanted to enter this place to dance or sing. The repressed and frustrated desires and exhibitionism are clearly seen at the end of the dream, while the anger and guilt appear in the first part.

11. On Thursday, February 2, when the patient was just getting over her menstrual period, she reported that for the past days she had been in a terrible mood, as was usual for her pre-menstrually. She had been angry at her fiancé, and her skin itched and was irritated. The preceding night she had *dreamed* that as she and her fiancé were singing before an audience, her belt and dress fell off. There was also something about her father's being shot—or only wanting to stay in bed. This too turned out to be a mostly transference dream; her dress falling off while singing indicating seductiveness toward the analyst; the shooting was her anger, on the pattern toward her father.

* * * * *

In summary, the most constant feature of her dreams was her being on the very brink of a longed-for satisfaction, basically to be loved, now appearing in the form of sex and marriage, but not quite achieving it, with resulting frustrations and anger.

Of course, it cannot be too strongly emphasized that the basic childhood emotional pattern does not appear neatly in all dreams, even in the early dreams in the therapy of a naive and previously untreated patient. Depending upon the repressions and the patient's reactions to the ever-changing life situations, one or another part of the pattern appears in the dreams, more or less fragmented and distorted. Nevertheless, if the analyst will keep a record of the first ten or more dreams of treatment he will find that in most cases recognizable patterns do emerge even if in bits and pieces which can be fitted together like a jigsaw puzzle, and they are invaluable for understanding the patient.

References

Freud, S. (1930): Civilization and its discontents: *S.E.* 21.
Saul, L. (1941): The emotional settings of some attacks of urticaria, *Psychosomatic Medicine* 3:349–369.

SECTION II: CLINICAL OBSERVATIONS AND EXAMPLES

To find the childhood emotional pattern and formulate it and to formulate the dynamic diagnosis briefly and accurately requires openmindedness and alertness and also concentration, study, and hard intellectual work. And so does using this pattern and diagnosis for analytic psychotherapy. To free the patient from the inexorable automaticity with which these patterns often determine his mental and emotional life can be a formidable task, requiring of the analyst enormous energy and a bulldog tenacity and determination to outlast and wear down a pathogenic pattern which constitutes the neurosis or other pathology. Therefore, the motto for this section is the old Blackfoot proverb:
Makokit-ki-ackamimat ("Be wise and persevere").*

The following clinical observations are notes on patients made and saved by the author for possible research use while he was at the Chicago Institute for Psychoanalysis from 1932 to 1942. One of these patients was seen for an hour or two after the war. All names are fictitious, and particular circumstances and other details have been altered. Any resemblance to persons in the present must be because of the universality of these patterns and is purely coincidental.

These notes were selected to represent the most common, typical, and frequently seen symptoms, situations, problems, and dynamics: deprivation, seductiveness, domination, gross preference for a sibling, and so on.

*From *Long Lance*. New York: Farrar & Rinehart, 1928.

10
SUMMARIES OF CHILDHOOD PATTERNS AND DYNAMIC DIAGNOSES

We now turn from the more sophisticated and laborious utilization of dreams to direct clinical review of the childhood emotional relationships as a method of discerning the childhood emotional pattern and dynamics.

The road between childhood emotional pattern and the (largely unconscious) motivational patterns of adult life is a two-way street, but unequally so. As analysts we are trained to discern these early patterns and their effects in the adult for health or neurosis. But in some small part we can travel the reverse route: if we see a person who is being given ample love and recognition but still feels unloved and deprived, we know that we must look for deprivation and lack of love in that individual's childhood, which has shaped his pattern. The same holds for the passionate rebel without a cause: the source is probably rebellion against some form of tyranny or mistreatment during 0–6 that has shaped this pattern. Thus the present dynamics provide us with clues as to what can be traced back to longstanding traumatic formative experiences in early life, particularly the most malleable period, 0–6.

In the following, after a review of the present complaint, life situation, and current dreams, we will concentrate on asking the two questions mentioned in Chapter 6, as this seems to be the most direct and rapid method for reaching the main dynamics:

1. First, the general question: "What is your memory or impression or what do you consider to be the main feature or features of your emotional life from birth to age six or seven?" The goal is to get the patient to select the main features.

2. Then the specific question: "Whom do you consider the most

important person or persons for you from 0–6?"—going on to ask specifically about the interrelations with *each and every figure of importance* during that early period, mother, father, each sibling, and any other individual who was of significance.

3. After this the earliest memories follow naturally. Some of them will already have been given, but usually more will be obtained if the patient's mind is directed to them.

4. Then follows inquiry as to dreams during childhood, especially repetitive dreams.

Very full notes should be taken by the analyst and studied or read over at leisure some evening shortly afterward.

In this clinical section, the effort has been made to select those patients for whom notes were available from the Chicago files who seemed most typical:

1. Patients deprived during 0–6
2. Those who were overprotected or dominated or both
3. The adored only child, the little "prince" or "princess" displaced by later siblings
4. The sexually seduced and inhibited, or those subjected to sexual seduction

These patterns are seen so frequently that the relatively few examples which follow should serve to make the point.

Usually it is extremely valuable to have in writing not only the dynamic diagnoses (the childhood emotional pattern and the current psychodynamics) but also summaries several pages in length, such as those presented in the following examples. The reason for this is that no matter how excellent the analyst's memory, he will find on reading his summaries that certain key details, important for therapy, have escaped him; also, bringing to mind this clinical picture of the essential dynamics of the patient will facilitate his therapy and increase its effectiveness. It is extra work for the analyst but well worth it.

In the following pages we concentrate upon the emotional pattern that causes the patient's symptoms, i.e., the pathologic patterns, the *patho*dynamics, and not on a formulation of the *total* personality with all its strengths and traits. We are alert to these qualities but need not necessarily analyze their sources because they are not causing the patient's suffering. Rather, if we reduce the symptoms and suffering, it releases these strengths and positive qualities to give the patient a better life.

In the author's experience it is almost always valuable for insight and therapy to use an hour or more after some months of treatment to *review* the patient's childhood pattern of interplay of feelings with the main persons of childhood prior to age six or seven. These summaries of the patient's childhood pattern can with some thought themselves be reduced to a few sentences written on a card, which provides a "dynamic diagnosis" of the main interplay of emotional forces in the patient which underlie his psychopathology and cause his symptoms. A copy of this card can be given to the patient, who can thereby see in black and white how the analyst understands his or her central problem. This dynamic diagnosis falls naturally into two parts: the childhood pattern and the current present-day dynamics. It can be a potent instrument and must be used with the usual analytic tact and caution. For example, Arlene Rodgers (whose case follows on p. 95) felt great relief when we entered on her card "loneliness" as a feature of her childhood pattern. "Why," she exclaimed, "I can feel lonely!" She went on to explain that this was a bad word during her childhood for family members were supposed to be one big happy family, and loneliness was forbidden.

We have defined psychodynamics very roughly as the interplay or dynamic balance (or imbalance) of emotional forces in a person's mind. Psychodynamics is not a certain structure of concepts in itself which can be learned from theoretical formulations. Understanding psychodynamics poses two difficulties: (1) the important interactions vary from person to person, are often similar but probably never identical; and (2) the interplay is for the most part unknown to the person himself, i.e., mostly unconscious. However, as a guide and an introduction to the study of psychodynamics what we *can* do is list and discuss the major emotional forces involved, and the most common of the interactions between these forces. (See Saul's *Emotional Maturity*, Part II and this book, Chap. 2, p. 7).

Familiarity with these basic universal human emotional forces and their most common constellations alerts the observer to what to look for. But easy perception is achieved only by much practice in reading the unconscious. The experienced analyst perceives and understands what is going on in his patient almost without regard to whether the patient is aware of it or not, so easily does he slip into seeing the forces and their operation in the patient's unconscious. Of course, his job as a therapist is to know with accuracy what is within the patient's awareness, but the experienced analyst's own understanding is not impaired because certain forces are unknown to the patient. Psychodynamics is learned by constant and varied practice in life as well as in the office. In this volume we must restrict ourselves to clinical observations in the office practice of therapy, but we give a sufficient number of illustrations for the perceptive reader to detect the similarities and differences in their dynamics, as well as to acquire some practice in reading the unconscious revealed through early history, first memories and dreams, symptoms, and behavior in life.

11

THE AGE OF 0-3

Scientifically speaking, the present state of psychoanalytic knowledge and of psychodynamics is, I think, one of first approximations, rather than precison. Getting the childhood pattern during the age period 0-6 is still a good, solid guideline or guiding principle. That is the important age period in the formation of personality and pathology which Freud so accurately observed. However, we have already pointed out the importance of not keeping to this rigidly but of examining and evaluating influences during 0-3 and 6-16 also.

Age 0-3 is of course part of 0-6. It is an important subperiod, for, as we have mentioned, it is related to the more serious emotional disorders. We can take 0-6 for neurotic disorders in general and 0-3 for the borderline, more severely neurotic and even psychotic disorders. An example is Wilma Blake. In this instance, we can be sure that the trauma did occur from 0-3, because when the patient was three years old the family moved from one town to another.*

* * * * *

I. Wilma Blake: The Princess

Wilma had dark eyes and blonde hair, was slender and somewhat above middle height. There were some things that the family thought she was too young to remember, which will be related below, but Wilma did remember them and afterward, when they went back to their old house and she told her parents about these events, they had to admit she was correct. Both parents were interviewed and confirmed the accuracy of these memories. On the other hand, I do think it is somewhat unusual for them to be so complete and so vivid before the age of three. In what follows we will go beyond the age of three, but these memories before that age will be readily recognized.

*NOTE: Material in brackets in this case and other cases indicates the analyst's thoughts during the interviews with patients.

I had seen Wilma a number of years before these notes were made; she had been so disturbed as to necessitate hospitalization on several occasions and had been cared for by a colleague and friend of mine who was so located that he could take charge of hospitalized patients, and had proved excellent at this, especially with these borderline young adults. In such cases he was often able to get them out of the hospital rather quickly, continuing them in treatment in the office and saving them and their families much anguish and expense.

Wilma's interview with me occurred at her request. She said it had been a long time since she had seen me and she had wanted to do it; I was delighted on several counts: I liked her and wanted to help in any possible way, and I was interested professionally to see how she was. I knew there were some unanswered questions about her basic psychodynamics and wanted to see if answers could be elicited. It was a good sign therapeutically that she who had been hospitalized with a psychotic regressive-passive withdrawal was capable of so sustained a positive transference.

By now, I had already learned the power of this procedure in questioning the patient in order to ascertain the main features of the childhood pattern, and proceeded as follows:

"Wilma, now that you have brought me up to date on what you have been doing and your present life, I would like to take the next hour to review your 0–6 because I have sometimes found that it is useful to do so."

She agreed readily. I said, "What do you consider were the main features emotionally of your very early years?" thereby starting off with the more general, less-leading question.

She replied, "I do not remember my 0–3, but I was told that I was very angelic and I was loved to death. Friends would come, and I was very huggable and lovable. The first thing I remember of 0–3 is the day my younger brother, Walt, was brought home from the hospital with my mother. [Clearly this is an emotional triangle with Mother and new brother, a natural reaction after being 'loved to death.'] I was then not quite two years old. I remember some woman, perhaps one who became a nurse for us, standing in the kitchen boiling the baby bottles. Then Mother was on the couch with Walt in her arms, and I reached out to touch him and Mother gently explained to me not to touch his head because it had a soft spot which would harden up later on. [This is possibly a faint hint of repressed hostility to Walt.]

"My next memory is of being on the couch and Mother putting Walt in my arms.

"My third memory was of the big room we had just off of Mother and Father's bedroom. I went in there and remember Mother sitting up in bed, and she suddenly said to me very sharply, 'Why are you up?' and I said, 'I have to go to the bathroom.' I assume that Mother was nursing Walt, but I felt as though I were being reprimanded for something that was not justified. [Some hostility from Mother, possibly playing into Wilma's hostility from sibling jealousy, and possibly guilt for it even at that young age.]

"My next memory, the fourth, was of my four-year-old sister, Alice, taking Walt for a walk. He was in his pram and it turned over. Alice said, 'Stay where you are,' and she ran back to the house. But I left and ran back too. [Another suggestion of hostility to Walt.]

[It must be here noted that I had not asked Wilma to give the main emotional features of her 0-3 but simply of her very early years. It was she who spontaneously spoke of her 0-3.]

"I have no memory of Father from 0-3, and I know it was age three because at that time he was transferred by the big company for which he worked to a nearby town and we all had to move. I guess we were very fortunate that the move was nearby and not at a great distance. Then I remember (fifth memory) the day we moved . . . Walt and I were sent to stay with two older women while all the preparations were made. I don't know for sure, but it was naptime I think and they wouldn't let me nap in the same room with Walt, and I threw a temper tantrum and ran outside and hid behind a bush. One of the elderly ladies came out and told me that the German sheepdog next door would get me if I did not come in immediately. I was scared but stubborn, and stayed hiding and wet my pants. Then the other elderly lady told me later that the little girl next door never did a thing like that. To me, it is all like a horrible, bad dream but it was real. Then Dottie came to take care of Walt and me. I vaguely remember something about her. I was supposed to eat my lunch with her, and I threw another temper tantrum because I did not want to. Then I went up to my mother's room, but Dottie came up there for me. She told me to come away gently enough, but I thought she was horrible. I just did not like her. Even today I have very mixed feelings about her. I used to have dreams about her being fired or killed by some young people, who then would take care of me and Walt. [Identification with and attachment to Walt and anger at Mother figures for its frustration, partly turned against self.]

"One of my older sisters said that Dottie was not warm, she never picked me up, but was very strict. But she taught me to read. When I was about nine she left and Walt and I were frantic. This was during the summer. Mother never told us that she was going to go, and it was not until fall that we realized she wasn't coming back and we had not been able to say goodbye to her." [These earliest memories all contain her brother Walt, signifying her close attachment to him, but also suggesting hostility to him because of jealousy for Mother. The second highly charged person is Dottie, the nurse, with dependence in her but also hostility to her because of her lack of warmth and her strictness.]

Now I felt it was time for the more specific question and asked, "Who was or were the main persons emotionally in these earliest years?"

Wilma was silent for awhile, knitting her brows, apparently trying to think. Finally she said, "I had no memory of Father. Of Mother, I have an image that is very . . . (she hesitated) well, not just all one feeling . . . that Mother was on a pedestal and unreachable. For example, Walt and I were taken for a walk by Dottie *every* afternoon, no matter what the weather. Then one day Mother said, 'Why doesn't Wilma stay with me for the afternoon?' and to me it was as though a queen had stepped out of the house. Mother was way up there. She was out of reach. I have no memories whatever of Mother ever hugging or kissing me."

I said to Wilma, "What you have said so far sounds like an intensified attachment to your mother because (1) there are no memories of your father so she was evidently the main one of your parents, and (2) there was a lack of closeness to your mother which probably increased the yearning for her, and (3) there was apparently her strictness."

"I think that is right," said Wilma. "For example, Mother never put us down for our naps . . . it was only Dottie. A little later, when I started kindergarten and first grade I would run home for lunch and the lunch would be with Dottie. I would just have time to say 'hello' to Mother who was busy with some sort of work in her study. Supper, Walt and I had with Dottie and then we spent a few minutes with our parents before going to bed at 7:30. I guess I had such great closeness to Walt because I was not close to Mother and did not like Dottie, but we also had terrific fighting, probably sibling rivalry.

"When I was seven, I was allowed to eat dinner with Father and Mother, and Walt came too . . . I had to wait till I was seven, but he was only five. He did not have to wait till he was seven. If anything did not go quite right at the table it was 'Go to your room until you can apologize.' Walt would return in fifteen minutes, all relaxed and apologetic, but not I. People said, 'Why are you so stubborn?' My brother Claude was six years older than I. He and I were close, and it was Claude and I against Alice and Walt. When Claude left I was devastated."

"Sounds a little," I said, "as though (1) because Mother was distant and (2) because you were displaced by Walt that when you did not get these strong persisting needs for Mother satisfied you went into a rage and got the stubborn symptoms. In other words, the need for Mother and a mother-figure persisted so strongly because of her distance and the displacement by Walt, the frustration was strong because the need was strong, and you became enraged and stubborn."

"Yes," said Wilma. "Mother kept a notebook about me, and she says I always tended to have an excessively close relationship with a single friend and did not get on with groups at all well. [Probably Wilma's pattern of the ambivalent but close relation to Walt.] Also, she recorded that a teacher said, 'Wilma is too good to be true. I would like her to splash a little mud on herself, than I would feel better about her.' [Probably the teacher sensed the too strict repression of hostilities by Mother.] When I did not get the love I wanted, I simply decided I would get no love. [Probably the pattern toward Mother.] When I went into the hospital the first time for my breakdown I was very distant from the nurses. They were all nice and trying their best, but I simply refused to respond."

At this point I asked Wilma, "What kind of love do you want and did you want?" The colleague to whom I had referred Wilma, who had been carrying on the therapy with her, was named Taylor. Wilma replied again, "Dr. Taylor said the kind of love I want is the kind that only an infant can get. It was a long time before I listened to Dr. Taylor, but when I started listening to him it made a big difference. It was then, when I listened to him, that I met Russell, my present boyfriend, in fact, the first relationship I have had since boarding school. Russell and I discussed this; he did not have such a good childhood either. If he is away for a day I sometimes become terribly depressed. Then one time I went away and when I returned Russell was in bed. I complained about this and asked him what was the matter. He said, 'Because I am so dependent on you and you were away.' I did not want to tell Dr. Taylor how dependent Russell and I are on each other. Russell did not really have a mother . . . she was there, but she was not there emotionally. She was not giving; she had lots of emotional problems and she was divorced. The children were a burden for her and she had an affair which led to a divorce.

"My older sister has such different memories from mine about her childhood with our parents, that when she talks about them it sounds like an entirely different family. She remembers Father and Mother teaching her to jump rope, to ride a bike and so on. I can't even imagine that they were ever like that! Also, Mother was so strict, had such high standards. My oldest sister—you know, I am the youngest of seven—asked me why I thought the next sister married one week after graduating from college . . . she explained that she was so dependent on Mother that she transferred this to her boyfriend. And also, that she married to escape Mother who dominates everything. Russell's family has taken me in completely, made me one of them, and my brothers and sisters have all adopted Russell into the family. But my mother refuses to accept him, and I am so angry at her."

We had now run out of time, and I took the last few minutes to ask Wilma some questions, to ascertain whether or not her mother was in reality so strict and so dominating, as well as what she had already described concerning her mother's being so distant.

Wilma confirmed that as best she could. I reminded her that in my only contacts with her parents, her mother was always very solicitous for her welfare, but Wilma answered this by saying, "She would not tell the truth about the early days."

I said, "I think she cannot, even if she wishes to, because she could not understand well enough what was going on in your feelings in those days nor how her behavior was affecting you."

Wilma then said, "Well, that is certainly the case with Russell. When I told Mother we were going together she became extremely angry and said that if we lived in sin it would kill her. My father, on the other hand, was very paternal, very fatherly. He understood and said he would try to win over Mother to his point of view of feeling that, whatever happened, I was his daughter and he would try to help me. I tried to talk to Mother very reasonably, but she became so furious and went so out of control that there was no use my saying anything; I just sat there and listened to her. Now Mother blames you and Dr. Taylor and the hospital for everything, and will have nothing to do with you any further."

Needless to say, I hoped that this was a temporary state of mind of Wilma's mother, and said so, adding that probably she would gradually quiet down and recognize that Wilma was her daughter and she must do her best for her. Certainly, at least at present, she could not face her own part in causing Wilma's problems, and if she could defend herself by blaming Dr. Taylor and me, that was perfectly fine with us . . . so long as Wilma got proper care and consolidated her gains. I think what precipitated Wilma's visit to me was the fact that her father had been her support through this, but when she confided in him that she and Russell planned to get married a few months hence he reminded her that she was not entirely well mentally and said, "How can you take on such resonsibility when you are not sure that you are sufficiently stabilized?" This, however, we hoped could be handled because it sprang from her father's true interest in her welfare. But at the moment Wilma was standing up to both her mother's opposition to living in sin and her father's opposition to marriage. Assuredly, she was gaining stability.

I talked with Dr. Taylor, and we agreed that the main thing was that Wilma should do what was wise in every marriage, if she should go ahead with it: namely, to wait at least two years to see how the marriage "shook down" before having a child. That was the responsibility and the biological experience which at this time Wilma did not seem ready for.

Other notes add that Wilma first had sexual experiences—actually of a slightly promiscuous nature—when she was in boarding school. This apparently was for three reasons. The conscious reason, as she had told me, was that it was a fine boost to her ego, the fact that boys wanted her. Also, rather than being in her mother's power she felt she was in command of the situation; she would have relations with a boy for a certain period of time and then get rid of him. However, she kept the relationship with one of the boys for nearly three years. When she met Russell she told him all this. He had a natural reaction at first of being very upset, but then was understanding; so she felt she had no secrets from him. The other reason for her promiscuity was the closeness she lacked to her mother in her home—in fact, the closeness she lacked toward anybody except Walt. But that was an intensely conflictful relationship, because of the hostility in it; she also had some closeness with her older brother, Claude.

Besides the ego boost, the feeling of having some control over the other person instead of being controlled, as by her mother at home, and the closeness she had lacked, there was also some element of angry rebellion out of frustration of her dependent love needs for being sent off to boarding school. This was a matter of mixed feelings, but it intensified the frustrated dependent love needs which she had had at home.

In this perspective, it might be that her relationship with Russell was a considerable advance because it involved a real mutual psychological relationship of identification and mutual love, and, in the background, mating as evidenced by their plans to marry. The sexual experience at boarding school seems also to have been at least in part a sort of declaration of independence, an attempt to emancipate herself from the emotional involvement and submissiveness and frustration which she felt within her family. It was a step for her toward independence in the world, even though a strict moral standards it meant a loss of virginity and therefore something to be deplored. At any rate, she seemed to have come a long way in her development from that time to the time when these notes were written, when she was twenty-one years of age and apparently had a perfectly normal, monogamous love relationship with Russell.

The analytic task that remained was to diminish the intensity of those elements in her childhood pattern which caused such a powerful flight-fight reaction as produced her symptoms of violence, mostly self-directed, and her almost total withdrawal, to the extent of having breakdowns with masochistic and suicidal trends which necessitated hospitalization. If the intensity of the feelings in this childhood pattern could be diminished so that she no longer had serious symptoms, then the outlook for Wilma's future life would be favorable. The severity of the symptoms, the necessity for hospitalization, and the difficulties in therapy did seem to stem from the fact that the childhood pattern was so strongly laid down, not only by the age of six but before she was three years old.

Just before Pearl Harbor she and Russell married, but I did not get to re-establish contact and learn the rest of her story.

Dynamic Diagnosis: Wilma Blake

Childhood: (1) Deprivation; Mother distant and turned patient and two-year-younger brother over to an emotionally distant, strict nurse. (2) Pushed out of little she had from Mother at age two by younger brother. (3) Mother's dominating, strict high standards led to hostile rebellion and stubborness. Items (1, 2, 3) led to patient's excessive needs for closeness to Mother (and Mother figures) and identification with Brother, combined with hostile sibling rivalry to him and hostility to Mother, causing guilt and anxiety with strong fight-flight.

Current: Patient's dependent love needs intensified plus rebellion against strict authority and control, leading to increased fight-flight; (1) hostility mostly turned inward as suicidal gestures and actual attempts, and masochistic exposure to danger plus over- or under-eating and stubborness, against own health and interest; plus (2) the flight as almost total withdrawal from people and regression with auditory hallucinations.

Strengths: Became evident only after complete collapse and hospitalization when finally (1) she could listen to analyst and (2) could accept human relations, especially with an eligible boy.

II. Terry Weston: Anatomy Is Destiny?

Terry Weston had been coming to see me on and off for several years. When I first saw her, she was generally unhappy; she had just broken off a relationship with a man whom she had admired a great deal and who was very kind to her, and she was also in the process of terminating her relationship with a woman. She had begun an affair with another man and was seriously considering marrying him, yielding to his wish for her. Her tension seemed to be so great that I feared she might have a breakdown. The beginning with her was very difficult because of this tension, which might lead to I knew not what, combined with a strong flight reaction—her tendency to want to escape it all and go to a foreign land. Also, she had considerable anxiety about starting any analytic work and an obviously strong tendency in herself toward independence and doing it herself. She finally started, however, not so much on the basis of reason but because of what I discovered later, namely some good positive transference from her early relationship to her father. That really is what carried the analysis, and I think without it she might well have had a breakdown. Now, some years later, she came in for a review of her 0–6. She had not been seeing me therapeutically for about two years. However I had found that these reviews of 0–6 in so many patients were extremely therapeutic and tended to tie together the main issues and give them a key to their lives in the form of a more clear understanding of their childhood patterns. Therefore I suggested this review to Terry. She hesitated and then refused and wanted to postpone it for many months, or perhaps a year, until various things in her present life might be settled. I did not know on the telephone exactly what she was referring to when she said this, but of course I agreed. However, she called me two or three weeks later and said she had been thinking it over and would be glad to come in.

When she did, I said, "Before we start the review of your 0–6 I would like to ask how you remember your first visits to me. When you first came, what were your chief complaints?"

She replied, "I think it was my problem in responding sexually. I am not sure, but I think that was it. I think that was the main thing." Terry was now in her mid-thirties, an extremely intelligent, attractive girl, married and with four children.

She went on, "I remember that when I first came to see you I was living with Gary and thinking of marrying him, but my mother was so set against it that I was not thinking clearly about it. I felt I was not sure whether or not I was in love with Gary and I wished I had someone I could talk to about these things. I feared I was not in a position to be in love, really."

I said, "Do you also think you had a feeling that things were not quite right generally?"

"Yes," she said, "but the discontent was mostly in connection with loving and not responding properly sexually, and if that is not O.K. then the rest will follow." [As it turned out, this was only partially true.]

I said, "What are your chief complaints as of now, today?"

She replied, "I wanted to wait some months before coming in to see you because still, in a certain way, I have the same complaints. I still do not respond as freely as I would like to Gary who is now my husband . . . I mean as freely sexually, and I still have some question as to whether I've made the right choice of husband. That train of thought can get pretty uncomfortable. But then, after thinking that way for some time, I get some distance from it and I feel that the situation has been the right one. And I begin to think that it is not somebody *outside* myself that makes my problems when I get unhappy and depressed and act in ways that are disruptive. But really I no longer act in such ways, and I no longer get that severely depressed, so that things are going along pretty well."

"Now," I said, "remember again to try to make believe that you are seeing me for the first time and we will try to review your 0–6. Who were the main people in your life, the main relationships, from your birth to age six or seven?"

Terry said, "My father, mother, and brother, particularly my mother and brother."

"Is it right," I then asked, "that there are really only three people, three main ones?"

She said, "The relationship with Mother was the most psychologically important. Next was the one with my brother and then the one with Father."

"With whom would you like to start?"

"Father," she said; "the relationship with Father is the one I remember with the most pleasure. Father was uniformly affectionate. He took me as I was; he took me places, gave me presents. Father traveled a good bit and was away about a week every month. What I remember is not missing him but his returns with gifts for me, and my being very happy . . . the holiday atmosphere when he came back. Mother always had lots of help in the house and she had a genius for getting people who were warm and reacted specifically to us as a family and toward me. But I have memories of no one individually. There were four or five different people during my 0–6. My memories of those years before seven were of going on walks with nursemaids or being fed by them. I also remember Father playing with me, but I have no memory of Mother playing with me. I guess Mother never did. She was pleasant to me, but from force of will because she thought that was how a mother *should* treat a child. Now I realize that Mother was under great strain in those days because of the difficult relationship with her own mother and possibly because of the relationship to my father; it might have been then that my father started having an outside affair. [Many patients cannot face the fact of neglect or rejection by Mother and excuse it or minimize it.] Father really liked me, but I have no memories of Mother because I don't think she really liked me but only behaved as though she did because she felt she should. I remember how efficiently Mother ran the house. I was never bored. I just went from one pleasant activity to another . . . this was because Mother had planned this all out carefully. I haven't given anything like that to my children; mine have known everything that has gone on, though.

"I have no memory of anything unpleasant with Father or Mother until I was seven years old, nor any fear, but I do have adverse memories of Brother. I have an old friend whom I've been friendly with since school. He was a classmate when I was ten years old and sometimes we meet and talk. He told me later that he thought when we were children that I was so precarious, so sensitive, so vulnerable . . . so vulnerable to anything going wrong in my environment. That is about all I remember of my 0–6 with Father and Mother, but I have many memories of my brother, all negative. I didn't like him, either as a baby or later on, but I have no memory of being shoved aside because of him. I remember only being negative toward him. From the very beginning I was interested in the different sexual apparatus that he had, compared with me, and I reacted to it with aversion. He was a little more than three-and-one-half years younger than I.

"I cannot remember anything nice about my brother. I felt that my own feelings and behavior toward him were bad, and the result was that I hid my reactions to him from Father and Mother and there was a fiction in the family of how devoted I was to my brother. I let that stand because I got praise for it and any other reaction would have been bad, so I dissembled my feelings and that set a pattern in me for dissembling my feelings. That about tells the main relationships to Mother and Father and Brother."

"Fine," I said. "Now will you tell me what your first memory is?"

"My first memory is of Mother coming back from the hospital with Brother. I was on the street when she took him into the house, and I was very curious to see the difference in the sexual apparatus. But I have no memory of going in to satisfy that curiosity. When I did, as I have said before, I reacted with great aversion. It is very hard for me to give these first memories because I was told so much and shown so many pictures that it is difficult for me to tell what I really remember and what is the result of pictures. However, I do remember definitely being in a small room, probably part of the nursery, and I was very stubborn. I did not want to sleep there. I did not want to be part of any joyful scene of Brother's arrival. It is from then on that I was shown all the pictures and told so much that I cannot be certain of what I remember myself, but I think I do remember that there were a few festive occasions when there was some element of competition in which I was involved. My inclination I think was to be ostentatiously absent. In fact, there was one such occasion only a week ago, and now I realize that is a pattern I have, dating from those early days. I did not object to seeing my brother, but I did object to being part of any joyful activity because of his arrival. The well-meaning pediatrician advised that after my brother came home I was no longer to be spoon-fed by the nurse; that is, it was time for me to grow up and identify with my parents and let my brother be the baby. But I refused to eat and I lost about ten pounds in weight, and then Mother broke down and gave in."

"Do you have any other of these early memories?" I asked.

"No," she said, "that's all I can be sure of." Then she was silent for a few minutes and I said nothing. Then she said, "Wait, yes I do. I was in that small room, and I was tying my shoe, and I took a long, long time to do it. Something was going on; perhaps a photographer was there, and they were hurrying me up and I was very deliberately tying my shoe slowly. That was part of my tendency from those early days, to be stubborn and to do it myself. Oh, yes, now I have another memory . . . that is, Mother telling me what a selfish child I was and in fact, that was more than a memory. That was a litany all during my childhood. For example, I would refuse to share a toy or a tricycle with a friend. There was never any problem about sharing with my brother, though. That never came up because there were always people around and that was part of the structure of the family—that is something one did.

"I have no memory of ever playing with my brother; for example, playing ball with him. I still have the stubborn tendency to do things myself, like when I tied my shoes so slowly and deliberately. [And, I thought, almost refused analytic help to do it independently.] Oh, yes, sometimes we would have a dog; I always hated it but that was another family fiction. I was supposed to love dogs, and if I didn't, something was wrong with me. Even Father thought that if I got close to a dog I would love it more, and I dislike dogs to this day. I have never had the free and easy feeling with dogs that other people have. The dog would knock me down and my parents thought that was so cute. They got a dog when my brother was born; my parents were so proud to have done this. He was supposed to grow up with us, my brother and I and the dog."

[The main issue seems to be that Mother was conspicuous by her emotional absence in spite of her physical presence. She organized the household with genius but was not herself emotionally involved with the patient. Perhaps it was because of this lack of her mother's love and closeness that Terry reacted so strongly as a child to the arrival of her brother. Where there is not a good secure relationship to the mother there seems to be a certain groundwork laid for intense jealousy, as for example in the case of Pat Ralston (see p. 185). Why, at age three and one-half, Terry should have directed so much attention to the genitals of her newly arrived brother and reacted to them with such aversion is not clear to me from this material. I do not like a purely deductive explanation, e.g., that it was the time of her oedipus. She was more or less deprived by Mother, and this deprivation increased her hostility to the new baby, but the interest and hostility seemed to be focused on his genitals. Possibly she had had some experiences with the nurses or other help which laid some kind of basis for this. However that may be, there is no question of this kind of material supporting Freud's observations of the existence of sexuality in young children, to say nothing of its tendency to peak at about three to five years of age. The other element that seems fairly clear in this hour, however, is that Terry's one good relationship during her 0–6 was with her father, the only one that seems to have been uniformly pleasant. I think that is what really saved her from a breakdown. It also made possible her transference to me as well as her remaining in analytic treatment. Without it, I think she might have been lost. Also, with it she had some basis for a continued relationship to a man which eventuated in her making a go, despite certain difficulties, of her marriage and being a fairly good mother to her children, even though she seemed to do it not on the basis of identification with her mother but on the basis of identification with her father. Small wonder, though, after hearing about her hostile aversive reaction to her brother and his genitals, that she had trouble relating to men and especially in having an adequate sexual response.

In the next hour with Terry Weston, reviewing her 0–6, I found material of some use developing from it, but it would have to be developed and tested thoroughly and frequently before one could be sure about it. We will mention it later.

The hour started in by my saying, "Would you like to review what has struck me as the highlights so far in your 0–6?"

Terry said, "Yes, please."

I said, "What I remember from the last hour was that in general your relationship with your father was uniformly good but your mother and brother, you said, were the two most important relationships; that your mother felt only what she thought she should feel toward you and this left certain unanswered questions, namely why you had such strong reactions to the birth of your brother and why the interest in his genitals was so intense?"

"Yes," she said, "that is correct, but to go back a bit, Mother took pleasure in the idea of having me as a child but not really in me. Mother was a passionate woman but not necessarily with Father. Father told me later on about Mother's rages. Mother's mother refused to meet my father because he was a divorced man. This grandmother made Mother's life a hell. She refused ever to come to visit us or to acknowledge the existence of my mother, my father, and myself and my brother. This put my mother under great stress. I can only guess that I was tense and anxious and hostile to Mother for all these things that I did not understand at the time, but I repressed my anger. Because Grandmother would not acknowledge our family, Mother felt she had to make the best family in the world, and I therefore fitted in and played the part of being the best child in the world; I repressed everything that could have interfered with that. I think one reason that I reacted so strongly to the birth of my brother, but I'm not sure, is that I was repressing so much already that when he came into the family that was just too much. My mother told me first that I was spoiled, but then she changed it to "selfish" because if I were spoiled that might be Mother's fault, but selfish might be genetic. When Father took up that idea, I was really crushed. I think the relationship between my parents was bad from first to last, although it had a few good moments. Mother spent very wisely what Father earned. This stimulated Father to earn and Mother enjoyed spending it, so that was good for both of them. But it was not a good relationship."

Now I asked, "Then why did you react so strongly to the birth of your brother?"

Terry said, "Mother was so unhappy that she was never free to play with me or understand me. When Brother came it threatened the little I had."

[This seemed to me correct; that rang true with all I knew of her. She still had not quite accepted the element of neglect and rejection or at least the lack of love from Mother. The arrival of Brother did more than threaten; it actually took away some of the little she had.]

All I said was, "Why would you say you had such a strong reaction specifically to your brother's genitals?"

"I have only a guess about that. I started masturbating at age seven and I guess I started my sex explorations when I was about three, and Mother felt such an aversion and was so disgusted and so against it. I reacted with increased interest because Mother made such an issue of it. My husband and I do not make it an issue with our children. In our view, their sex explorations are just part of their general interest and curiosity and other explorations; it just makes a part in the overall of their play. It is not an issue of itself. But my mother was so embarrassed about it. Once I remember I was sitting with my hands folded in my lap and my mother thought I was masturbating but I was not, and she made such a face as I would never make to a child. But I think all three-year-olds have some interest in exploring the sexual parts.

"That about covers my 0–6, but that's because my memory began at age seven, so from then on I remember a great deal. I remember Mother's irritation and sarcasm and episodes, the likes of which must have happened before. For example, her authoritarianism with me. I started school at six and always liked my teachers very much; they were all gentle except one. My relationships with adults were good because I was smart and I learned well, but my relationships with my peers were not good because my mind was dominated by expectations and demands. [And, she might have added, they mostly follow my pattern toward my brother.] I was never close to my brother except for possibly an hour at a time. Once I remember reading to him, but mostly we just went our separate ways. I was easier in my personality than my brother, who was abrasive, but I acted easier mostly just to put him down; anything to get him into trouble. I remember being spanked twice, possibly more, by Mother. Once Mother was giving a dinner party and I was on the third floor and I called down. Mother was angry because of my interrupting her party.

"Father spanked me once in a situation that was very traumatic. I had been rollerskating on the sidewalk outside of the house, and of course I was forbidden to come in with the skates on, but once I did. Father and Mother must have heard me, or noticed the marks on the rug, and accused me of doing it, but I lied and said that I didn't. So they sent me upstairs, and my father was coming up to punish me and I was terrified. He did spank me and I felt unjustly treated even though I had lied. You should not make any kid that frightened.

"My sexual fantasies since that time have always had a coercive element." I asked Terry what she meant by that. She said, "I mean I feel forced to have sexual pleasure, feel seized and bound and forced to have sex; but of course that idea might go back further than that time."

I said, "Have you any idea to what time?"

Terry said, "Maybe to the atmosphere in the home, that I was supposed to be happy, but usually because of pleasures that they arranged for me and not from listening to me and knowing what I wanted—not that they didn't listen some; for example, I wanted skates and I got them. But the atmosphere was that I was forced to enjoy pleasure that they arranged, while I was really very angry at another level."

"Do you think that your mother's disgust with your masturbation played a role?"

Terry answered, "That's for sure. If sex is forced on me, then I am relieved of the responsibility of going against Mother, which I didn't want to do at that time. There were some positive things at home, too. For example, I was once excluded by my peers from a playhouse, and once I was really ostracized, and I broke down and cried for two or three hours and Mother (and my brother too) were very nice to me. I was crying with a lot of unhappiness and anger (here Terry was silent for a moment or two), and I guess you had better steer this conversation now because I have run out of thoughts on my 0–6."

I said, "Our next task in these meetings is to try to see the main points of the childhood pattern and also their relation to your present problems."

Terry said, "Yes. If my children or my husband make demands on me I do not react well, but I feel I have to cope and I *do* cope— but in an angry, uptight way. Mother never took demands upon her well. Once I was visiting Mother after being married and I had one of the children with me, who was then a baby. I asked Mother to pass me a paper towel, and they were right next to her, she had nothing to do but reach out and give me one, but Mother was at a loss and she called someone else even for a little thing like that. Mother always had demands on me: to go get her eyeglasses and things like that, but I never could have any demands on her. Mother's energies all went into organizing the house with all the help she had. But all these energies went into her living our lives for us, organizing her house. It's been hard for me to give to my kids. I feared that I would give birth to a child and that would be signing my death warrant. I'm afraid of giving too much, and I have trouble with giving children's parties. My husband does not relate on the level of giving children gifts, and he is right. Father liked to give presents and gave them all the time; that was his way of relating to people. So on my birthdays, for example, I always got too many presents. Mother had trouble giving, as I have. Mother would plan in advance so as not to be caught up in a situation where she would have to give to us."

"Do you have an example of that?" I asked.

"Yes, for example, summertime on vacation. She would have plans of going to the lake, but if a day that she had not planned for turned out to be a very hot one she would never say, 'Yes, it's a hot day, let's go.' She would always say, 'I can't go, I have things to do at my desk.' She would have to arrange for us to go to the lake in advance. She would never do something with us herself, and that's one of the most difficult things I have to do with my children."

I said, "Would you say that the difficulty of you and your mother both, in giving to children, is an identification of you with your mother?"

"No," she said; "I don't think so. Oh, wait a minute . . . yes, in a way I think that's so. Mother had all the help and structured it all, but it cost her a lot and she had migraine headaches and was under great tension. In fact, life cost her a lot. Father and Mother had no close friends, so I never saw how other families work. It seems the friends that I have selected, like Giselle, are much like Mother. Giselle plans, organizes like Mother, yet I feel that something is wrong with that, and I try to see that my own children get a fair shake in life. Unlike Mother, I can play too. Mother never played; she read books and did play the violin very well, but she always played set pieces. She played as part of the atmosphere; she had a beautiful living room and books on the shelf and objects of art and played the violin. For her it was more an accomplishment and that is a big part of my problem, to get out this element of doing something because it is an accomplishment instead of just doing it freely."

I said, "Is that also identification with your mother, or more completely, one of the identifications that you are fighting?"

She said, "Yes, it certainly is."

[An idea that I got out of this hour with Terry which I think is worth testing and which I would like to try further with other patients is this: We now had a pretty good idea of her 0–6 emotional pattern. The first task would be to organize it so we could both express it concisely and be in agreement about it. The next would be to see what parts of the pattern are making problems in her life today; for example, the identifications with her mother that she is fighting, namely, the difficulty in giving to children and in a narrower way, her difficulty in letting herself go and just doing things freely. Now the idea is that if we can even intellectually discern as clearly as possible the childhood pattern and can see the parts of it that are making problems in the patient's emotional life *today*, it may save a great deal of psychoanalytic time in dealing systematically with the problems that are disturbing her today. This will not eliminate the need for the emotional experience of working through—which we are all accustomed to and know—but may help speed up the process, although the start is an intellectual one. Terry could already see from our review together how she was fighting her identification with her mother. Now of course that comes up in daily analytic work; but the question is, will it not come up much *faster* if we go after it than if we simply sit back and listen to the patient's associations?]

In the third hour of review of her 0–6 Terry Weston said, "Unless you have something to say or ask, I will start off by saying that I was not satisfied with the last hour. I think I theorized too much. Once I thought that my problems came from my mother and brother, I made it worse. I was then so provocative, I needled them so; only my relationship with father was relatively calm. I can see it in my youngest daughter in relation to me. When I was seeing you, I was so angry at my mother this anger colored the history I gave you of my past."

I said, "Yes, these vicious circles are very easily set up."

"Of course," she said, "but when I am here telling the history I tend to exaggerate my grievances. But there were a lot of things that were quite nice. I don't tell my children, for example, not to tell outsiders what goes on in the family. This is perhaps my reaction against my mother who was always telling me not to do that . . . not to tell anybody what I observed in the family. The difficulties in my life right now are that I'm very fond of my husband, I admire him, but I wonder how much of a high-flying feeling of love I have or ever had. I can see why, in terms of him, in terms of his makeup . . . in other words, I can blame him, but what of it is in *me* is the question?"

I said, "Exactly. What parts of *your* childhood pattern are influencing you today?"

"Yes," she said, "I can see something. When my husband is home I feel his presence, no matter where he is in the house. I always feel judged. I feel a current of being criticized and that I am not quite right and that I should be doing things. He is so efficient. But if I give in and start doing things, then I feel I am doing them because they are expected by my husband and then I get very angry at him. This is very much the pattern toward my mother. Mother was critical, dominating, directive. She wanted me to *do* things. She had my life so organized anyway, but if a few extra minutes came along she would call for me to do things. I may exaggerate because there were times when I could do what I wanted but . . . only within certain limits. I never had a peaceful place in my house as a child, and it's the same now. I feel better only when everybody is away. I have never been able to put out freely for my kids (three daughters and a baby boy), and this is my weakest point. I have tended to blame my husband because he is not flexible, but there also is a pattern to my mother because she was very unflexible."

"You told me when you started this review that your problems today were chiefly in loving and in sex."

"Yes, she said, "and also in giving to my children. This is certainly connected with my mother, who always conveyed somehow that I was not quite right, but that if I did exactly what she said I might turn out O.K. anyway. Yet there were moments when Mother did love me unconditionally, but she had a hard time of it and I brought out the worst in her, whereas I think my brother brought out the best in her. He gave Mother presents and that sort of thing. It took me a long time to realize that I had been provocative with my friend, Lydia. She irritates me in ways that Mother did, and I say things that irritate her. But now that I have seen that it is a repetition of the pattern toward Mother, I don't do it as much anymore. I don't know if I still do it with my husband. I see better the patterns that are mine. The relationship with my husband is better than it has ever been. He will not initiate sex but I do, not because I feel like it but to please him and to hold our marriage together. But then I get angry at myself. But if I do not initiate sex, then my husband never does and says it's better that way because he doesn't need it anymore and I'm not free enough about it anyway. Then I get furious.

"But I can't quite get a handle on what is my part of the problem. Mother kept saying that I was selfish and maybe I eventually said to myself, 'O.K., I'm supposed to be selfish, then I *will* be selfish.' Father preferred me to Mother and that frightened me because Father and Mother did not have a secure relationship to each other as a unit, so I feared to express myself sensuously with Father."

I said, "Do you think your relationship to your brother has contributed to this problem of loving and sex?"

She said, "Brother irritated me. He had more freedom than I had, and I resented him so and transferred some of this to my husband and then looked for areas in which the resentment would fit. That is, I transfer the resentment to my husband and then look for areas that justify the resentment. Mother would be critical and hostile to both Brother and me, but Brother could have temper tantrums and raise hell and run out of the house and seem to not be hurt by it, while I *was* hurt by it. Mother reduced me to tears at least three times a day, although a little less after I was married. Talking about this churns up my anger and that does no good in life. It's better to control the anger."

I said, "Of course it is. We churn it up here for a purpose . . . not to keep it churned up, but to understand it and reduce it; exactly as you said about your friend—that when you saw her you were irritated by her and you irritated her following the pattern toward your mother. But then you said you don't do it anymore. That is exactly what we are trying to do, reduce the hostility after we see it. And also you said the same thing about your husband: as you see that the hostility toward him and your friend are simple transferences of the pattern toward Mother, then you realize there's no use taking out on your husband and your friend today your reactions to Mother when you were a child. Therefore, it is better."

"Yes," she said, "that is true. It has worked out that way. I am angry at my husband because he seems freer than I am. Mother would push the bell and I would have to come. In other words, I had to take orders from her. Now my youngest daughter is the only one who is like Mother and insists on these instant demands upon me."

I said, "Do you think that way back, when your brother first came from the hospital, that what you called your aversion to his genitals plays any part in your present problem of loving and sex?"

She said, "I can see it intellectually. I had so much aversion to him that it would have been the same if I had had a sister, because when he arrived they stopped taking care of me. They stopped spoon-feeding me three times a day, and I had to make a place for Brother in the family, but these are not sure memories."

"Still," I said, "You seem to be saying that there are at least two elements: number one is the aversion."

"Yes," she said, interrupting, "there is no doubt of that aversion at all."

"And," I continued, "the other question is, why do you think the aversion was directed so specifically to your brother's genitals?"

Terry said, "Mother disliked the physical care of babies. Once she had to care for a friend's baby boy, for some reason. She cleaned his penis very carefully. What is that? I understand that boy babies have something that forms a sort of crust that must be cleaned? And Mother cleaned his very carefully but with a very perceptible aversion, and maybe I took over her aversion to the male genitals. To this day, if I had to change a baby I would rather change a girl than a boy. But I don't see this in relation to my husband. I like my husband's sexual appartus, to see it and to feel it, but I have an aversion to the sexual apparatus of other men. I think that their penises must be more boyish, more childish. I am really working these things out very well myself in life. First I *establish what it is that I am feeling when I am distressed and upset, and then I look for the childhood pattern. I am doing this all the time in life. Of course, I can only do this when I am not hurting too bad; but I realize that I must not simply blame other people, that I must see what it is that I want* . . . like my desire to be alone in the house. I must look for the childhood pattern of why this is.

"I was a little depressed after talking to you the last two times." I asked Terry why that was. She hesitated for a moment and then said, "Because Mother was a good listener. But I felt that I had to tell her things to get her love. In other words, I had to tell her things to get from her the love I should have gotten unconditionally without having to tell her things."

I said, "Then is not this the very same thing we are talking about? It would be a shame to let this old pattern toward your mother when you were a child get in the way of a good relationship to your husband and children and to me in the transference." She agreed fully. I thought in my own mind that she would work this all through more rapidly and effectively if she went on with some analytic work with me and had the advantage of the transference to carry her working through, but she felt that she was making so much progress in working it through in her own life and her husband was so opposed to her returning that I felt it would be incorrect to press the point and try to get her to resume. It would be better to let her go ahead, making this progress on her own. This would be satisfactory because we agreed that we would stay in touch; this was easy, because basically we had a friendly relationship in the transference and countertransference and, in reality, because I admired her a great deal as a person and I think she liked me also. So we let it go on that note, that we would stay in touch and see how things developed. There seemed to be no reason to doubt that everything would continue to go well and that she got something out of this review of her 0-6; she was an emotionally honest, courageous young woman, and would not hesitate to call and come in any time for whatever was needed.

As it turned out, Terry did come back to see me to work through her dynamics further, especially the transference. She came only once a week in this final stage, but with much movement and progress in every hour. After the war she wrote me and has done so about twice a year. Things are going well between herself and her husband, she has friends, and her children have developed nicely. She has come from homosexuality and danger of breakdown to a stable life that is as satisfying as that of most.

Dynamic Diagnosis: Terry Weston

Childhood: (1) Deprivation of dependent love needs by Mother. (2) Pushed out of "the little I did have" by birth of brother at age three and one-half, leading to hostility to brother. (3) Excessively criticized and blamed by Mother. (4) Excessively controlled authoritarianly by Mother. (5) Distant but good relationship with Father.

Current: Feelings of being deprived, unsuccessful, controlled; fighting identification with Mother; rebellion, suppressed fight-flight, repressed hostility and guilt leading to impaired giving (especially to children), loving, and sex.

Strengths: (1) Drive to independence. (2) Courage in facing own motivations. (3) Physical vitality and fighting spirit for improvement and happiness for self, husband, and children.

III. Arlene Rodgers: "Cinderella"

This patient is a housewife, about forty years old, who has a number of vague complaints, all of which boil down to one word—"unhappiness"—which is not readily defined. She was the youngest of six children. As usual, a review of her interrelationships from birth to age about six and of her very first memories gives information that makes her world rather clearly intelligible and which also gives the emotional atmosphere in which she lives. Before I asked Arlene to give her impression of the main emotional interrelationships with the members of her family from 0–6, she began recounting her earliest memories, so I followed her in this:

"My first memory," Arlene said, "was at about the age of three years. I burned my third and fourth fingers badly when I reached up and put them in some hot sauce which was just off the stove. It was put to cool on a high place and I could see what was in the pot. The next thing I recall was that my mother and I were in the bathroom upstairs and she was treating my fingers and that was very nice because she was paying attention to me, and that I liked. [Suggests hostility, self-directed, and very strong needs for attention.]

"My second memory is that I was looking out through some bars; therefore, I think it must have been a crib. It was lovely out, sunny; I have no memory of ever having had a playpen so I think it was a kind of crib. In other words, as I see now, I was confined by these bars looking out into the beautiful day. I remember that my father would say in the evening, 'Pipe down and go to sleep.' It was Father who would spank me for not going to sleep, but also it was Father who would take me a glass of water at night when I wanted it. [Feeling confined and butt of some hostility, and again emphasis on getting attention.]

"My third memory is of when I was a little older—five years old and had my tonsils out. I was given ether out of a lighter can poured on a piece of gauze. It was very primitive. I felt sort of a detached wonderment. I think that four families had arranged for the doctor to come and do all the children at the same time. I was placed on a table. It was not really horrible, though, and when I woke up my mother was there beside me, and I don't know whether or not she was sleeping." [Again, butt of hostility and need for attention.]

I asked Arlene if she had any further memories. She said, "I do not recall any more early ones, but at the same age of about five I remember (fourth memory) we were in the barn with a knife grinder with a crank, and we worked it a way that sounded like a siren and we played fire engine." The patient was now 'warmed up,' so to speak, and went on to give other memories. "Also about this time (fifth memory) some kidnapping was in the news, and I had great fear because of it. When I would go to bed I thought I could see the top of a ladder at my window and two hands on it coming to get me. [Again, theme of hostility to patient.] I remember about this age some Japanese beetle catchers in a rose garden (sixth memory)."

She said (seventh memory), "Also before the age of six I remember Father burning leaves in the driveway." I asked if she had any further memories. "Yes," she replied and proceeded to give memory number eight. "Two things are strong in my mind. I remember the soap dish which was indented in the bathtub, and I remember my mother ran about two inches of water in the tub to give me a bath and I always froze; I was so cold, but my mother washed my bottom with soap and it always stung and I hated it." [Again, hostility to self.]

"Any further memory?" I asked.

"Yes," she said, and gave memory number nine: "My grandmother always lived in a room of her own in our house. She was always darning socks or something and she was always available. I would get on her lap and we would sing together. This is a very pleasant memory. Grandma always liked me." [Strong appreciation of receiving attention.]

Of course by now I had a pretty clear impression from these memories, but it is generally best to get the patient's interpretations first; therefore, I asked Arlene if she had any impression from them. "Yes," she said, "I do. I feel that all these memories show me as helpless and hopeless; wandering around without any protection searching for a safe place and finding no connection. There was no protection at all . . . none at all."

"Like a hobby horse we had . . . there was no protection, because all six of us would use it and there was no supervision at all, and I had a lot of fear. [Theme of self-directed hostility causing anxiety.] For example, I would go into the hall toward Mother's bed but there was nobody there, nobody around. [Lack of loving attention.] I always slept next to my sister. We shared a room . . . she was a few years older. We had separate beds; she was in a bed really, and I was in a crib, but no one was ever available, the house was empty and lonely. There was no contact with anybody, only fear that a person would come in that window. It was all so empty; the hallway was empty and Mother's room was empty too. It was clean, but empty, no people. Grandmother was on a different level; that was good, but the basic level was empty. I did not really have any close contact with my father. He helped me get water at night but that was all. Father and Mother had a double bed but it was empty. There was really no contact with Mother nor with my older sister until much later, nor with anyone until much later. There was the contact with Grandmother at about age three. At about age five or six I would sometimes sit on my father's lap, but I don't remember any connection with Mother. The only connection was with Father, Grandmother, and my older sister. All that I learned was defensiveness. Here we were, a household of nine people including two live-in maids, but still it was so lonely. My only way of coping was to defend myself against my older sister, my two brothers and my mother, but mostly against my mother. It was really to defend myself against Mother and to physically survive the onslaught of my sister and brothers. Also, I had to keep up with them."

"I think I know," I said, "what you mean by no contact, but just to be sure, will you please explain it to me?"

"I mean," said Arlene, "that I got no notice; no attention was paid to me; I was ignored, nobody gave me any notice or attention. I think my mother was not capable of it; I doubt that she contacted anyone in her whole life."

"Do you see," I said, "any connection between these memories and your present life?"

"Yes," she said, "I certainly do." Before telling her response, however, let me review here what these memories meant to me, the analyst. Her first memory was of getting attention from Mother but only because she had burnt her fingers. The next was of being confined by the bars of her crib and shut off from what was pleasant in life. Also, the big feature of having her tonsils out at the age of five was not only the unpleasantness but having her mother near when she awakened, which was what she craved and missed. Being bathed in the cold water and freezing was similar to the burnt fingers. Then her grandmother was the one figure in her childhood who seemed to be friendly and onto whose lap she could climb. Then later, she could climb on her father's lap, and this meant a great deal to her also. The picture of her relationship to her father was similar to that toward her mother, in that he spanked her for not going to sleep, but still she remembered that he brought her water when she needed it. The memory of the fear of being kidnapped is susceptible to different interpretations, and probably if I had the time in this hour to treat it as a dream, we would have clarified some of them. In the first place, Arlene may have felt she was kidnapped and not in the home as a wish to be taken away from the home that to her was so depriving. And also, the hostility and the fear may have been a repression of her own anger with possibly also some guilt. However, instead of telling the patient all this, I asked what *she* thought and what the relationship was, in her mind, to her present life.

Arlene said, "As I see it, because no one made contact with me, I felt I was not allowed to make contact with others, and I have lost closeness to many lovely people in my life because of that. It is sad and maybe too late but I did contact my oldest child, my daughter, but not the next child, a son. And I did make some contact with my two youngest children, both daughters, but they are defensive too."

What I have failed to convey in presenting this hour is the tremendous impact it had on the patient. Her unhappiness in life, her chief complaint, stemmed almost completely from her isolation from the community and her relative isolation from her husband. She complained that she did nothing but work, that she carried the family. She felt that the community was cold and that she did nothing but work, work, work and got no help, that she was all alone and *nobody cared.*

Then I said, "You see now how much of this is not the fault of the community, but is in your own feelings, because you continue at age forty with the same pattern of feelings toward the community that you had at age three and four toward your family."

"Yes," she said, "I see what you mean. It is not the fault of the community, but it is not my fault either . . . I can see that. It is the fault of the way I was treated as a child."

"You are exactly right," I replied, seeking to give some support and appreciation for her insight. "That is very true, but of course our concern is not in placing blame or fault but in recognizing the nature of the problem and trying to solve it."

This interview, it turned out, dealing only with these first memories, in a patient who already had considerable analytic work and insight—this single interview turned out to be a turning point in her treatment and her life. She used to rage to me against her husband, and against her neighbors and was filled with anger. After this interview, she understood the situation enough to begin to take things with more calm and more consideration for me. Before this, in spite of my interpretations of exactly the same thing—namely, the deprivations of childhood and its effects on increasing her demands and also her feelings of frustration, of anger—nevertheless, she would be extremely demanding of me, although she always tried to be considerate. But after this interview she showed some true identification with me and some true consideration—and also, more importantly, increased consideration of her husband and children.

In all, or nearly all cases, after a while—maybe a year or two of analytic treatment—I have found it most beneficial therapeutically to use an hour or two for the patient to go back and take the early history as though we were seeing each other for the first time and there had been no treatment. The results of reviewing a patient's 0–6 are not always so dramatic as in Arlene's case, but I have found the method usually to be effective—because it is so often able to clarify the basic childhood pattern which has caused the patient's problems and which needs to be altered and outgrown.

Dynamic Diagnosis: Arlene Rodgers [as worked out with the patient]

Childhood: Last child of six; deprivation of attention, untaught, unencouraged (especially in personal relations) but depreciated for not knowing. Used by Mother as slave labor, for menial tasks, and also for Mother and Father's own interest, through patient vicariously; patient not respected as an individual, no concern for patient's (and siblings') future careers. *Loneliness*, repressed (not permitted) because it had to be one "big happy family," except Sister cried much and had terrible headaches. Lonely despite hubbub, all chaotically busy, six children in nine years, emphasis on food and clothes, with scrimping regarding money. Neglect by Mother led to *excessive attachment* to sister, more than to Mother. *Inferiority* and *envy* toward siblings, all siblings, especially sister, preferred to patient; patient was *Cinderella.*

Current: Excessive needs for what she did not get—attention, approval, acceptance, valued, appreciated, encouraged, taught; *envy* of others who seem to have these, and *give-get imbalance* leads to frustration, leads to fight-flight as almost chronic hostility and tendency to some actual withdrawal from friends and social contacts, mostly turned against self, causing anxiety and masochism. Tries to give her children what she lacked.

Strengths: (1) Patience and perseverance. (2) Devotion to her children. (3) Narcissistic drive to win out in the end.

IV. Hortense Thompson: Emotional Nutritional Deficiency

Hortense Thompson was a tall, slender, attractive, blonde woman with great vitality and energy. She was in her early thirties, married, with three children.

At the end of about three years of analytic work with her, I asked Hortense to come in to review her 0-6 before leaving on a summer vacation. She did not do this, however, and I did not hear from her, but of course I saved an hour for her in the fall. As September arrived and I still had not heard from Hortense, I phoned; she said she would call me back in about a week and come in to review her 0-6. That time also passed without word; finally a letter arrived, saying she had stopped work on her graduate degree and that, although some people were clearly helped by psychoanalysis, she was not one of them . . . she had decided to stop treatment.

Hortense had come because of difficulty with human relations and also because of a severe writing inhibition, so that she was unable to write even simple themes for her classes. Also, she suffered from examination phobia. Now she had made so much progress that she had successfully passed her examination for a Ph.D. and had nothing to do but write the dissertation. In other words, having come this far and on the verge of success—of obtaining a degree, which for her meant being able to pursue a life interest and career—Hortense decided to stop treatment and give up the effort to obtain the degree.

Of course I discussed none of this with her on the phone but simply said I would like her to come in for a review of her 0-6. She agreed and I set up the appointment. I made it for a relatively early hour one morning so that we could have two or even two and one-half hours, if necessary, for making the review. This is worth reporting, because by now I had learned the tremendous power of reviewing the 0-6 after a period of analysis: it brings the issues into focus for the patient with special clarity, force, and therapeutic effect.

Hortense had a good marriage, got along well with her husband, and had three half-grown children. This is *not* to say that she had no problems in the marriage or with the children, but she recognized what a good man her husband was and wanted to do right by the children. She assumed her family duties, but under a certain strain, which is not surprising in view of her problems with human relations. During her analysis she was always embroiled in all sorts of problems including those of passing her courses. This, I recognized, was to some extent a resistance. On the other hand, it was so important to her to pass the courses and get on with her progress in her career that I was willing to take time to go into the problems with her and expend much energy giving her ego support to get through these problems. Now we stood at the verge of success.

When she came in I said immediately, "I am not going to ask you how things are going. I do not want to hear in this hour all the realities you are always embroiled in. I think we should plunge in and do our job first in reviewing your 0–6. Later, if you wish, you can bring me up to date. I am going to ask you two questions about your 0–6. The first is a general one, and that is, 'What were the main features of your life from birth to about age six or seven?'"

She replied, "Separation, isolation, loneliness, littleness."

I said, "Would you tell a little more about these?"

She replied, "Your question makes me feel very bad because it makes me think of what the loneliness and littleness consisted of. In the first place, I recall when I was two years old my brother sitting on a closed toilet seat in a bathroom upstairs, being forced to eat something. Sometimes I think it was not my brother but myself, and it was a big governess making him or me eat something. But mostly I think it was me standing there watching my brother and not being able to help him. The point is, Brother and I were eating upstairs, separated from our parents who were eating downstairs. Also, I know the dates of these things because we moved from Denver to Chicago when I was three years old, so there was also a time (when I was about two, in Denver) that I saw some veteran paraplegics and I felt very strange and small. I thought of them as being big, as though they were on stilts. I was not with my father or mother, to be protected by them, but felt very lonely.

"Also, in Denver, there was a big bedroom and it was dark. I wanted to be in the other room with the people. I was all alone in that big room and I was frightened. Also in Denver and therefore before the age of three I think of picking some sort of berries. There was a beautiful blue sky, but again I was all alone. It was still there when I had my tonsils out . . . I had anxiety, helplessness, terror. I had a vague feeling of being in a bed and then in an operating room with a cloth on my face. They did not use a mask.

"After we moved to Chicago, I have some recollection of not feeling so little, small, and helpless but of feeling different, isolated, and separated. When we moved into the house in Chicago, I felt very small in relationship to the house. Father was around somewhere when I was in the house for the first time. I remember there was a pantry and I was in it, and the doors were small enough that I could open them. Also I was so skinny then that Mother kept milk in the refrigerator for me to drink. Once I went to get some; it came in glass bottles, and I spilled the whole bottle.

"When we first came into that house and I was just barely three I measured myself against the height of the windows in the living room, and I think of all the incidents which happened in that living room which led me to run away from home when Father and Mother were angry at me. The time I ran away I was about three or almost four. Also, between three and four I had trouble with my ears and had treatment for them. We visited my grandparents in St. Louis. They had twin beds, and Grandmother always wanted Grandfather to move out so that the children could sleep in the room with her. It was at that time my eardrums burst; blood and stuff came out, and I was taken to the doctor and he seemed very big and I felt little and afraid of him. I had bad ears at age three; at that time I remember eating some bad Easter eggs and I thought that was where I got my bad ears. For a long time I refused to eat eggs.

"Somewhere a little later, about age four, I had radium treatments for my ears. Along with them came horrible things. At age five or six, after one of these procedures, I was dizzy and fell off a chair and broke a tooth. About then I had a baby tooth that was abcessed and had to be pulled. I am trying to remember how I was put to sleep . . . there was a man and a mask and I was put to sleep but it did not smell horrible, yet I was terribly frightened. This was partly because I had had another mask once when Brother closed a car door on my finger. I was in a panic; it was some sort of picnic and they all went off and left me and a nurse took me to the hospital. It was terrible; I had several stitches. I fought, screamed, vomited, and had to be forcibly held. At five, or maybe six, I ran away from home all alone. I put everything in a sheet and wrapped it up to take with me. I ran away to an uninhabited house and just sat there on the porch.

"When I was still three I had a girlfriend. I had some friends and some enemies; I have not seen any of them since. There was one of the boys I had terrible fights with, but I have happy memories also of the school in Chicago . . . that is, from age three to four. I loved painting on an easel and I loved cleaning the paintbrushes. We napped on cots and there was someone who ran around and rubbed our backs briefly as we tried to nap. That was very nice. About a year later, though, the other children used to chase me down a hill and throw stones at me and I recall nothing else of that school.

"As I neared six I learned to read, and I loved to read. I had one friend, and she and I would sit and read together. Again, it was physically near to the door, maybe so that I could get out before the other children did and get to the office and be safe.

"I don't know when the relationship to my brother started. He was three and a half years older than I, but I do remember the day a phone call came from the school to Mother saying that he had been hurt playing soccer or something. Mother went to see him and I went with her. Then I have a vague memory of Brother, the nurse and I eating at a small table. I don't know who was at the big table. During that period I had a lot of nightmares . . . once the nurse came into my room and once I went into my parents' room. I had many nightmares of falling, and if that is not separation I don't know what it is! I had them so frequently I dreaded it.

"Also, before the age of reason—that is, before six or seven—I ate some pills. I climbed up on the bathtub and from that onto the sink and examined all the pills. There was a garden party going on outside and as usual I was all alone in the bathroom. I don't know the timing of the beginning of sex play . . . I assume it was between five and six."

The patient had answered my first question of the main features of her 0–6 by giving 17 memories of these years but especially of her 0–3. Now she was silent, so I said, "I will ask you a more specific question. Who was the most important person emotionally in your life during this 0–6 period?"

She said, "I don't know." She hesitated a little and then added, "But my instinct tells me it was Nanny. That recalls a few more memories . . . at about five, they had a photographer in and a painter, to make pictures of us. From age two I had bad eyes and had eye exercises. I was taken somewhere for them. They tried to get me to read print of the size in an encyclopedia, and that is the first time I read an encyclopedia, and I remember reading about elephants. I thought of this because the nurse was the one who groomed me; she got me all washed, combed, and brushed my hair and my clothes just right for the picture."

I said, "You told me your nurse was the most important for you. Tell a little bit about that relationship."

Hortense said, "Well, she groomed me as I said. She was there when I returned from school. She also took me to the dentist. I had braces from the time I was four years old."

I asked, "Who was next in importance for you, besides the nurse?"

"Your question makes me feel so lonely," said Hortense. "There was no one else. Except maybe that one girl who was my close friend, and we played together. She had no brothers or sisters, so maybe I was important for her, too. More often we would go to her house to play rather than her coming to my house."

I asked, "How about your mother?"

She replied, "I don't remember her. She was probably there and probably important, but only just flitting about, especially in St. Louis. I can't really remember my mother in Denver or my father or brother, but they must have been around. Of course they were, when we were in Chicago. I remember Mother taking me to school when I was four or five, and I told you about remembering the day when the school called and said Brother was hurt. It is not that she was totally absent, but I didn't relate to her. I did have a comforting sense that she was there, but there was no developed or defined relationship." [Which suggests the present problems in relationships.]

She was silent, and I asked, "Is there any more you can say about the relationship to your mother?"

Hortense shook her head defintely "no." Then she said, "I felt she was there in the crisis moments . . . that is, if the school called about Brother, or if I had to go to the doctor or the dentist. Then she was there, and met her obligations; more than met them.

"I remember first grade in school with absolute clarity. It is really the teacher that I remember. She was a wonderful, warm person. Her name was 'Jane' . . . ."

Hortense ws silent again, and I said, "Do you remember the times you ran away from home, why that was?"

She replied, "I only remember a terrible anger with Mother, but I have no memory of what it was about." [Possibly in reaction to frustrated dependent love needs for her mother?]

"I don't want to leave the topic of your relationship with your mother," I said, "if there is any more."

She hesitated and then said, "No, there is no more."

"Who, then, was most important for you emotionally after Mother?"

"I can't answer that," Hortense said. "There was no one . . . no one emotionally important for me. The only one I know is Jane. That does not mean there was no one; I just don't remember. Maybe I am just covering everything up."

I said, "Let's go to Father."

"I remember him with a sense of warmth," she said, "but he was never around. He never beat me or belittled me as he did later."

"Is there anything else in relation to Father?"

"No," she said; "there was a beloved dog, but he was a little standoffish, a little dignified. Since then I have had much more success with dogs."

I asked her about her relationship with her brother. She replied, "When I was about five I have just that one memory of school calling to say he was hurt; nothing else in that period. Of course, there was that very early memory of his being fed on the toilet seat, but the real memories of my brother started much later. In that first memory I was two and he was five and a half. Later on, Brother had friends over and they had games and they would tease me. That was when I was six or maybe seven.

"Oh . . . wait a minute; I do have a memory of my parents, at least Mother, coming in when Brother and I were saying our prayers at night. We did not sleep together but we said our prayers together."

"Was there anyone else who was emotionally important for you?"

"There must have been cooks and maids," she said. "I think Bridget, the sewing lady, was there from the beginning. She only left when I got married, and she refused to come to the wedding because for some reason she was so angry with my mother. She was very loving toward me and felt that I was not properly cared for. She came once a week on cook's day off. I remember her visually, more than anyone else. Sometimes she took me to her house; she was very poor. I have some vague recollections of being with servants before the age of seven, but after that the servants were of a different type."

"Did you have repetitive dreams in childhood?"

"No," she said, "no others except the nightmares of falling."

I asked, "Any recurring dreams since then?"

"Well," she said, "I had the falling dreams all through college. No one pushes me, but I am falling off a cliff or building. I awake, not because I am about to hit the ground, but because of the terrible sense of aloneness which makes absolute panic, and in the panic I wake up. Usually when I wake up I feel cold."

I said to Hortense, "You indicated that maybe all you have told me is not true and only a cover-up, but what and why would you cover up like that?"

She answered, "Hostility . . . maybe hostility: maybe anger at my brother for jealousy or at Father for not being there, or at Mother for having other interests. Suppose as a developing child I want to express reactions but lack command of language and cannot express feeling and I use makeshift ways that are dysfunctional, and no one will listen, and I am frustrated at not being able to communicate my feelings, and the family does not realize that this is a block, so I am incapacitated in this. When something is wrong, Father expresses himself with an infantile rage. I don't mean like a small child, but really like an infant. I consider both Father and Mother handicapped people and Brother the same, so maybe I tend to be like that."

I said, "You raise a very important question . . . what about your identifications?"

She said, "I did not identify except when they came up to hear our prayers because that was close and warm, but I must identify with them some because I mirror their behavior."

"Do you have any feeling in yourself of a lack of your own identity?"

"Sure," she said, "of course . . . if I was so angry with them I must have been ambivalent about identifying with them, but there was nobody else to identify with." We discussed this briefly, and I remarked that some people do not fight off identification with one or both parents but actually want *more* identification . . . they want to be more like them, and feel that they do not quite live up to them. So that maybe Hortense's dissatisfaction with her own identity is in part because of that ambivalence.

She said, "Are there *really* people who want to be more like Mother or Father? There are things I admire tremendously in both my parents, but for the most part, no. But even if we have learned this over the last three years, it doesn't seem to be therapeutic to me . . . it is not useful."

I replied to that by saying that I thought the reason it was not therapeutic and the reason she was stopping work on her degree when it was practically within her grasp was perhaps that she was repeating the pattern toward her parents with me in the transference, and there was so much hostility to me that she was bound to defeat me even at the cost of her own failure. I thought there was a residue of masochism there. To this she agreed, and without my saying anything further asked if I still had time to see her and if she could continue in regular treatment.

This I mention because it shows the great power of these reviews of 0–6. I really made no interpretations of the material and did nothing but question her as indicated in this report; but in the process of her answering the questions, she saw her own dynamics with an increased clarity and understood what remained to be worked through.

Of course, I also indicated to Hortense that analytic therapy did not solve the problem in three years because the problem was not really so much one of 0–6 as of 0–3. The trouble dated back practically to birth and we could document it from her memories before the age of three. Thus, by her simply reviewing 0–6 her resistances for the most part collapsed, and she wanted to go ahead and work her problems through. At the very end she said something confirmatory: "You remember how often I expressed some concern for your health? Now I can tell you that I have been worried about your dying, and in view of what you have told me about the transference, it seems to me this might be direct hostility to you as part of my pattern of feeling so alone and little and frustrated." By this she related her childhood pattern directly into the transference, and also showed an insight into that part of the pattern which was chiefly repressed, namely, the hostility. In her fight-flight pattern to the loneliness, isolation, and littleness, we see that the fight part produced the anger, which was almost entirely repressed; she turned it against herself masochistically, and the flight part, joined with this, made her tend to withdraw from people and from achieving the Ph.D. that was almost within her grasp.

Dynamic Diagnosis: Hortense Thompson

Childhood: Deprivation in 0–3, and "only the little one" from 3–6; lack of a relationship with Mother, although Mother more than adequate in meeting her obligations, e.g., taking patient to dentist. Some warmth from Father, but Father never around. Gross parental preference for Brother, three and one-half years older. Felt Brother and his interests important and patient not at all, patient only the "little one." Patient too hostile to Mother, Father, and Brother to identify with any of them. Patient felt separation, isolation, loneliness, littleness.

Current: Difficulty relating to people; inhibition in academic writing, e.g., writing of themes, etc. Feels what Mother, Father, and especially Brother do is important, while patient's interests are of no importance, are just play, which is still attitude of Mother and Father, who still value Brother far ahead of patient. Feels insufficiently loved, leading to mobilization of fight-flight reaction: the hostility, mostly repressed, leading to inhibitions with people, in work, and in psychosomatic symptoms; and the flight causing tendency to withdraw, give up.

Strengths: Superior intelligence and sense of reality, vitality, courage and honesty, determination, perserverance, independence of mind.

V. Dottie Reardon: Psychotic Personality

Dottie was a young matron in her late thirties, not petite but below medium height, a black-eyed brunette who could only be described as charming and beautiful. In addition, she was intelligent and energetic, and had held some responsible jobs in the field of education. When Dottie came to see me she was pleasant to talk with, and evoked a sympathetic response. But she was the only patient I did not miss when I left Chicago. I had been asked to see Dottie in consultation by another analyst, a friend, who complained to me that she woke him with phone calls at all hours of the night. Then, like the "Ancient Mariner," she hung onto him on the telephone, disrupting his sleep and that of his wife.

In her first interview Dottie buttered me up for the future slaughter. She was beauty in distress, and how fortunate she was to find me, the one person she now felt could help her after the abuses to which her other psychiatrists had subjected her! The first ones, she indicated, were not trained in psychoanalysis, and the analyst who referred her to me had made grave mistakes. She knew I could not treat her myself, but was sure I could refer her to the right person.

I tried to discern her childhood pattern, but her volubility was a successful smokescreen, and I could not get answers to my two main questions—except for feelings of extreme deprivation from 0–3. She had been very attached to her mother, but Mother was preoccupied with her own social life and severely rejected Dottie. This certainly fitted the pattern Dottie was developing in her present life. She was aflame with intense demands for attention, and when she could hold someone's ear, she would pour out an endless torrent of abuse against another person.

The first casualty was her marriage. Beating on her husband with her insatiable demands for attention combined with hostility so venomous that it seemed ready to burst into violent action, she finally drove him off. He realized that she was severely ill emotionally, but she had no concept of the reality of this. For her, it was only another example of how someone had abused her. Dottie's needs for attention and rage at not obtaining it followed her pattern to her mother, and were so intense that they disintegrated her sense of reality and her controls (in technical terms, her "ego" functions of reality testing and executive functions). I referred her to Dr. Taylor, mentioned previously in this book in the case of Wilma Blake. He was excellent with this kind of borderline problem. Of course, it was not long before she acted out her childhood pattern toward him—calling him at midnight, awakening him after a long day's work, feeling rejected if he said he could not talk at that hour. She also used the threat of suicide. In reality, Dottie was so aggressively demanding and hostile and so remote from reality that people did not notice her charm and beauty but found her to be obnoxious in the extreme and were provoked into hostility toward her. This she seized upon, and she complained that people hated her.

At first she phoned me only during her lucid periods, when she was in control of herself—ostensibly to have someone sympathetic to talk to for a while. But after she had seen two more psychiatrists and repeated the same pattern toward them, my turn came. She phoned one evening, typically during dinner, and hung up in a rage when told I would be free in one-half hour. She called back later to say:

"You just don't know what that Dr. Taylor did to me! Because you referred me to him I assumed he was able and would help me, but you just don't know how he hates me . . . ."

I broke in to ask, "What about the other psychiatrists you have seen?"

She was barely in control enough now to respond, but did say, "They all should go and study some more," and then she continued her torrent of hate, rationalized and justified by the rejection and other abuse she had suffered. Again I managed to break in with, "What can I do to help you?"

She was now, after a half hour on the phone, quite wild and unrealistic and proceeded to direct her rage at me, but in a somewhat restrained and oblique way: "You—I used to have faith in you—but not now. I have no faith in you anymore."

I replied, "I'm sorry, but that is not the point. The point in my mind is, "Can I do anything to help you?" With this she vented a sort of yell and hung up with a bang.

I considered her a psychotic personality, for the childhood pattern came out not as a paranoid trend or a circumscribed paranoid psychosis but pervaded her entire personality, swamping her "ego," i.e., her reason, controls, and sense of reality. There was not enough "ego strength" for her to be treatable psychoanalytically, at least not out of an institution. The poor girl was so obnoxious that she was isolating herself from every human being. If the last libidinal tie were broken, she would probably commit suicide or become flagrantly psychotic. Of course, she had reacted to advice that she spend a period of time in a hospital as though the advice were a form of violent abuse against her.

No approach seemed to work. If a person were distant with Dottie it was proof of rejection and justified her rage. If a person were sympathetic, as I had been, it stirred up her childhood pattern to her mother of expectations and demands, being frustrated and engendering rage and hate, exemplifying the old advice, "Never give a paranoid anything."

A few years before seeing this beautiful and tragic figure, I had seen in treatment a man who complained of unpopularity. He was only neurotic, not psychotic like Dottie; that is, his "ego," his perception, reason, and controls were intact and we could talk over his problem. At first he seemed likable enough, but with time he became irritating with his long, pointless phone calls, his lateness for appointments and his reluctance to hang up, his dragging in of mud and dirt on his shoes, his smearing of dirty hands on the walls, his hostile innuendoes, and so on. Clearly he was a most obnoxious personality—but only a neurotic one, not psychotic. We could analyze. He had enough sense of reality to recognize how his hostilities were being acted out and to see how these hostilities must antagonize the people with whom he wanted to be friends and to be popular. And, in time, we were able to "work through" his childhood pattern, reducing his demands and hostilities that were antagonizing people instead of winning them. But poor Dottie could not even realize what she herself was doing in every human relationship. Every attempt to reason with her only precipated a blast of rage and hate, destroying the relationship and herself.

IV. Irene: Healthy Dynamics

Infrequently, if not rarely, one meets an adult so fortunate as to have been raised from birth with love, understanding, and respect for his or her personality so that the individual is assured of a good healthy 0–6 and a healthy core of dynamics for its adult life. Irene was one of these fortunate individuals. At thirty years of age she still had excellent relations with her parents and siblings and with her husband and children. Seldom does such a wholesome person come to see me professionally.

When she contacted me, Irene had two children, ages one and four; she was finding that the responsibilities and demands made upon her by the children were very strenuous, and she in turn became irritable and angry. In addition, she was angry with herself for what she considered a lack of strength. These dynamics were not known to Irene at first. All she knew was that she would have sudden crying spells, which would make her feel ashamed.

After we talked for only one hour, Irene began to realize how difficult the job of raising children was, how demanding and how confining, how interrupting of her previous freedoms, and how demanding the two children were of her time and attention; and she began to realize how legitimate her inner protest against it was. She also saw that it was simply not realistic to expect to handle all this responsibility without some irritability and protest, because it was a day-in-day-out, month-in-month-out job. With this realization Irene was tremendously relieved emotionally, and there was no need for further treatment. Her life went on well. But a year later she again found herself pregnant. This meant that she soon had two children in diapers at the same time. The youngest was not quite six months old and the next child just over a year and a half when Irene again came to see me. In addition to her physical depletion by two close pregnancies, her oldest child was very active by temperament and even tended to be hyperkinetic. He was outgoing and loving, but so active as to upset the entire household and quite difficult to live with. This situation, combined with the two infants, was a tall order for anyone to handle. Irene was aware of her heavy responsibilities and was trying to cope. Yet she also realized that she was full of anger and hostility. In fact, her opening remark at this interview was, "What do you do with your hostilities?"

I asked for details; she particularly emphasized that she wanted to save her wonderful relationship with her husband. Irene felt that the two of them had something rare in life: they were both very much in love with one another, it was an unusually fine relationship, and she did not want it to change in any way. Her husband, who was with a large company, was ambitious and overworked. He left for his job early in the morning, came back relatively late at night, but without being asked would pitch in and take over whatever household chores needed to be done. He, too, was carrying too much responsibility, and it was hard for him to do his job and return home without any emotional support and recuperation. Irene recognized this, and it hurt her. She felt that she should have more to give to her husband, and when she found herself behaving irritably, she hated herself. Above all, she was afraid to lose the close, loving relationship between them.

How do you help a person therapeutically to handle *consciously suppressed* hostilities when she already knows her own dynamics so well? It is probably a matter of working through. I reviewed with Irene her entire situation so that she had it clearly fixed in her mind. We discussed the fact that responsibility for husband, home, and three young children—one overly active and two still in diapers—was really enormous. To carry that burden indefinitely without some angry protest would be asking too much. But the situation existed, and she would have to arrange as best she could to get some time off from the home. She would have to talk things over openly with her husband, which she had already begun to do.

This paraphrase of an old quotation seemed appropriate for Irene: "Young love, too, is beautiful, but the most beautiful is the love that has weathered the storms of life." Both she and her husband saw the wisdom in that, and it helped them realize that they were in the midst of a most stressful period in their life together; if they could keep their love in spite of the excessive responsibilities and demands for a few more years, then they would be over the worst hurdle. This situation would not last forever—soon the children would be more grown up; the parents' sleep would not be interrupted each night by the baby.

Irene told me about another young couple, friends of theirs whom they had met socially. They were in a somewhat similar situation. He was overworked and just beginning to climb the ladder; his wife was burdened by responsibilities for home and children. They had four children. This young couple—Lloyd and Candy—had become irritable under all their responsibility; they were getting on each other's nerves, and hostility was generated between them. Unhappily, it seems that within most marriages each partner tends to take out his or her feelings on the other. With Lloyd and Candy, the hostility was beginning to diminish their love for each other; and Irene, a keen observer, was aware of this. The situation between her young friends precipitated her visit to me. She did not want the same thing to happen to her marriage. At the time of her second visit with me, Irene said Lloyd and Candy's love for one another had so diminished in fact, that they felt there was not much sense in continuing the marriage, although Candy felt it was only fair to the children for her to stick around until they were more mature and could stand the separation better.

It was gratifying to have Irene come to see me, not with the goal of so many others—preventing a breakdown—but with the very positive motive of trying to preserve a fine marriage, by handling anything that might interfere with the love between herself and her husband.

We have stayed in touch, and Irene writes that now, many years later, the marriage is still excellent and her two sessions with me were a turning point in her life; she saw that everyone, including herself, is not infinitely strong but has limitations and must know them and stay within them. Plenty of stress and demands continue in her life, but it is a devoted family and the children are maturing in a loving atmosphere. It was Irene's basically healthy 0–6 that enabled her to react so well to the insights she gained from only two visits. She was internally sustained (Saul, 1970).

References

Saul, L. (1970): Inner sustainment: the concept, *Psychoanal. Quart.*, 39(2).

The emphasis of this book is on learning, intellect, and skills rather than on emotional development, but it is a valuable and important guide:

White, B. (1975): *The First Three Years of Life*. Englewood Cliffs, N.J.: Prentice-Hall, Inc.

12

THE AGE OF 0-6

I. Rachel Rosewell: The Princess and the Princes

A young, attractive, tall, and slender woman came to see me because of a very simple complaint, namely, a tendency in the past few months to gain weight, which she had not been able to control. As usual, when one endeavors to look behind symptoms to their causes, one gets into a hitherto unimagined world.

This patient, Rachel Roswell, was an intense brunette, in her late thirties, married, and with three children. It was soon evident that she was highly intelligent and had many diverse interests. After I asked a little about her family and the medical aspects of her weight gain, whether she had a history of it and the results of her recent physical examination, we came to her childhood pattern. I asked the general question, "Please tell me the main features of your life from the time you were born until the age of about six."

Rachel replied, "I started to tell you that I was afraid of being alone and that was the main feature, but then I thought, 'No,' I used to have a constant battle to keep my mother from being angry at me and I think *that* is the main feature. I remember once being on the back seat of the car with her and thinking to myself that I must be getting older because there now seemed to be longer periods of time between my mother getting angry at me. My mother felt that selfishness was the main negative motivation in the world, and that anyone that had it, especially women, must be constantly fighting it. My mother was often angry with me for the way I talked. She thought it was an unpleasant voice.

"She became angry if I used the word 'I' too much, but I don't recall her getting that angry at my younger brothers. I am the oldest and have four younger brothers, but I don't recall them being penalized in the same way as I was. I was also afraid of the dark; I remember a desire to be free and to be free meant running freely and talking with friends. It was also a desire to be alone. I even built a little shelter in the woods near the lake where I could go alone and no one else could get there. (Rachel grew up in a northern suburb of Chicago, near Lake Michigan.) I remember my birthdays—Mother was good at birthdays; that was the biggest day in the year, even bigger than Christmas. There were always presents and people seemed to be there all day long. I remember a lot of fighting with my four younger brothers who seemed to challenge everything I said, and I wanted to be left alone. My baby sister played no part in my life until I was twelve years old. I remember that Mother said I must have a bowel movement every day after breakfast, and maybe because of that I was constipated for months. She insisted that I nap after lunch which I never could do, and I developed insomnia. She also insisted that I keep my room neat and therefore I kept it a mess; I think that Mother really loved me, though. She was always glad to see me when I came in. When I was small she used to come with the car to pick me up and she always seemed glad to see me."

I then asked Rachel the more specific question: "Who were the main emotional figures in your life during your 0-6, birth to about six?" and Rachel replied, "Mother, Mother, Mother."

"Unquestionably it was Mother," she continued. "Mother insisted that Father must be the most important person in the house, but I felt that he was distant, disinterested and unconcerned, so it was all Mother. Later I had an intellectual relationship with Father when I was preadolescent, but all during childhood Father came home late every day and then he and Mother talked with each other and I felt left out. On the other hand, I was glad to be left alone. Father was just not there. I simply could see no reason for being so loving and attentive to Father as my Mother wanted me to be. I felt that Father never approved of me because he was never there—in fact, I felt he disapproved of me, and that if he approved of me he would have done things with me."

"What about the relationships with your brothers?" I asked.

"I remember Ron, who was the next younger child to myself in age. I remember him the most. He *hated* me, and I was glad to see him picked on at school. Once Ron said, 'I am going to kill you,' and went into the kitchen and got a knife. He and I fought so; when he had appendicitis I kicked him in the stomach. Ron and I would fight over who would hold Mother's hand and we fought over who was the older, but Mother always took Ron's side."

"Is there still some hostility between you and your brother, Ron?" I asked.

"I don't know," Rachel replied; "Ron went out of my life when I became a teenager and went away to boarding school. I have sometimes thought of going into the same business he was in because there was an excellent opportunity for a woman there and I could have filled it well, but I worried whether those old hostilities would come back or not because they were so strong. However, you asked about today and I think today I have made my peace with the brothers, and we all think of Mother as the common enemy."

"How does that work?" I asked.

She replied, "It has something to do with Mother's attitudes toward us. I think Mother was quite hostile and took it out on us. But I always felt that she did not take my side. There is very little of all that left inside me . . . now today, in the present; now I adore my brothers, but maybe that is because there is no longer any need to not be friends because Mother is no longer part of the picture."

"Why is that?" I asked.

She said, "I think Mother was a lot of the reason we fought so much. If she had left us alone we would have been much better off."

"Can you give an illustration?"

She thought a moment. "Yes," she said, "I once had a conversation with Mother over what would happen if she or Father were to die. Who would take care of us? I did not want Mother; I wanted my grandmother, my father's mother. I did not want to hurt my mother, but I guess I did so. She thought it was not an unreasonable idea, though; I fancied living with Grandmother and realized it would be much better than living with my mother. Grandma was easygoing, never said anything about my mother, but my mother said awful things about her. It was probably part of Mother's trying to direct everything. We did not want to think badly of Grandma, but Mother insisted. Grandma was important for us . . . she cared about how she looked, how the house looked, and about feminine things, but Mother's house was always a mess and Mother was always talking against everyone. I think my own enjoyment of my house comes from Grandma. She liked to have the linens neatly stacked and to have nice clothes, etc. Grandmother was a very religious person and active in the church. We used to have church services in the house— her house—every Sunday morning for everybody, but particularly for all the grandchildren, and my mother made fun of it but I liked it.

I liked the structure of it because my mother's life was so damn messy. I have always thought that concern with appearances is a negative thing, but now that we talk I begin to see that was because of my mother's attitude toward my grandmother, because Grandmother loved nice things—Sunday dinner, flowers, and so on. When I thought of marrying my husband, my grandmother said, 'If you do it I will give you a beautiful present.' But Mother said, 'If you *don't* do it I will give you one equally beautiful.'

"I wanted to be a cross between Grandmother and a man whom she liked very much. Grandmother's closets were always so neat, they always smelled so good. My mother's closets have always been a mess and smelled. I hardly remember my grandfather at all. He was so gruff and played very little role in my life, but he did share Grandmother's love of the good life. He would bring home lots of people—friends, business associates and so on. They had lots of family feeling. I have often wondered how anything decent could have come out of me because my mother was so neurotic, and now I think it must have been because of my grandmother. However, Mother was often affectionate, but she is not someone I want to emulate. I guess I did not like her."

[This seems to be a good illustration of how a parent's handling of her child provokes sufficient hostility to prevent the child from identifying with the parent; although her mother was often affectionate, yet she did not want to identify with her, to emulate her, because as she said, she did not like her. However, the tendency to identify is so strong that to this day Rachel was fighting against it.]

I said, "Why did you not like her?" and she replied, "Probably for the same reasons as today . . . I never thought about it. I think she does not have worthwhile goals in life. Mother never has done something with somebody because of liking them. I think there is no love in her life; it is only obligation. 'You must greet your father at the door. When you grow up you ought to live your husband's life.' She never thought that a person did something because the individual wanted to do it for himself. Now I seem to be unfair to Mother, because she did seem to have some warmth. Mother would gather us in her arms; you could always count on her. It's just that I liked Grandmother much better."

"Why?" I asked.

"I guess because she was a nicer person."

"Even from 0 to 6?" I asked.

"I think so," she replied. "I used to spend a lot of time at Mother's knee. During cocktail hour I often would sit and listen to Mother and hear how grownups handled life, ourselves, each other and so on. Mother was a dreadful gossip . . . I never remember her saying any generous thing about Grandmother or anyone. I am not like Mother; I like most people.

"Why this is amazing. There seem to be no men in this story. I think it is not me blocking it out; they just were not there. Father was so distant and Grandfather was even worse. The brothers younger than Ron I barely remember, and the next youngest one to Ron always teamed up with Ron against me, so it was those two against me. But the next youngest one was not so intense as Ron, and therefore my hostility to him was not quite so bad as my hostility to Ron. The very youngest one was a spoiled brat and has turned into quite a character. They were all a strong influence in my life, though, but in a negative way."

"In what way?" I asked.

"Because we fought so, and I disliked it so, but Mother loves a good fight."

I explained to Rachel about the earliest memories and asked what the first one was that she remembered. She told the following:

"The first memory must have been when I was less than two years old. I was being vaccinated for smallpox and I was very sick; I remember a white-tiled bathroom and someone carrying me. Was it because I could not yet walk, or because I was sick from the vaccination on the leg? At any rate, the room was very big . . . or rather, the room itself was not so big, but the ceiling was so tall, the feeling was of a great deal of concern about me, how sick I was and that somebody was taking care of me. [Something had happened to patient plus getting care.] [This sounds rather like the first memory of Arlene Rodgers, the patient in the previous chapter.]

"My next memories, all before six, were of the summertime: (2) when I was barely three we lived in a yellow house with an enclosed porch all the way around it, and I could remember it, and my brothers and my mother said that was impossible for me to remember. But later on I pointed it out, and my mother said, 'Ye gods, she really *does* remember it!' (3) I think it was the summer following that there was a great storm, and we were waiting for a boat, and Mother was afraid of the storm, refusing to take the boat and wanting to take the train. Father agreed. I did not feel well, I may have been carsick. [Danger and something bad happening to patient.] Grandmother and Grandfather were with us. (4) Then the next summer I remember Father teaching me to count, how to clean eyeglasses, how to open a new book, and tricycling around the porch. [Attention from Father.] (5) Also I had swallowed something which I think may have been a cherry pit, and there was terrible concern over whether they would have to operate. [Again, something bad happening to her and concern about her.] (6) I never wanted to nap but was always forced to, and so as a result I never took one, and this made Mother angry at me. [Hostility to Mother, and Mother to Rachel.] (7) The household help changed very fast, always, in my mother's house, because they did not get on with her I guess. (8) Then Ron, I remember, got into a hornets' nest and was badly stung." [Hostility to Brother.]

I asked the patient what she thought of her description of her childhood in general and of all these memories she had given, and she said, "I think it boils down to anger at Mother. I think there was anger in Mother which seemed to come out in part at us, the children, and I was afraid of that anger, and maybe that's why I wanted to be alone but was afraid of being alone. I could not meet anger with anger. Today it is a little different. When Mother is angry, which is all the time, I tend to get angry back, but as a child if I got angry I was afraid Mother might leave me and I needed her. Also, I think there was jealousy in Mother of Grandmother, and I wonder if this does not still have impact today, because I feel it is not right to take pleasure in my house, although I really do. I realize that at 0–6 I was mostly taken up in avoiding Mother's anger, and I wonder if that is why it is so hard to talk to my husband, because he gets angry; because I feared Mother's anger or anyone's anger and now, especially, his. He does not become very angry openly; it just festers. I am even afraid to discuss important everyday matters or various decisions in his life with him for fear that he will get angry with me. Once, for example, he wanted me to sign some papers. I refused because I thought it was my right to understand what it was I was signing, but I went to a lawyer and the lawyer said I definitely should not sign. I am struck by the fact that there was no real relationship with men in the story of my early childhood."

"Is that really true?" I said. "For there *were* males, at least certainly your brothers, even though your father and grandfather seemed to be mostly out of the picture. Is there anything more about them shaping a pattern in you? You have already described your mother shaping a pattern and your tendency to repeat this toward your husband. Are there any patterns toward your brothers or other males from 0 to 6 that still persist?"

"We fought a lot," she said. "Was it sibling rivalry, or maybe that I was bossy? At any rate, there was hate between the brothers and myself."

"Can you give me any examples?" I asked.

"Yes," she replied, "one time after dinner we were playing in a swing and it broke and they laughed at me. That was, of course, mostly Ron, but the others followed suit and laughed too. Then I remember swimming in a dangerous mountain stream with rapids and I was caught by the current and swept out of the swimming hole and over the rocks and I yelled and they just stood there and let me go by them. Once I was in a car accident and was taken home. My mother insisted on hearing all the details. Mother defended me, one of the few times she had done that, when Ron kept interrupting me. She told him to be quiet while she asked me."

Then I asked Rachel this: "Did you not say that the fighting might be from sibling rivalry, and now from this memory are you not implying it might be from seeking the attention of your mother?"

"I think," she said, "that I got all of the attention at the beginning when I was the only child and none after the brothers arrived. I was the firstborn, and very much the pet and center of attention. I don't remember it and had not thought of it, but now I think it must have been the arrival of the sons . . . I remember Mother and Father discussing the addition of a new wing on the house; it may have been a nursery wing. We all lived in that wing; it was incredibly messy. It was typical of Mother. She didn't mind if we drew on the walls, but at the same time she insisted on the bowel movement after breakfast and the nap after lunch, and when I couldn't do either Mother was furious. I remember once a baby crying and seeing Mother change its diapers in the bathroom. I remember many nurses, many, because they never stayed . . . we were such awful children. One of them washed out my mouth with soap and my mother was furious. When I got a haircut the hair would get down the collar and itch all night. I would have terrible dreams, so much so that I could not sleep. I consciously decided that I would ask people in the dream if it were a dream, and also that I would fly. There was always someone chasing me and the fright was terrible, but often the surroundings were magnificent. A friend of mine is an expert in mind control. I guess that's what I did then when I determined in the dreams that I would definitely fly and ask people if it were a dream.

"I guess I also had some resentment against Father, because when he came home he took Mother away. I thought it was silly, but Mother always said 'Daddy is coming home,' and 'Kiss Daddy good-night,' when I had no feeling for it. But I loved it when he would read to me. The best way to relate to a child is to read to him."

"You said you were often chased in dreams," I said. "By whom would that be?"

She replied, "I started to say it was always an animal, but now I am not so sure. Sometimes it was people, sometimes it was men, and that was always very scary. One man was in a suit of armor, a sort of knight. Sometimes it was in jungles, all kinds of vines and branches grabbing at me. Sometimes it was in castles, men in armor. I said to one, 'Can you tell me if this is a dream?'

"I remember another childhood memory, however. This was at our lake cottage; Grandmother came to visit and I was playing with her ring. I dropped it. There was a great search and finally we found it. She said I should not lose it because she would give it to me when I was eighteen, and she did."

Rachel continued, "My mother's mother came to visit, but it was not happy, because she and mother fought. I think I had no brothers then. It was before the betrayal, before I was pushed out by them.

"We had a dog, and she went up the beach and returned with four or five other dogs of the same breed. Mother got so angry once at Ron that she threatened to put him out of the car. About that time I had a nightmare of an owl. Owls swallow mice and regurgitate the bones. I saw little piles of bones. The summers were great, though. Someone once asked me why I liked trains, and I said because they took us away summers. Father was supposed to rule the house. Mother would say, 'Your father thinks this,' or, 'We must ask your father; wait until your father comes home, don't do this because your father will spank you.' But my father taught me to read, to count, and all about stars. I think Father never liked children and still doesn't. Ron was full of scars because he never cared about hurting himself. He was a cute devil, but I hated him at times. I remember a photo of him and myself, with me all dressed up. I remember me going for a walk once, in town. I hated it. I hated my clothes; I was not allowed to dress casually. While we were there on vacation, there were crowds of people on the main drag and my brothers would get lost. When Ron disappeared, my mother hardly knew that he was gone. I knew that if I were separated from Father and Mother I would never see them again. I would be swallowed up by all the people and taken away into loneliness. I remember playing with the brothers and how delicious it was to thwart them."

Here our time was up, so I took the last moments of the analytic hour to review these memories with Rachel. It was quite evident that they dealt with getting rid of the brothers—getting lost on the avenue, the owl eating the mice (and the mice might well represent young children) and spitting out the bones—and certainly these memories showed the hostility to them. It raised two questions: (1.) Was the hostility to the siblings and also to Mother and Father so intense in large part because of frustrated dependent love needs toward the parents, especially Mother? (2.) Did all this hostility and the hostility to Mother and Father not cause a great deal of anxiety, either directly for fear that if the patient expressed anger she would be punished or deserted or anger her mother even more, or her father, or even by a guilt? For she kept apologizing for her hostility to Mother, saying that perhaps she was being unfair to Mother.

Careful study of these memories confirmed this. The next hour we returned to the patient's chief complaint, namely, the gain in weight. I started by asking her all her present complaints, and she said, "The weight is at the top of the list. I overeat almost deliberately, almost defiantly. Also the second problem is . . . and I don't know if it's really a problem . . . figuring out a way to reconcile my need to be myself with my husband's career—my own identification. I feel dissatisifed all the time, I can't seem to do anything on my own, and I don't want to be merely an appendage of my husband."

"Do you think," I asked, "these two complaints might be connected?"

"Yes," she said, "my eating was my way of expressing myself and a way in which no one could stop me."

"Please tell me the whole history of your overeating," I asked.

She said, "I have struggled with my weight all my life, but it has been a false struggle because there was really no problem and I was never fat at all until recently. Mother was more hung up on it than I; Mother made me have the medical tests."

[At the very beginning of the hour the patient asked if I would suggest her having a physical examination, and could I recommend an internist who was a specialist on obesity. I said I went along with the idea of a physical examination completely because occasionally some simple thing such as a small dose of thyroid might alter the metabolic balance and help an individual stop weight gain. Then she discussed where to go, and I said that the best thing to do was for me to phone an internist known to be excellent, and perhaps she should go into the hospital for a few days and have him order all the tests. She reacted to this with great anger, which I did not understand; then she told the reason—the thyroid test that her mother always bugged her to take—and my mere mention of this was taken as my trying to force her to do something. Also, it was Rachel's mother who kept insisting that she go into the hospital, and she was angry with me for suggesting the same thing. Of course this happens all the time, and one never knows, especially as an analyst, when he will suggest something in perfect innocence and with simple good sense only to find it striking an especially vulnerable point in the patient. This example is an unusually clear one.]

"When I had the tests they were always normal, but nevertheless Mother always bugged me about them. Mother said it was the mark of a lady to have thin wrists and ankles, and criticized my grandmother. I identified with Grandmother and I think that Mother tried by these means to break up my relationship with Grandmother. It was my mother who insisted that I go to a doctor who was supposed to be an expect on obesity, and I hated him. It was also Mother that insisted I go on a diet when I was eighteen years old. Yet it was possible that Mother force-fed us, that is, forced us to eat when we were young. Possibly my weight gain now is my protest against being forced to do anything . . . I want to be my own person. In a way, I have thought I have sold my soul to the devil, that I might do something outrageous to prove I could not be controlled."

"Like what?" I asked.

"Gaining a lot of weight, or taking risks driving a car, and I've even had suicidal urges. Once I had an urge to throw myself off a boat into the lake when nobody could stop me, and every once in a while I awake at night in severe terror with an urge to run away and be free. I feel something in me saying, 'You cannot stop me; I can do what I want.' And now I think of Mother's influence being so strong that I was angry at Mother and wanted to be free. If I think of beating

Mother to death in my head I feel free, but I also feel somewhat the same to my husband."

I said, "As in the last hour, the key seems to be hostile rebellion to your mother. She tried to force you to have the bowel movements after breakfast and the naps after lunch and now to be thin. But Mother force-fed you and also wants you to be thin."

"Yes, I see that," Rachel said. "I never made that connection. That is very good of you to point that out. I rebelled against all that and I was constipated and could not nap, but today I like all the naps I can get and I have forgotten about all the bowel movements and they take care of themselves. But must I do something rebellious to prove that I am free? Suicide, car accidents, and so on are socially unacceptable."

"It looks as though the obesity is connected with your marital problem," I said; "you tend to repeat toward your husband the same pattern of hostile rebellion you have toward your mother, and perhaps you also repeat toward society this hostile rebellious pattern toward your mother. Doing something rebellious and outrageous would get back at your husband and, in a way, at society."

"Right!" she said, "and now I think of it often. I think too of *another first memory*. We were never allowed to cry as children. Mother used to say, 'If you do not stop by the time I count three you will get spanked,' and then she would try to shame us by saying, 'You are feeling sorry for yourself.' I did everything Mother and Father expected of me; I did well at school, I married well, but I never struck out to have a life of my own. Now I frankly discuss everything with my brothers, and they are very supportive."

"Why do you suppose they are so supportive?" I asked. "Because they were subjected to the same kind of control themselves?"

"Yes," she said. "I'm sure of it, and Mother still controls me. For example, I am not thinking of divorce, but I also could not think of it because Mother said she would not taken me in or side with me at all, and of course I have the children and it would help a lot if she gave us enough money so that we would have some financial security.

"It seems," she continued, "that all these controls by Mother are physical—bowel movements, nap, not being allowed to weep—they all have to do with physical conditions rather than psychological, although one of them was psychological, namely how long can I go (three days?) without making Mother angry at me."

I have remarked that it seemed that this young woman was so treated by her mother that she was hostile to her mother, therefore failing to identify with her. It is more correct to say that she did not consciously accept an identification with her mother, for I think there is always some degree of identification with a parent. There may be reaction formations against this, but some degree of identification exists. In this case, I think it was evident in the strength of the patient's personality; her mother was a strong, dominating, and controlling personality, and the patient tended to be this beneath the surface. She was a great organizer. She did not take it out on her children, but it was evident in her social activities, where she was a leader and a dominating personality. This she probably did not get from her father, who was mostly absent from her life, but who was somewhat withdrawn and shy.

The point I am trying to make is that identification with the parent always exists to some extent, even though it may not be immediately evident, and even though the patient might be unconscious of it. As an example of reaction formation against it, I recall a man who organized a large, successful business and was running it very efficiently. He was a good father, very kind and understanding with his children, both boys and girls, and an outstanding husband. One would never think from this that he had run away from home as an early adolescent because of having been beaten by his own father beyond his tolerance. He suffered so from this that he vowed consciously, and apparently also developed an unconscious reaction formation, to always be kind to his wife and children, definitely *not* the way his father had been to him. The reaction formation was supported, however, by a positive identification with his loving mother. His identification with his father therefore did not show toward his wife and children, but it did give him a certain strength and force in his business relationships. This was evident as two sides of his personality: at home, he was quiet, shy, and obedient to his wife, the loving husband and parent. But when he crossed the threshold to run his business, this shy, retiring man became a forceful leader, even though always with a gentle manner.

Probably all human relationships are made up of object relations and identification. For some reason, it seems (from my teaching and supervisory work) that students are able to grasp the object relations much more readily than they are the identifications. It is evident that if the child is rejected by a parent, dominated, or made the butt of the parent's hostility, his reactions against this treatment can often be readily seen. So much for the object relationships. What is more apt to be overlooked, however, is the tendency of the child to *identify* with that parent.

A young woman was ignored by her parents. She insisted that she had been loved up to the time her father was killed in an accident and her mother had to go out and take a job. But her first memories— this powerful tool of insight into the unconscious—showed almost nothing of her relationship to her mother. What was most evident when she first came to see me was her rage. Her complaint was acute anxiety. Her dreams were all of blood and thunder, of rooms collapsing and killing or injuring a lot of people, usually including herself. And in life she had a very hot temper which she did not hesitate to vent upon her husband—even, in a somewhat paranoid way, unrealistically accusing the husband of all sorts of things. But beyond this underlying chronic anger and anxiety there was a coldness to everybody that prevented her from making friends. She did have a few friends among her own age group, patterned after the relationship to her sister and two or three cousins when she was a child. Basically, though, she did not have much in the way of love and affection to give. She disliked almost everyone and disapproved of practically everybody. She was not given enough love as a child, and therefore did not have enough to give out as an adult. But what was more difficult to see and became evident in her analysis was her identification with her mother. In a single sentence, her mother ignored her; therefore, identifying with her mother she ignored everybody else. This is identification with the aggressor, but more broadly, it is simply identification with the parent. What the parent did to the child, the child tends to do to others. Sometimes because of other forces, this relationship is covered with reaction formations, as I have said.

The object relationships must be seen, but also the identification must never be overlooked. This was confirmed in the very next interview with Rachel Roswell.

Two hours were spent with her on her childhood dynamics, which came out quite clearly; then in the third hour came a good example of the difficulty but importance of discerning the identification with the parents:

"That session with you a week ago," Rachel said, "was a very insightful one. In fact, I was elated after the insights of that meeting. Then it wore off, but I have not made any bad slips in eating since. It seems incredible, but that seems to be more under control already. But I tend to control as my mother once did, and still does. In mentioning my chief complaints, I said the first was overeating. Then everything about my interest in opportunities for women seems to be part of my efforts to be free. But also now I have a fear of being like my mother, of growing old and being like her. Yet my control is not all that bad. I control the house, I keep the house well organized. What is that? What should I do?"

I said, "I think the first step is to give it a name, and that name is 'identification.' We have already seen a lot of your object relationships to your parents, which we have discussed briefly . . . your resentment of your father being absent, your appreciation of his helping you to read, and a few other things, and your defenses against your mother's hostility and your resentment of it. But now you are afraid of being like your mother, and that is your identification with her. That is something that must also be understood and—if need be—outgrown."

Rachel replied, "I still feel hopeless about not being like Mother . . . maybe because I have been aware of being like her for so long. I even treat my oldest son so much the way my mother treated my brothers, but I also try to be nice to my children and this is confusing for them. Jack, my oldest son, and I have a very strong relationship and it worries me. But now I see that Jack reminds me of Ron, my oldest brother, the one with whom I fought so. Jack is the oldest of the three sons, just as Ron was the oldest of the four brothers. Jack agreed to cut the lawn all summer. We had so much rain and we said to keep it properly he would have to dash out to do it when the weather was nice, but he does only a little at a time and I get angry, but I don't want to be controlling. I cannot see any solution. I see the control but I can't see any way of solving it."

I said, "I think the solution lies in insight first and then in practice in living in order to outgrow the handicapping childhood pattern. First we must see them, and then we must talk over how to solve and resolve and outgrow them."

Rachel said, "Jack has not done his shopping yet for camp and we are going on vacation in a few days, yet I fear to insist that he do it and be controlling."

I replied, "Is that not a matter of how you say it . . . with tact? Can you not treat Jack as an adult, as a reasonable person? For example, if you say 'Jack, look, these are the things you need before going away to camp; we have only a little time left, what do you think we should do to solve this problem? How will we get this job done?'"

"Yes," Rachel said with some enthusiasm. "I can see that I can say almost anything I want if only I do it right. But still my biggest problem is the overeating. Is this connected with my treatment as a baby? Yet I like to cook . . . I never thought of this before. Mother never liked to cook nor could she cook. I love vegetables; I would rather grow vegetables than flowers. I like arranging them, but still overeating is my biggest problem."

"No," I said, "I don't think so. What I mean is, the overeating is your biggest symptom, but it is only symptomatic of your biggest problem, and that seems to be the relationship to your mother."

"Right!" said Rachel. "I can see that. My mind now seems to be going back to Jack. I have remarkable children. With all of our problems, yet not one is neurotic. Jack went to a school where he had great energy and often got into trouble. The school only punished and never tried to understand him. Therefore I went to consult our pediatrician who said, 'You'd better change schools.' Now, obviously that is not so easy. But the pediatrician suggested a school and I looked into it thoroughly, went to see it, and spent some time there. I thought it was wonderful. To some extent the students run the school. There is not an excessive amount of homework, but the students take a good deal of responsibility. I spoke with Jack about it and he agreed. He transferred there, even though his own school had already begun, but everything went fine. This was an important step in Jack's life. He began to feel as if *he* had some say in his own life. [Which is what Rachel was seeking for herself.] It improved his relationship with me greatly, and he spontaneously began to kiss me good-bye mornings and also when he came back in the afternoon. Jack then began to have a new respect for me and saw me as not all 'nagger.' Each of the children go to different schools, but all have reports that are excellent, are popular, have leadership, and so on. It's really been the best luck."

I said, "I guess you and your husband did a good job in their 0 to 6's."

She replied, "Why is it so important to me to have everything in order? I have no help now at all and will have none on vacation, but I do not like to see the dishes lying in the sink. Would that be because my mother was so messy? She left everything lying around and therefore did I rebel against her because I couldn't stand it?"

"Not only possible," I said, "but likely, and it may be that you got the strength to rebel against your mother from your grandmother."

"Why, yes!" said Rachel. "Grandmother was so neat, I can see that rebellion, but why do I feel that I must control?"

I said, "Usually the child sees only two possibilities—either to be like the parent or else to be suffering at the hands of the parent as a child. In your case, it would be either control like Mother or be controlled by her."

"We must go and visit my parents for a few days, and I fear that when I am with Mother I will fall into the old pattern and start excessive eating again."

"Very good," I said, "then you recognize that you are afraid of the mobilization, by proximity to Mother, of part of your old 0–6 pattern?"

"Yes," said Rachel, "I think I see that, but I don't want to be hurt by Mother's attack either. Shall I just stay silent? I don't think it helps any for me to be nasty back. Should I just ignore her?"

I replied, "This is very good because now you are doing it by your ego instead of by an automatic, unconscious reaction. Now you are aware of your reaction and are thinking of the best ways to handle it. Even if you do the same as you have been, and stay silent, at least it will be with insight and with judgment. You see the problem, we talk it over first and judge the best way to handle the situation, and then you try that. This is using your higher faculties of understanding and judgment rather than having an unconscious, automatic response. And you learn from living. Your development is then reopened." We discussed this for a few more minutes and I think that Rachel saw the point very well. She was highly intelligent and highly psychological, and I think she got a new idea from this of the nature of analytic processes. She saw more clearly what it was we were trying to do.

I did not want to influence in the slightest Rachel's flow of memories that were so revelatory of her childhood pattern. But eventually she would have to render to the past what belonged to the past, and get her relationship to her mother out of that child-mother pattern and onto an adult-to-adult basis. Therefore I reminded her that when her mother came to see me to give her view of the history I had liked her very much. Whatever she (Rachel's mother) had gone through during her own children's 0–6, she *had* tried to be a good mother and was, I thought, a rather heroic figure. She had come through a very difficult time in her own life, and although her children were not entirely unscathed, she had meant well and had given them such sincere love that the children's problems were not seriously handicapping, and all were doing well in their lives, rearing good children of their own. Working with Rachel we saw only what was wrong in her mother's raising of her children because of the pressures that Rachel's mother had to endure from *her* mother, in turn. Thus we did not get a balanced view of all the positives she provided, which gave Rachel and her brothers their strengths and superior qualities.

"... For I the Lord thy God am a jealous God, visiting the iniquity of the fathers upon the children to the third and fourth generation ..." (Exodus 20:5). In medical school we were immersed in the world of the body and its physical ills and assumed that this Biblical statement referred to congenital syphilis; it never seemed to fit quite properly. But it describes perfectly the transmission of the emotional problems of the parents down through the generation, and in this sense is rich in meaning. As we trace each patient's emotional problems to his relations with his parents in earliest childhood, we glimpse the emotional problems of the parents; if we interview the parents, we see the origins of *their* problems in *their* 0–6's. If the analyst lives long enough, he sees the transmission to the younger generation as well of the emotional disorders which plague psychologically suffering humanity.

Dynamic Diagnosis: Rachel Roswell

Childhood: (1) First grandchild, cynosure of family, *displaced* by siblings, all boys, who were preferred by Mother. (2) Controlled by Mother through dictatorialness instead of winning over by love. (3) *Distance* of Mother and Father. (4) The displacement by siblings, overcontrol, and distance cause increased dependent love needs, frustrated, especially toward Mother and intensified hostility to Mother and siblings.

Current: (1) Feelings of deprivation lead to increased demands and hostility and feelings that men are preferred over women; jealousy, especially of husband. Anger and competition with men. (2) Feels dominated, leading to defensiveness and domination to prevent being dominated and to impulses to flight. (3) Struggles against identification with Mother and cannot identify with Father or Brother figures. Therefore striving to achieve own identity without knowing how; some dissatisfaction with being a woman. Fight-flight leads to anger and a little masochistic regression including tendency to over- or undereat, and fantasies of being free from control by withdrawing, by running away.

Strengths: (1) Superior intelligence. (2) Drive to help self vicariously by helping the underdogs. (3) Determination to stand up to any- and everyone.

II. Walter Burton: The Oedipus

Walter Burton was a good-looking, blond, successful young lawyer of thirty, already somewhat portly, who came to see me because of simple anxiety, primarily about his marriage, although, more broadly, his love life—his relationships with women. He had a mistress, which made a situation to which his wife objected vigorously. So his home life was in poor shape; on the other hand, he was not very happy with the mistress, who was insisting that he get a divorce and marry her.

After asking in detail about his present-day life situation and pattern, I inquired about his 0–6. I asked who were the main figures in his life from the time of his birth to age about six or seven, as best he could remember. [This was before I learned that it was better just to ask for the "main features."]

He said, "My mother. I am an only child and I think it was my mother. As a secondary figure, my father and my mother's mother—that is, my maternal grandmother. Also, possibly my mother's sister. But the most important was my mother."

I said, "Should we start with the relationship to your mother when you were little?"

He said, "My first memory is like a Polaroid picture. I was about two years old. Early one morning I had gotten up for breakfast; I had gotten out of my crib and onto my mother's lap and her arms were around me. She was nuzzling me, saying something to the effect that she loved me and my response was, 'I love you too.' [Satisfying, loving closeness to Mother.] I also have memories of Christmas about this time. In other words, from about the age of two. And these memories were also very warm and happy." He is silent as he thinks further, and I said, "Apart from these discreet memories you are telling, what is your impression of the basic emotional interrelationship with your mother?"

He replied, "It was very loving, but it changed when I was about two and a half to three, although it was still loving. But at that point my father took a new job in the next town; then we moved, and we lived with my grandmother. My mother went back to work as a secretary. She had worked before marriage, and now she went back to the same work. All that occurred over the space of a year. I was not happy about my mother going to work and about my being taken to my grandmother's every day. That is, every day until we moved in with my grandmother. When we were at my grandmother's, my mother did not ignore me when she was there. Also, if she went out, she took me along—if she went out shopping or walking or anywhere I went along. So the relationship changed, but I am not sure just how. I think it became too intensely one-to-one."

[This is somewhat similar to, but much milder than, what happened to Pat Ralston, p. 185: the intensification to the mother because of the father's absence.]

The patient continued, "Grandmother was nice to me but was basically a baby-sitter, basically to care for my physical needs rather than anything else. I forgot to mention my grandfather. He died just about that time. I was told later that grandfather was very stern and authoritarian, but I do not remember that. I think he was always good to me. One day he came into the kitchen and sat down and said he did not feel well. With that, he was dead. The doctor came and confirmed it. I was not especially upset about it; I guess I did not understand it. But about a year later the younger sister of a friend of ours died, and I saw her and that *did* upset me.

"I think my very *first memory* was of being chastised severely for urinating in the street in front of our house. That was before we moved to my grandmother's, that is, just about the age of two. A year or so after that, when I was nearly four, I was bothered by some side issues. One was that Mother would tell me her problems, that were way beyond my ability to understand or help with, and I was upset because Mother told me her financial problems. Then she cried, and that made me afraid that Mother would be taken off to the poor house.

So I did all I could do; I gave her my collection of five or six dollars that I received for birthdays and Christmas and so on, and she took them. Mother would tell me her other problems, for example, her troubles at work, her fights with her sister, Diane, and I did not understand that either. I only knew it was bad. I guess Mother was a quite dependent person and had to tell someone, so she told me. I also got a feeling that Mother may have been trying to substitute me for Father and I felt uncomfortable. That impression seems to have been substantiated, because at that time I slept in the same bed with Mother. Sleeping in the same bed with Mother provided a physical proximity that was nice, but it was too intense and there is no question but what it was sexually stimulating. On the rare occasions when my father came home I was put back in my crib, and I said, 'Why can't we all three sleep in the same bed?' but I was put down on that issue. Except for this one matter of wanting to sleep in the bed with them, that was a rather happy time for us, a good time. Mother was still working, so while Father was there he would take me to a tavern. I thought that was great and had a good time.

"Once Father was home after he had an accident, and he was in a hip-to-foot cast, and it was wet. He came home and was sitting in the kitchen and took a hammer and chisel and took the cast off. I was afraid he would hurt himself, and then I saw the unhealed scars and that made it worse.

"I don't know exactly when it started, but I had been wetting my pants, and about this time it was pointed out to me that doing so was unacceptable."

This was by no means a complete review of Walter's 0–6, but even this much made it quite evident that we were dealing with a very mild edition of *Paradise Lost*, mild that is in comparison with Pat Ralston. Not only was it more mild, but it was qualitatively different in that, when his father left and his mother went back to work and tried to put him in a position of being leaned on instead of given the love to mature in his own way, the main effect was an intensification of what Walter called "the one-to-one" relationship with his mother.

Even this much knowledge of 0–6 at least suggests without absolute proof that part of Walter's current problems with women stemmed from the overattachment to his mother, which made him put women too much in a position of Mother figures to himself. I suspected that when he married his wife, he tried immediately to make her into a mother and then when she began to have demands upon him he turned from her and started an affair with another girl. But at this point I merely hoped to continue this review of his 0–6 in order to get the dynamics more clearly and certainly.

At the next meeting with Walter Burton I said, "You told me not to forget where we ended the last time. I have not forgotten, and can easily summarize that hour for you. If you like, I will do it briefly, and perhaps you'll get back into the mood of it more rapidly. As I recall, everything was apparently quite idyllic, with much love between your mother and yourself, she having you on her lap with her arms around you, nuzzling you, until your father went away to a new job in a different town. At that point you did not like being taken to your grandmother's every day while your mother worked, and then after that she moved in with your grandmother and was not around much, but still took you out when she went places. During this period you got used to sleeping in the same bed with Mother, and when your father came home you did not like being sent back to the crib. However, with your mother still working your father took over some of the care of you himself, and you enjoyed going out with him to a tavern."

The patient interrupted with, "To several taverns. That happened more than once, and I thought it was neat."

"Then our session ended," I reminded him, "with your relating how your father came home with a broken leg, and with a hammer and chisel he took off the hip-to-toe cast; this frightened you and you were upset at seeing the unhealed wounds. Also, at just about the same time," I reminded him, "you started having a urinary problem and were punished for urinating in the street outside your house. You were just beginning to learn what was unacceptable."

I said, "I guess I should not comment, but if I wanted to be Freudian, at this point I would mention the fact that this memory of your father is reminiscent of castration and might refer to it, since it follows so immediately upon your associations of being in bed with your mother and being displaced by your father. And this also is followed by the urination incident and its unacceptability, which might mean there was some displacement of the sexual problem to the urinary problem. You were learning that wetting and sex were both prohibited and punishable."

Somewhat to my surprise the patient said, "Yes, I think it's true.

My uncle (who was not then my uncle but was dating my mother's sister) was visiting in the house. I was getting in my pajamas down in the kitchen where everybody was, and I wanted to be with them. My mother started chatting and said that I was wetting my pants. With that my uncle whipped out a switchblade knife and said if I did not stop it, he would cut it off, and I got the hell out of there! That was about six months before Father came home and cut the cast off his leg. I was leery of Uncle for a long time after that. Now, thinking back over it, I believe that he never gave it a thought. I think he just believed he was being cute, but it sure scared the shit out of me! The enuresis was a problem in the daytime as well as at night, mostly because I was doing something and did not want to interrupt in order to go to the bathroom. This continued until Father came back home permanently when I was about six. I don't mean that it stopped in one day, but it was around that time it stopped. I always had a lot of jealousy when Mother was with any male. For example, when she was dancing with Father or when she was sitting for a picture and my uncle put his arm around her. There was one picture, I remember, in which my uncle had his arm around Mother and I was in the back ready to hammer him over the head with a toy, and I was not kidding; I really meant it. Once Mother and Father took me out, and when they were dancing together, they left me at the table. I got up and tried to break them up. These things did not happen just once but a number of times. It was as though I had staked out Mother as my territory and would not let another male near her. Mother and I took a lot of trips, about a half dozen after Father came home permanently.

"My mother's sister and my grandmother lived in the same house but I do not remember anything specific in relation to them. They were always very nice to me; only my aunt and my mother would fight at times, and Mother would tell me how she had fought with her sister; that upset me because Mother was upset. Once I saw scratch marks on Mother, so it was probably more than just verbal fighting.

"Once my aunt picked me up and I purposefully grabbed her breast, and she became quite upset and I did not understand why. My grandmother I remember well. She was very quiet and kind to me. But she was not warm, because I never felt close to her. Once she would not let me do something or tried to make me do something . . . I forgot just what it was . . . and I had a full-fledged temper tantrum. I threw myself on the floor and kicked. One of my shoes came off and I threw it at her. Then I got frightened because she didn't do anything. I just think she felt hurt. Right after that, it clouded up. Clouds came overhead, it became very dark and in a little bit it became very stormy with terrible thunder and lightning. I thought, 'That's what you get for being a bad boy.' I thought the Almighty would punish me.

"As I mentioned before, sleeping with Mother was very stimulating sexually. It was not only sleeping with her. To get me to go to bed Mother would race me to see who could get into their nightclothes and into bed the quickest. I always won and was in bed first, and Mother would be nude with the lights on, putting on her nightgown. This, too, was not an isolated occurrence. It was not only sexually stimulating but very anxiety-producing. Even now, just the thought of it is anxiety-producing. I remember a few times Mother saw me staring at her completely nude, and then berated me for staring. That made a lot of anxiety. The desire to watch her was too strong to control, but if I showed it, she would see me stare and berate me, giving me a ration of shit. Mother would say, "Why are you staring at me? There is no difference between men and women, both have bodies.' Who the hell was she kidding? Both have bodies, but they are not the same. I think I knew that even then, at age four. At four I was already playing Doctor with the little girl next door. I knew the difference, but I did not know the utility of it all. Even to this day, I find watching a girl take off her clothes in front of me is more stimulating than anything I can think of."

The patient was silent for a few moments; then he said, "I was just thinking whether there was anything more about this that I can bring to mind, but at the moment I am drawing a blank, as though telling you this has exhausted me. Now I only think of something trivial, a few playmates, nothing to do with anything."

"Go ahead," I said, "and tell the trivial things anyway."*

"There were two little girls next door who were cousins. We played together and had no difficulty; the only problem was that we had some sex play, but that was only exposure, probably limited to three or four times. I don't seem to remember anything about them. I do remember their names and what they looked like, but there was nothing more in our relationship, only how I related to four-year-olds. I recall a woman next door; she was eccentric, if not psychotic—

*Remember, "free association" means completely free, no censoring whatever.

I think psychotic. If you got near she would come after you with a hatchet."

[Here, again, the memory of the sex play with the little girls was followed by what sounded like a castration threat, cutting with a hatchet.]

"I think of my grandfather. He used to save soap chips and I would help him cut them up. This was good because I could do what he could do, and we could do it together, but what was *not* so good was that every once in a while he would kill a chicken for dinner. Maybe it would be a poor layer. He did it by chopping its head off on a chopping block, and I did not like that too well. There was blood all over the place."

[Possibly here again is a measure of the patient's anxiety and fear of punishment, and possible guilt for the sexual feeling, plus some repressed hostility.]

He continued: "I went through a series of dogs, mostly strays. One dog followed me home; he apparently belonged to no one, and I talked my mother and grandmother into letting me keep it and I got very attached to it. I think my mother and grandmother had most of its care; they fed it and kept it clean. Then one day a neighborhood girl teased the dog and he bit her. And they (I don't know who 'they' were) said they would take the dog to watch him, and they never came back with it. After a couple of months they told me he would not come back ever again and I was greatly upset. This occurred about two more times with different dogs."

[A comment on this material: here the material is generally about transgression and threatened punishment, but is mostly focused on sexual feelings toward the patient's mother that produced considerable anxiety in him and fear of bloody, probable castrative punishment. He spontaneously reports a connection to the present time, in that to this very day the sight of a woman undressing in front of him is the most stimulating experience he can imagine, a direct repetition of the experience with his mother. Probably being an only child with no siblings provided no means of diluting this intense, sexually stimulating attachment to his mother, which was further intensified by his father being away for a time, his sleeping in the same bed with his mother, and the mother's exposure of herself to him night after night.]

With this fixation it is not difficult to see why, as an adult, he has an excessively strong attraction to women but also difficulties with them, but the details of this have not yet appeared.

The next hour we continued the review of the 0 to 6. He said: "When I was about seven, my father returned permanently. Father, Mother, and I moved into a new house. My father's mother came to stay with us because her husband had died, and so instead of just the three of us there were four of us for a number of months—probably three or four months. We moved into a new neighborhood where I knew nobody. It was meeting new friends. I had my own bedroom now, so that was the end of the daily exposure to Mother. My father's mother—my paternal grandmother—was with us for only a few months . . . she was very unpleasant. I felt as though she was my jailer, but maybe that's being too harsh. She was nothing more than a baby-sitter. She pointed out that I was somewhat spoiled. Until then, if I asked for anything such as a toy, I got it, from Mother, Father, or Mother's mother—but Father's mother put her foot down on that. I think she left after a few months because my parents did not like her. Father never commented on it.

"In a way, although I didn't like leaving the old house, I did like it better in the new neighborhood. It was a nice area, nicer than the old one, with a big backyard, and we were near a public playground. But I had left all my friends. What I liked least about it was, at first there was no one near my own age. The kids were too young, not much more than babies, and the other ones were too old, too sophisticated for me to handle. We moved there in June, and I resumed school in September, and at that time I began meeting kids my own age, but I was new, and felt that I was an outsider. In fact, the very first day the teacher had no seat for me at all, so she had to sit me double with another boy, but it worked out all right because the boy and I, we became fast friends for years. That was good, but I had trouble with the teacher. She was an old biddy. You could tell how old she was because she taught my father when he was ten years old, at least 25 years before. Also, the school was more advanced than the one I went to before, and the work was a lot more difficult."

I said, "Now you are very normally getting into your relations with your peers, the relationships outside of the family, and I think we should come to them shortly, but first shouldn't we finish up your relationships within the family—that is, only the relationships with your father and mother now there were only the three of you again?"

"Yes," he said, "that's right. I began to feel less dependent on my parents. I guess it was a typical latency period sexually, but not completely. I felt real good about having Father back. Mother was O.K., I think, but that seems a blank to me, remembering back, because I was beginning to get pissed off because Mother was still working and was not there when I came home from school. But I channeled away some frustration and loneliness by finding some things to do. But still, the other kids' mothers were always there when they came home. I do not mean that my mother was derelict about this; the neighbors knew and were watching out for me, but the neighbors were not Mother.

"But now," said Walter Burton, "I would like to leave this for a moment to catch you up to date on what's been happening. I am still separated from my wife, but we are getting along much better, and I think the children are doing well. But Mary, the girl I've been having an affair with and trying to end, was very upset and just to make her feel better I took her to dinner. I took her home afterwards; I had some work to do, but it worked out like this: I came in and finished the work at her place. She was still very upset, rather hysterical, and I tried to console her and ended up spending the night with her. She said, 'You seem to be unwilling to make any commitment to our relationship.' I thought this over for a moment and then said, 'I'll have to think about it.' She said, 'Well, call me in three days and tell me your decision, but if you will not make a commitment, then we are finished.'

"After three days I did not call her but I wrote her a note saying that my mind had not changed, that there was simply no future in the relationship between us. The next day, but before she got the note, she telephoned me and talked for nearly an hour and at the end of this time told me that she had taken an overdose and would I help her. I thought for a minute and said that I would and I would come right over. I called a doctor and we went over and he pumped her stomach, but she seemed in pretty good shape . . . it was not a fatal dose. She is in analytic treatment with a relatively young man, and I only hope that he is good and able to help her. You know, before I came to see you I really always thought when I was with my wife and there were things to be done, 'My mother wouldn't do it this way,' or, 'She would do it that way.' In other words, I was really unconsciously, as you pointed out at the very beginning, trying to make a mother out of my wife, and it never really occurred to me that she had needs of her own. Maybe it was from the pattern toward my mother, but it seems that I have wanted every woman I see, and also I never realized the intensity of their own needs. Now I've got Mary, with such intense needs toward me that if I don't satisfy them, she threatens suicide. I guess I don't need two women making demands on me."

I said, "There's a well-known saying; 'It's hard enough to take care of what you've got,' namely your own wife and children."

He replied, "I certainly see the sense in that."

[This patient saw pretty clearly both his dependence on women and also his more or less following the pattern of sexual arousal toward his mother and the inhibition of it because of her scolding him for staring at her. He was only very rarely actually impotent sexually, but psychologically he was intensely desirous of having a girl, and then when he got her was not satisfied by the relationship. Thus he was a sort of Don Juan, and continued this pattern by trying to make his wife into a mother so that he had a home and still could go out and have an affair with another woman. At this point he was reacting well to the analysis; there was a diminution of his anxiety and he was getting much more satisfaction out of his relationship with his wife. Whether this suicidal attempt of his mistress would lead to ending that relationship remained to be seen. He felt that if he could adequately be satisfied by one close relationship, namely to his wife, that it would be good for him and for his children and ease his conscience about them, whom he seemed to love. This probably followed a pattern of identification with them, and also of identification with his parents, who despite their faults did love him, their only child. But he felt that if he could get more satisfaction out of his relationship to his wife, then he really would not need these outside affairs and would have a quieter life.

He enjoyed the relationship with his mistress, but it was becoming too strenuous, especially with her suicide gesture. But he was never sure that she might not make a mistake and really take an overdose, and that she might leave a suicidal note blaming him. As we were to learn later, his mother was rather strict and restrictive, and this too had been worked out in his marriage, because his wife was very unrestrictive in actuality; yet insofar as he made her into a Mother figure, she *seemed* to him to be restrictive.]

The next meeting with Walter Burton found him silent for a few minutes. After waiting to see if he would start with some particular topic, I said, "I think that we did not quite finish your 0–6. We got about as far as six, but then there seemed to be other important emotional material which you never quite got to tell. Should we try that now?"

He said, "Well, may I digress first about something which I forgot to tell you and should have? I remembered it; I guess I just repressed it."

I said, "Sure, go ahead."

Walter related the following: "A few weeks ago I spent the night with Mary and she was very demanding, and in the morning we were both in a hurry to get to work, but we fought. She said I did not give her consolation enough. I really do not know what it is she wants, and I grabbed her by the throat and almost strangled her. I guess that was because I wanted to get rid of her. Then there went through my mind immediately the thought of Mother and death wishes to my mother. That was, for example, when I wanted to marry Jane ten years ago and my mother opposed it. Maybe I want Mother dead because then I would be completely independent and not controlled."

[This supports the possibility that the associations we have reported, which have often followed his memories of Mother, were in part expressions of his own hostility.]

"Is that realistic," I asked, "or are you really trying to be rid of your own attachment to your mother?"

"That's a thought," he said; "there might be something to that." He was silent for a few minutes, and I said, "Could this be connected in any possible way with your mother's early seductiveness to you and the sexual attachment to her?"

He said, "I don't know; maybe. Since Mary took the overdose a week or ten days ago I have seen her only a couple of times and just to say hello; a very distant relationship. Oh, yes, I just thought of another thing. My wife Sylvia and Mary got together last week. I heard my wife on the phone making the appointment. I don't know their idea; maybe they just had curiosity on both of their parts, or they wanted to get a different view of what they get through me. After it Mary was pretty upset and phoned me. I guess she was upset because the conversation with my wife confirmed what I had told her, that we were through, but I was angry with my wife. I don't know exactly why. I think because Mary is so precarious with taking overdoses, and I thought my wife would trigger her off some way."

"You mean another overdose?" I asked.

He said, "Not necessarily that, but some other form of craziness or hysteria. If I had known where they were eating together I would have gone there and told them both to fly a kite!"

"Why were you so angry, do you think?"

He said, "That is what my wife asked. I think because they were both interfering with what I am doing; I am doing the best I can in my own way, but there was a dream which I would like to tell you. It occurred two nights ago. That evening my wife had had a baby shower for one of her friends and I came home in the middle of it. There were women all over the place. In the dream, like reality, I came home to a shower which was just breaking up. I found that Jane had been there. She is the girl I dated for a while about two years before my marriage. It was quite an affair. She was eight years older than I, divorced, not rich, but fairly well off financially. We had a very good relationship. She was very attractive and very seductive. In the dream she had already left the shower and had forgotten something, and I thought, 'Great, I'll take it to her and thus see her again.' But then it turned out that someone was going to come for it and I thought, 'Great, I'll be here and see her when she comes.' But then it was a man that came and I was angry, angry that she had another man in her life, and he told me to stay away from her. Then the rest of the dream was all trying to find her. I got a street number but that was not right; I got a phone number but that was wrong. Then I found her house but she was away on a trip. Her two daughters were there. They were six or seven when we had the affair, so now they were pretty well grown up. I feel as though there was more to the dream, but that is all I can remember. When I woke up, it took a long time to realize that this had not happened, that it was ten years already since I had seen or heard from her. The last I heard she was having all manner of emotional problems, and I never answered her letters.

"The thing about Jane was that she was the closest thing to a mother, as well as a fine sexual partner. Like Mother, anything I wanted she would do for me. Not only sexually, but if I should come home, for example, at nine or ten o'clock and want a steak and french fries, she'd make it. If I should come home and tell my wife that's what I want, she would tell me to go make it myself. Jane had the habit of undressing right at the foot of the bed just as my mother did. That was very exciting to me and I have other associations of Jane with my mother."

That took us to the end of the hour, and I remarked, "It seems that in having troubles you do what many people do, and that is, try to go back to Mother, which in this case in your dream is Jane. But then of course you run into your problems with Mother, meaning the emotional pattern which developed in childhood toward your mother and which you are now trying to be free of. As you see, in your unconscious the balance of forces is such that your wish is for Jane, but the mother pattern also blocks that wish so you really do not find her and do not go back to her."

He said, "Yes, I can see that and I think that in reality I am making some progress in getting my relationships with women in a little better order. I find it is really all I can do to keep my own life reasonably happy, and I certainly do not need the emotional disturbances of another woman in addition."

With Walter Burton, it seemed that a 0–6 review was of at least some immediate benefit. A regular hour wth him soon afterward went like this:

We sat down and I waited to see if he had anything urgent on his mind to start with, but he didn't. He said, "How should we proceed today?"

I replied, "Well, if you want to continue as we have been, we will go back and ask what your complaints were when you first came to see me, nearly a year ago."

He said, "My personal life was getting screwed up beyong comprehension; it was so chaotic, so unorganized, almost unlivable. I was torn between two women, one of whom I was married to and the other with whom I thought I was in love and with whom I was having an affair. The situation could not go on indefinitely unless I changed it or my wife did. That is pretty much the main reason I came to see you."

"And what do you consider your chief complaints are today?"

He replied, "To some extent, the same. I have resolved some things in my own mind, but now must resolve them in reality. I have accepted that my wife is not a perfect wife, a perfect mother, or a perfect human being, but I realize how many good points she has. At the same time, I know that Mary needs a friend until she can find someone else, so I continue to give her some support by talking with her. She has tried to get me to bed with her, but I have not done it, because if I do, then I am back where I started. My wife and I are on a semi-separated basis. I am living in an apartment, but I spend all of the weekends at home and two or three evenings a week there without staying overnight. This has helped lower the tension when I go out after dinner to work, to see a client, or when I have to go back to the office to finish something up. My wife always was certain when I went out after dinner that it was to see Mary. She is still jealous because she equates my being out at night with my seeing Mary. My wife and I have now resumed our sex life, at least of sorts. Certainly more than it's been in the last five or six years. There has been considerable progress, in other words, but some problems still remain, although on a smaller scale. Also, the problem remains of my attraction to every female that passes by. It is better, but the potential for trouble is still there. It is now a matter of keeping it under control."

I said, "Well, perhaps everybody has to control it, and Freud wrote a book about civilization, saying that certain restraints were needful for its existence."

"I understand," he said, "but why should I control my impulses?"

"That is certainly a legitimate question," I said, "and I think there are a number of answers. One, of course, is the children . . . they are always the first to get hurt."

"True," he said, "but sometimes the impulse becomes very over-powering and you don't think of the problems and the price you will pay. For instance, last Friday I saw a middle-aged man and his secretary together, and the girl turned out to be his daughter. Before I knew it, she was all over me, and it was a great temptation to take her out for a drink and go on from there. It would have been very easy. Maybe she was just happy that I was trying to take care of her father, but I did not interpret it that way."

I said, "I think there are at least two points involved here: the one is realistic. If you get into these affairs, what troubles will they make for you, your wife, and the children? Then I think the other questions are psychological: what is the relationship to your 0–6? Does your pattern of early childhood exaggerate these impulses toward women, and does it tend to make the relationship masochistic, i.e., involve suffering for you?"

He said, "Yes, so far as the trouble is concerned, but whether it is masochistic I don't know. Since I have been twenty-one years old I get into these involvements . . . about half a dozen of them, further than I would like, where I cannot get out of them gracefully without hurting somebody. Of course, then I was single and the girls were not married, but it usually ended with trouble for them just the same. In fact, you could almost say it was sadistic, if that use of the term is correct. I would get involved to the point where I was sure the girl was in love with me, and then I would drop her."

"That sounds like a question of the direction of the hostility; whether you hurt them, or whether you directed it toward yourself," I remarked.

"I knew one girl, Sheila, and after I seduced her, she broke off the relationship with me and I was hurt, and wanted to get even with her. I never told you about her. I dated her about fifteen years ago and we had an affair. I met her by chance two or three years ago and she invited me up to her house, and I thought about going, but didn't. It doesn't fit my pattern somehow."

"What do you mean?" I asked.

"If I wanted revenge, that was the time to do it. Now she is married. When I saw her, she was still very attractive, but I felt no impulse or attraction to her."

I said, "Maybe that was your revenge, that you had no interest in her. Is there something in your pattern of 0–6 that makes these relationships so strenuous, or at least, not as satisfying as they could be?"

He said, "The attraction is strictly sexual and not to the personality."

I answered, "Is there a clue to this in your 0–6?"

"Yes," he replied, "I think so. It might be in the intensity of my relationship to my mother, or at least, the strong sexual overtones in relation to Mother."

I said, "How do you think that affects your present relationship with women?"

He replied, "What do you think?" with a shrug.

I told him that I could only guess: "Perhaps you react to every woman something like you react to your mother. She is an attraction, but sex with her is forbidden so the relationship is never satisfied."

"Yes," he said, "I think there is some of that. It was when my wife was pregnant with my daughter ten years ago that our sexual life ended. What could be more of an indication of 'mother' than having a child? So perhaps I did equate my wife with my mother."

"That leads to another guess," I said, "and only a guess: you were attracted to your mother, but sex with her was forbidden so you tended to turn it to another woman, but then psychologically each time you did that you made the woman you were attached to love you, which meant partly turning her also into a mother, leading you in turn to feel resentful and inhibited and to reject her in favor of still another woman."

He said, "Probably. That seems to be true, and my wife is the only one of these girls who is a mother and has given me two children. Most of my relationships with women until I was twenty-one fell into two groups: the very casually sexual, the once-or-twice-and-then-an-end; the other group was mostly composed of "good girls," although why they are called that I don't know, whom I had to work at very hard to get them in love with me. When that worked, then I dropped them."

I asked, "What is the relationship of that to your 0–6 pattern?"

He answered, "In my childhood mind I did feel rejected by Mother. I felt rejected somewhat by Father's leaving, then by Mother's going to work and leaving me with Grandmother all day, but then even more after my Father returned and Mother continued to work and left me entirely on my own after school."

"Are you saying that this is partly identification with your mother?"

"What do you mean?" he asked.

"I mean that you seem to do to the girls what you felt your mother did to you."

"Yes," he said, "I think that is correct, because even on a conscious level I have frequently had fleeting thoughts that this was my revenge. I was revenging myself on the girl for what Mother had done to me. And I always felt controlled by Mother. She simply could not comprehend my having tastes or opinions different from her own. Even today she can't understand why I wear a certain kind of tie, or shirt, or shoes. It was not only her arousal of sex and the forbidding it, but also this domineering. I can't be close to her without feeling that I am losing my identity, my integrity, my independence, being my own person."

[It seems to me that this actively engaging the patient's cooperation in going after the connections between the childhood pattern and present-day feelings, thoughts, and behavior actually saved us time. We got more out of the hour than if I had sat back passively and simply listened to the free associations, trying to understand the material. I want to be very clear, however, that I don't at all mean to abandon free association; I simply mean it is worth trying the active investigation of 0–6 as a supplement to the routine basic free associating. Needless to say, I think it is much harder work for the patient, but certainly also for the analyst. I think it saves time, which is of the essence. Also, of course this supplemental technique does not work in every patient, but only in certain patients and only at certain appropriate times in the therapy. With these limitations, it seems to be—if used carefully—an effective therapeutic supplement.]

In practice it is advisable to go beyond the age of six or seven; and if nothing traumatic or nothing formative for the personality is turned up, it is still worth doing just for the sake of ruling it out.

This is illustrated by Walter Burton, whom we have described thus far through age six. In his particular circumstance, after age six the family moved to a somewhat nicer house. Then things were relatively quiet. There was still some contribution to his pattern, because he resented his mother's continuing working even after his father was back, which prevented her from being at home when Walter came home from school. The mothers of his friends were all at home, waiting for their children. This he took as a feeling of neglect and of being pushed somewhat prematurely into independence. This situation took place when he was seven years old, and he felt that after that things were relatively calm. But we decided to go ahead and take the history, looking for the pattern after 0–6; thus in the following discussion we cover ages seven, eight, and nine to see what they reveal. He started off as follows:

"I was reading a book about a little boy who had a great deal of anger but was afraid to let any of it come out, and eventually he developed asthma. He could not let it come out because he was afraid of losing the love of his parents and so on. That made me think that in my own past I could recall very few instances of *my* hostility coming out, except the incident of throwing the shoe at Grandmother. Otherwise, I recall no manifestations of outward anger. I do recall one or two times when I took it out on the dog, and then immediately I felt very guilty after hitting him. I think it must be significant that I never expressed the anger. As you know, at age seven we moved to a nice area which meant leaving my friends, but it did not take me long to pick up others. One of them I was especially close to for ten years. In a way, it is curious that we became friends . . . I think it happened because I had some trouble with the kids in the neighborhood . . . being beaten up by them, only not seriously. Never any bones broken or anything like that. I think it was largely because I was the youngest and the smallest. Jack, my friend, was smaller than I but built like a truck, he was ready to take on anyone at any any time. I think our relationship was somewhat symbiotic because he was not too smart but he did have the muscle and I leaned on that relationship. I had considerable fear of being beaten up, and he kept me out of trouble more than once just by his presence. This is getting up to the age of eight or nine.

"I remember nothing spectacular in relation to my parents at that time. They were there in the evening. It was my job to set the table, to clear it, and to do the dishes, and I felt rather put-upon by this because the other boys I knew did not have to do it. If my parents were not going to be home in the evening because they were going out bowling or visiting or something, I had to go the fifteen miles alone by streetcar or bus to my grandmother's. I thought this was quite much for the age of eight, at least that's how I feel now, but I may not have felt it at that time. Actually I never got lost, I never lost the money or anything like that—as I got older I got a little streetwise in that regard. My parents gave me money for lunch at the school cafeteria, and often I would keep the money and 'con' the kids out of some of their lunch. I would not be too hungry and would save the money and then buy something after school, like candy, that was much more pleasurable.

"I did not like school much. I hated spelling, and I still don't spell very well. What I hated most about school was the long walk in the mornings. That was about a mile and a half. It was not rural, it was all urbanized and it was mostly along a main street, and I was not allowed to take my bike. But if my parents left before me in the morning, I would take the bike anyway. One day my father came home a little early and found me returning from school on the bike, and they raised a little hell, but after that they pretty much let me ride it.

"I do not seem to be able to remember a teacher I liked until I was in the eighth grade, that is, about thirteen years old. Some of the teachers I downright disliked; I thought some of them didn't like children in general and did not like me in particular.

"The things I liked best I excelled in and got straight A's. But I disliked English and spelling. I almost did not get through high school because of the English. There was never any question, though, as to why I did poorly. I just did not do the work. Sports were a big thing. I thought that to be somebody, to be popular, one had to be good in a sport . . . anyway, that was my feeling at the time, so I tried out for football but did not stick with it.

"I think I did not continue with the football chiefly because of the fear of football and in part because I did not want to put the work into it. It was probably fear of failure more than anything else; I cut it short and stopped trying. I took a newspaper route, but I probably did that mainly to have a reason for quitting football. I did not like the paper route much either . . . I liked the money, but I hated making collections. I hated having to badger people for the forty-five cents or whatever it was for the week's papers. I guess the chief reason I did it was to make my mother happy. I put the money in a savings account and never really spent any of it until I was a sophomore at college . . . well, maybe a little bit here or there, but basically I didn't start to spend it until then. My mother never asked for it . . . she was content to let me save it.

"I also did not like the paper route because it cut into my afternoon time. I guess this was my first lesson in 'You can't have everything.'

"I told you the last time that my wife talked with the woman who has been my mistress. I guess they were both very cautious as to what they said, and I don't know if it really had any effect, but overall things are rather better with my wife. I'm learning to accept her as a person in herself. I'm beginning to see that she is not an extension of me nor of the children, and that she is not my mother and will not do for me what my mother did. Which doesn't mean that there are not occasional moments of friction . . . for example, my wife asked me to take the children out for hamburgers because she did not have enough food in the house. I said O.K. and took them, but when I returned there was not any dinner being prepared for my wife and me either. She just didn't want to cook dinner that night, and she should have said so. If she had said she did not want to do it, I would have said, 'It's O.K. with me to go out to eat.' Anyway, I think I do see the whole marital relationship and my wife a little more realistically."

* * * * *

Dreams help in making a formulation, and vice versa—the formulations, if they accurately represent the main childhood pattern of the patient, help in understanding dreams. Here is an example of this, which Walter Burton reported spontaneously the following hour:

"I am in another city at a convention. I am walking down the street with someone, I think a colleague, and we enter what we think is a cafe, but in it is a stage like an arena or auditorium, with seats, and on the stage there is an orgy. There are three nude girls and also two or three men, also nude. The audience is watching them have sex on the stage. I sat down and started watching it, but felt rather uncomfortable. It was sort of gross and I was not enthralled by it. A girl was lying down and a man was on top of her, but not much was going on, and then suddenly I was in the driveway of my own home. Somehow my old roommate was there. I thought, 'What are they doing having this show in my house? My God, they will all come back here, the girls will, and I must stop it.' Then a car pulls up and the people all seem to be foreigners. I ran inside the house and thought I had to stop somebody else who was running in or else he would tell my wife, and I hit him and he hit me. It didn't hurt me, but I saw blood coming out of my belly. In the next scene I am in a jungle, as though on a safari with my old roommate, or with somebody. We have a great load of stuff that we must carry through the rain forest. It is on a platform. My roommate or the other man, whoever he is, turns out to have his end of the platform on a truck, and he himself is not carrying anything."

I looked at the patient, waiting, and he spontaneously told the following: "The convention, the dark street, going to the cafe, the orgy, to all that I associate the fact that I am planning to go to a convention in about a month . . . it's in New Orleans. I've never been there. I thought I would like to see it, and I have thought of having a fling there with a high-class call girl. Then back in the driveway and my wife's finding out about the orgy—that is obvious. That refers to her finding out about my present affair that I am having with Mary but trying to end, finding out about my extramarital sex life, or maybe it is fear of my mother finding it out . . . I think more likely my mother. My getting hurt is probably retribution. Perhaps the jungle scene is just an escape because the dream is starting to overwhelm me. But there is another possibility; it also makes me think that I am overworking and my partner in our firm is not carrying his load."

[It seems to me that this dream follows roughly the formulation we have already made and confirms it: transgression and punishment, sex and its repression; rebellion against being controlled; anxiety because of fear of retribution and the resentment of the work and feeling some deprivation of dependent love needs. Thus, knowing the childhood pattern gives a clue to the latent content of the dream and the dream suggests some of the childhood pattern. Of course, not all dreams show these connections as clearly as this one; they are more apt to reflect the childhood pattern in bits and pieces. But as we have pointed out, if the dreams are well analyzed and a series of them read by the analyst at one sitting, the basic patterns usually emerge. Sometimes they emerge even from the manifest content alone, although it is always better, if not essential, to have the associations. Nevertheless, I think it must be recognized that the secondary elaboration of the latent content by the ego itself is influenced by the latent interplay of emotional forces. In this dream, Walter neglected to notice the transference; he is also anxious about what I think of him and will think of him in the future if he has his fling with a call girl. His overworking connects with his being forced by his mother into responsibilities for home and paper route. The violence is probably also an effect of his anger at his mother for the partial neglect and for her control of him. This came out clearly in his later associations, in which he repeated his fear of being close to his mother because she tried to force him into thinking and acting as she wanted, and threatened his individuality, his sense of "being my own person."]

A formulation could be summed up in these very few words: Walter Burton had an excessive attachment to his mother, sexual, dependent and submissive, combined with hostility toward her and withdrawal from her as a defense. This is the pattern that he feels and is acting out toward other women. The form taken by the hostility is doing to the girls what his mother did to him—seduction and rejection. Expressed on a card as a dynamic diagnosis we arrived at the following:

Dynamic Diagnosis: Walter Burton

Childhood: (1) Only child, Father mostly away (age 3–7). Seductiveness and repression of sex to Mother leads to excessive sexual needs toward Mother, forbidden and causing fear of punishment. (2) Some deprivation of dependent love needs toward Mother. (3) Some excessive overcontrol by Mother. (1, 2, and 3) cause: (4) Fear of closeness to Mother because it threatens independence and integrity of his personality, because of (a) arousal of sex which is forbidden and (b) domination of patient's thinking and feeling by Mother; avoids Mother in "trying to be his own person."

Current: Wants every woman, but fears closeness. Leads to frustration and fight-flight; anger mostly at Mother with rebellion, revenge, displaced onto women and self. Can't stand being dependent on a woman or having a woman dependent on him. Marital difficulties; fight and flight pattern toward women—sees them as objects of hostility and as refuge from life.

Strengths: (1) Strong therapeutic urge. (2) Courage in facing himself. (3) Independence of personality with high intelligence and professional competence and success.

III. Leila Smith: Risks of a Nurse and Trials of a Wife

Leila Smith was a charming, blondish woman, slightly under middle height. She came to see me because she had been living in a rather unhappy marriage for a number of years; she had adolescent children, and had been divorced and remarried, but now the second marriage was also not going well. Yet, she did not want to get a divorce if her marriage could be improved in any way.

As usual, after spending most of the hour getting a picture of the present-life situation and the present marriage with its difficulties and strong points, I tried to obtain a picture of her 0-6. After explaining what I was trying to get, I asked her for the main people in her life between birth and the age of six or seven. She said, "Mother, Father, Sister, and Nurse."

"Which," I asked, "was the most important?"

She replied, "I guess Mother was, but I think of my nurse who never should have had the care of children. She was a very strict woman, and if my sister who is a year and a half younger than I did anything that was not right, we would both be spanked, not given a meal, or supper would be withheld. We would be sent to bed as a punishment. I was so upset by her that at dinner I would throw up every evening. She would force the food down me, and then I would be put to bed as a punishment. I was then about five years old. She was only with us a little over one year, but it was long enough to do a lot of damage. That year for a while we visited my grandfather and grandmother, and years later my grandmother told me that she had advised my mother and father to get rid of that nurse because she was so cruel to the children."

"How about before the nurse came?" I asked.

Leila said, "Before the nurse came I had no fear; I don't remember if it was happy or unhappy. I think I just was fed and slept and felt a sense that everything was perfectly adequate. Mother was the one person who was my joy, whom I was glad to see when she was there. But Mother was not there as much as she should have been. I think my mother should never have had children, because she was more interested in her social life than in the children. I did not know that then, of course; it is only my opinion in retrospect. And Father was a complete introvert, but Mother was the opposite. They had a rather good marriage; Mother led Father by the nose, but he liked it that way. She wanted a lap dog for a husband, and he was content to be that way."

"What do you mean by that?" I inquired.

She said, "Mother ruled the roost. She said where we would go, when we would go, and what we would do. I think Mother had imagination and Father had none. Father was completely dominated by her. I think if he ever really objected to anything, he would have stood up to her, but he went along with things as they were, apparently feeling satisfied."

"How did this affect your relations with your father and mother?" I asked.

"I had pretty good relations with both of them, but my mother was more interested outside of the home than in the home; she was not of the temperament to spend time with children. As a result, when I had children I spent a lot of time with them, reading to them, playing piano and singing with them, and so on, because I thought it would be so important for them in their older years. But Mother was not a dictator the way my first husband was. I am well out of that marriage with Sam; he has had all kinds of trouble with the company and is now out of a job. He has remarried but not in the way I would like it to be—he goes his way and his wife goes hers. He had a broken ankle and was in a cast from his knee down and then he had some sort of emergency at work. His wife would not cancel her tennis to drive him, and he had to scrounge around—because of course he could not even move by himself, let alone drive a car—in order to get somebody to drive him. In fact, I had decided that I would drive him myself if need be."

I said, "Shall we return to your basic emotional relationships in your 0-6?"

She answered, "With Mother I had a good relationship but she was not there enough to give me a sense of security and comfort. And of course the nurse was sadistic. Father was just nondescript."

"What do you mean by that?" I asked.

She said, "Unimaginative, withdrawn. It was difficult for him to show any kind of affection or emotion. My sister was always fighting with Mother, but she played ball with my father and got on well with him. She was bolder than I was; I would not have dared fight with Mother. Sister was smarter than I, quicker, had a good mind; but when she was still quite young, just after graduating from college, she started drinking and really died of alcoholism only a few years ago."

"Anything more about your relationships with your father?" I asked.

Leila said, "Nothing unpleasant that I can remember, just sort of neutral, relatively normal relations, a little better than neutral. But then Mother died when I was fourteen years old and then Father became much more withdrawn, really entirely withdrawn from my sister and me. He showed no signs whatever of any interest or affection. He never did a single nice thing for us; I think he was inadequate. When Mother died, his world collapsed, and I think he was not very smart. I never cared much for my sister. What I mean is, when she was born she got all the attention. She and I are entirely different. She was hard and tough, and could take care of herself in any situation, and I was the more sensitive and insecure. As I said, she was never afraid to defy Father or Mother, but I was."

"But in the end," I said, "she killed herself with alcoholism, so you turned out to be the stronger."

"Yes, I guess that's true," said Leila.

"What were the effects of all this on your emotional makeup, do you think?"

Leila responded, "I never really thought I was insecure until my teens. It was not until Mother died and Father became so remote that I realized all was not as it should be. I saw friends whose parents did things with them, but Father was not made for family life. He never took us on a trip or did anything for us. And I think also as a teenager more responsibility was put on my shoulders than should have been. Because of that, I was not able to grow up at my own natural pace. Sam, my first husband, was the opposite of Father. He was very active and amusing. I would not want to be back with him, but I'll give him credit by saying that life with him was never dull. My present husband, Jack, is more like Father although much more interested in the world and has more ambition and drive than Father ever did. Jack is much easier than Sam. Our only disagreement is over his excessive permissiveness with his children, especially when they upset my own life. Jack is excessively dependent upon me for his children."

What had become evident from this interview but also from all that I knew previously about Leila's marriage (but did not include in this summary) was that, because of her own deprivation in early life, she had become very sympathetic with others who were similarly deprived. She had the very positive reaction of not neglecting her own children, but tried to read, sing, and do things with them for the sake of their futures. In other words, she did for her own children what had been lacking in her own childhood. When his wife would not drive the first husband—Sam—to the dentist for extractions, Leila even thought of driving him, although they had been divorced for a number of years. She had done an excellent job with her own children, who seemed to be turning out healthy and stable. This admirable tendency to give to the deprived with whom she identified made her sympathetic in helping the second husband, Jack, with his adolescent children. But Jack's former wife had no interest in them whatever, no control over them, and neither had Jack. They became excessively demanding; they would save up their laundry when away at school, all arrive on the same weekend, and expect to have Leila make all the beds, run the laundry for everyone, put on the meals, and do the cleanup. If Jack suddenly wanted a party for 12 people, Leila accepted it and had some of the food prepared in the afternoon, to be served later; then Jack's children (especially his son Joey) would come in, raid the refrigerator, and eat up what Leila had set aside for the party. When they had a number of weekend guests, the son would say he was coming to visit but would not be there on Saturday night; he would be visiting a friend from Saturday morning to Sunday night. But then he would turn up with the friend and expect Leila to bed down and feed the two of them. In other words, the very positive reaction Leila had of wanting to help those who were deprived was being exploited shamelessly in the marriage with Jack. He, apparently, had no realization of this whatever, but always sided with the children in making their excessive demands upon her. As she rightly said about her own childhood adolescence, more was put upon her than should have been. After the death of her mother and the withdrawal of her father, Leila had enormous demands made upon her; the situation now in her marriage to Jack was a comparable one—everything going out and almost nothing coming in by way of support.

My next meeting with Leila began with my asking about her relationship to her sister. She said, "My sister was 18 months younger than I. Our relationship was not too good; I felt jealous and left out when she entered the family. You would not think I could remember from that age, but I remember feeling pushed out. My sister was always sleeping, and I couldn't see her, and then when we were a little older, she was still too young to play with. We were just the opposite: she was a tomboy, tough, secure, while I was very quiet and feminine."

I said, "You have told me about your general memories from 0–6; now can you forget about those relationships you have been relating and just tell me your earliest memories?"

Leila replied, "(1) The first was that of my sister arriving and I was not allowed to see her or play with her. I felt rejected, put aside. Probably that was only temporary, but it seemed to me like forever. (2) The next vivid memory was at age five, of that nurse who was vicious. Her cruelty stands out in my memory. I think it was because she made me timid."

"Do you have any memory," I asked, "between the arrival of your sister and the nurse?"

"No," Leila said, "the rest was very ordinary. Just of things going along. (3) I do have a memory, though, of about age four, of preschool. We lived near by the school and I was happy there. There were other children, there was a routine, and there was security. Sister and I were very restricted, much more so than the other children. For example, we were put to bed at 6:30, very early. We were never allowed to have children come in or to spend the night at our house; we were not allowed to go overnight to visit them. This was the opposite of what I have done with my children. From age three, they have had little friends come in and sleep over at our house, and have also gone out to visit. I remember that at age eleven I thought that Mother was not right about a lot of things. Our friends all went to neighborhood movies at night, but we were not allowed to go unless there was an adult with us."

[It sounds as though Leila's mother was possibly overanxious and may well have been conveying her timidity and anxiety to Leila. Or, put another way, Leila may have identified to some extent with her mother's overanxiety.]

She continued: "(4) I have another memory of before the nurse came. That was of going to stay with our grandparents. I always enjoyed that a lot. Oh, yes, (5) also at about age four I was terrified of the dark at night, and also I had a fear of being kidnapped, and had to have a light on at night in the hall or the bathroom, or somewhere nearby. Our life was very regimented. We ate at certain hours, had to be in bed at a certain hour, but really we did not see much of our parents. It was a real treat when we did. (6) I remember one Sunday, I think it was in February; at any rate, there was a lot of ice and snow. We were out walking, and we went around some trees that had stone rims circling them to protect them and we thought it was fun to walk on these stones from one tree to the other. My sister managed it, but I fell into the icy water and got drenched and went home. I was severely chastised by the nurse, although obviously I had not done anything bad . . . it was only an accident. The relationship to the nurse was chiefly punishment, always being scolded or punished.

"The families of my friends were more Edwardian; they were more permissive. In our house we were forbidden so many things and punished for things that I would never dream of punishing my children for. That does not mean that I approve of overpermissiveness. Once I phoned a boy and my mother was outraged and said, 'Girls don't phone boys.' That was ridiculous; of course they did. They chased boys! My mother had a lot of kooky ideas about children. When I was about ten years old I asked my mother about the facts of life, but she never told me. Yet I enjoyed being with my mother; she was always amusing. We always had a lot of laughing and good times together, but Father was very dull. He had no sense of humor at all, although Mother thought he did. But I never saw it.

"Now I would like to tell you about my marriage, which is the present problem. Mostly we get along fairly well. My husband is more content with the marriage than I am. The problem is the children. After a visit from his son, Joey, it takes us a month to get back into a good relationship. Joey's mother washed her hands of him when she was divorced from my present husband. She just turned him over to us, and Jack never made Joey spend any time with his own mother at all. He only spent time with us, and Joey's attitude was, 'I'd rather not, so why should I?' He is a very egocentric, uncooperative, and inconsiderate boy, and I have been forced to live with him. My daughter tells me that the trouble with me is I won't stand up, but if I said no to his coming to visit on a busy weekend when I had 12 guests here, Jack's whole family would have been down on me and made my life very unpleasant. Jack has never said no to his children or to his former wife, but he has said no to me. A while back, Joey needed an operation and Jack asked me if I would mind his staying with us the week before the operation. I said it would be all right, but I couldn't have him convalescing with us because he would be in a cast and is so demanding anyway. Then it was all agreed he would stay with us a week before the operation and go to his mother the week after it. We all agreed to it, but then she welched out and refused to take him, and Jack insisted that he stay with us.

"My bitterness has built up over the years, not from any one single incident. Fortunately, my own children are fine and get along well with Jack; but the children by his first marriage were the problem, but now are all pretty well grown up and away from home. The youngest girl lives with her mother, who is some distance away, and does not visit us often, but I've always had a quite good relationship with her."

"So it boils down to Joey?" I asked.

"Yes," she replied; "he is the one who has tried to break up Jack and me, and I think he has done so deliberately. Jack says the trouble is mine because I never had a brother, but I had male cousins. I think the trouble is that Jack is afraid to say no to Joey or to his ex-wife. But Jack is very tough in business and dosen't hesitate to say no to me."

I asked, "Is it oversimplifying matters too much to say that Joey is now the problem?"

"No," said Leila. "Joey is basically the problem now. He is away at college and has a job also. I hope he does not come home before the next semester. Jack believes anything that the children say. I can tell the truth—but when Joey lies, Jack believes him. For example, I once showed Joey six pounds of hamburger that I had ready for dinner and told him that if he wanted a little for lunch he could have one pound of it but not more. He ate four pounds of it. I had done the shopping, I bought it, I planned the supper, I put it in the refrigerator, and I knew how much it was. But Jack believed Joey's denial when I accused him of eating four pounds."

[Leila has not finished telling the story of the problems in her marriage, but what seems to stand out is what her own daughter has told her, namely, that she is afraid to stand up for herself or to take any firm stand. Why this is can be suggested if not proved by her 0–6. Her mother was seldom around, yet she had a pretty good relationship with her. Leila's father was almost totally withdrawn. I think that is why the memory of the nurse is so strong and vivid, and seems to her to be her only memory of importance: she got so little support from her parents that the intimidation from the nurse was a traumatic experience which left her shy and timid herself. That is why she cannot stand up to her second husband, Jack, and why she dreads his family being down on her and making life unpleasant. So strong is this fear that she is actually seriously considering divorce rather than making a go of the marriage by having the courage not to let herself be exploited by the stepson, Joey, through Jack's always siding with him. The overall trauma of 0–6 was her mother's distance and lack of interest and also her father's lack of interest, plus being pushed out of the little she got from Mother by the birth of Sister, and pushed prematurely into too much responsibility. This caused intensified jealous hostility to Sister and made her vulnerable at age four or five to the specific trauma of the sadistic nurse; her vulnerability was increased by the mother's death and the almost total rejection by Father from age fourteen.]

Dynamic Diagnosis: Leila Smith

Childhood: (1) Excessively strict, sadistic nurse. Excessive restriction; deprivation. Mother rarely there and little interest in patient and sister. Father emotionally withdrawn, completely dominated by Mother. When Sister born, 18 months later, felt pushed out; Sister got all the attention; jealous hostility to Sister.

Current: (2) Feels insecure, timid, tends to be submissive. Unable to stand up for self; takes excessive responsibility but resents it; rather isolated from people. But tries to give her children what she did not get.

Strengths: (1) Dedication to her children. (2) Determination to not be dominated beyond a certain point. (3) Relatively free in loving and being loved.

IV. Amy Colton: Love with a Hook

Amy Colton was just past thirty years of age, an attractive woman I had seen for nearly a year. She came because she felt her life was at loose ends, a mess; that she had no organization, did not know where she was going, and was isolated, and no one really cared anything about her. When she met a man who was nice to her, she thought there must be something wrong with him or some mistake. Yet, the present reality seemed to be that a number of people were good to her, her life seemed organized, and although past thirty she had finally begun to work on a graduate degree at the University of Chicago. Her 0–6 went as follows:

As usual, I asked who were the main figures in her life from the time of her birth to about the age of six or seven. She said, "Mother, Father, and Brother." Her brother's name was Johnnie, and he was two and one-half years younger.

She went on, "Also there were two friends of my father who would spend a lot of time with us."

I asked, "Was any figure in your 0–6 more prominent than the others?"

She replied, "My mother certainly, because my father was away working on his job. I was the firstborn, not only in my family but in all my father's brothers in the area, so I was a princess for nearly two years. I had a great deal of attention. It's strange, but I remember Father's family much better than Mother's. I don't seem to remember my relationship with Father—only two things, and they both are not good. (1) One was when my brother was born and I was left with my aunt and I was looking out on the street and it was empty. There was no one on the block, no cars and no people, but at the end of the block—at a distance, and I think when one is a small child things may look much further than they really are—I saw cars passing by. And then I would look at myself, and I would see my frilly dress. [This memory conveys emotional emptiness, an absence of feelings for people, and a withdrawal into interest in herself.]

"(2) Secondly, I remember that after my brother was born Father came home and left the gate open, and I ran out with my doll and no clothes on, running away from home. I was told later that Father ran after me and gave me a spanking. I guess I've been running ever since, running away from home. [She is correct; in the emotional background is the implication of hostility to her, transgression, guilt, and punishment.]

"Mother was always there; for example, she was always at the dancing lessons she took me to. I think she was trying to make a Shirley Temple out of me. I was on the stage before I was five years old, doing recitals. There was a dancing teacher and I was taking lessons from her, but when she left the area I quit, and I never danced again. The teacher's leaving broke my heart. [Probably because insufficient love at home made the longing for the teacher and the sensitivity to rejection so strong.] Mother was always there like a pillow, very soft-skinned, very white-skinned, very vain but with good reason, because she was pretty and attractive. I was terrifically attached to Mother. [Probably overattached, as are so many rejected and therefore anxious children.] I was coy, shy, frightened of strangers; I always invited people to dinner when Mother was not prepared, but Mother got used to it.

"At about age six I had a vegetable garden, but it was really Mother who grew it. I remember once striking my brother, and Mother taped my hands behind my back and put me in the corner for hours, only for me it seemed like days. Mother used to play a Bing Crosby record and then sing along with it. When Mother smiled and liked me, the whole world was quite good."

[When I first saw this patient, her mother had been dead for over five years, but she wept uncontrollably almost the entire hour on mention of her mother's name.]

"The next most important figure in my life I guess was my father. He worked on three different jobs; he would leave at six in the morning and sometimes not be home until long after dinner in the evening. In other words, he worked from about six A.M. until nine or ten P.M. If he had time in between jobs, he would come home and Mother would shoo us out—my brother and I. Father was too tired to be with children, but Father had two men friends and they used to bring us all sorts of things. I thing Father was hardly in the picture at all from 0–6. I don't remember his being around. His brothers ran a family business and would send us all sorts of junk . . . candy, nylons, all sorts of things."

"It sounds as though they were very nice to you," I said.

"No," she said, "they were not, because I never knew them. And they all died within a few years of one another."

"Are you saying that Mother was always around and Father was never around?"

"Yes," she said, "it was me, Brother, and Mother. But when I was seven years old we got a new house and moved in, and Father took over Brother. Father then began coming home at seven o'clock instead of nine or ten P.M., so he was around more. Father took over Brother because he thought that Brother was too soft, too feminine. Now Brother has entirely changed. I used to beat him up all the time. I used to pinch him until he was purple. Then he was a sweet disposition, a nice kid, but if he did anything wrong I was the one who got blamed."

"What do you mean by Father's taking over Brother?" I asked.

"I mean he would take Brother out of the house. That would be mostly every Saturday and Sunday, or if they were in the house, they would be together in the workshop. Father was raised with three brothers, and he felt my brother should be with men more. When my father took my brother out, my mother was apt to beat me up. She was so crazy for a while; she was looking for any kind of help that she could find. She tried Christian Science and many other things. Father was not very nice to Mother. Mother had an operation, and Father refused to get her and drive her home. She started her menopause in her late thirties and had terrible migraines. My feeling is that I've not emphasized the part of my brother in my life enough. He grew up and ran a business which became very successful. In a way, he took the place of my father; he has been my father, in fact the very worst father I have ever known. He is so mean to me in withholding money that is rightfully mine that I don't even know how I will pay for my next meal. Last night I had fantasies of killing him. I just beat the pillow."

[We can easily see why Amy has feelings of no direction and has no close human relationships. She was greatly overattached to her mother, and when the mother died, Amy's emotional life collapsed. But even in this close relationship to her mother, she was often beaten by her mother. For her father she apparently had no tender relationship, or very little. Toward her brother was hostility and guilt for her meanness to him, which was a natural hostility in reaction to her excessive, ambivalent needs for her mother and also was provoked by her being blamed for everything the brother did wrong. Apparently the brother pushed her out of the position she described as being "princess" of the family. Hence, there is not a single good relationship in her 0–6, and it is something of a question as to how she turned out to be as stable as she is, able to organize her life, get a graduate degree, and have some kind of human relationships even though she feels they are most ungratifying. Her 0–6 is sufficiently confused and lacking in steady love and tenderness that one can see why today she has a pattern of feeling confused and has no stable relationships. Also, there was no one with whom she could satisfactorily identify, and I think she has no satisfactory feeling of identity herself. With her pattern of being beaten by her mother and having very little emotional closeness from her father, and a pattern of being displaced by her brother and reacting to him with her own sadism, but then suffering at his hands when he has grown up, it is small wonder that she feels she has no satisfactory relationships with men, nor is it surprising that she has not married.]

Amy Colton came to see me on a regular once-a-week basis which seemed just about right for her; more often, I think, would have been too intense, and time showed that she did very well on this basis. In our hour together a week later I said nothing, not knowing whether she would start off with present-day material or whether she would continue with her mind on her early life pattern. She said, "I think of my neighbors. They lived two houses away from us. I remember the front of their house better than my own. Now, after our last hour I think I know why my brother is so important to me, although I had not realized it.

"When I left my last hour with you a week ago, I was so very depressed for two days. I think it was connected with Father's taking my brother away from me. Brother was the only male I knew well until I was six or maybe seven years old. The other males—the uncles, the friends—were like mythical males. They appeared and disappeared, but my father's taking my brother away does not fit with my brother taking my mother away, or rather my brother dividing my mother's time and attention and taking that away from me. I felt that Father and Mother gave Brother more love than they gave me, that they only gave me 'things,' and you can give things to any fool. It's all still a muddle and a mush. I feel I can't unravel the yarn, unravel it, undo it, and get things rolling again. But I have consulted with two lawyers about hurrying up the settlement of my inheritance so that I have something to live on and can pay my bills, including yours. I got two diametrically opposed views. I really talked with bank people and am finding out about attorneys. I would rather work through them with my brother, because on the phone with him we both get so emotional and hostile. The bank prople are working on a partial settlement soon. I am thinking less of my brother, and I have passed the examination and am to start in graduate school next semester, a few months from now. I will try to get a full-time job until then, and after I start school I will try for a part-time job. At school there is a woman who is an assistant director, and I have rapport with women more easily than with men. I don't get into a lot of strange situations with women as I do with men."

[This is not surprising, because Amy had a strong although ambivalent relationship with her mother, but apparently almost no relationship with her father, who ignored her or beat her, or with her brother, which was fight and be fought. When they were young she used to beat up on him, and since he had grown up he had beaten up on her financially. Of course, I said nothing at this point.]

Amy went ahead: "So tomorrow I see this woman and I think that in a few years she will not be just the assistant director but the director. Those neighbors I mentioned . . . the woman had a job with a very good company. I guess she was a friend of my mother's. She used to make lemonade and other drinks, which were always available. There were two girls who were her daughters, and she had a son too, who was eight or ten years older than I. Apparently she got along all right with her daughters, but she used to say that she was having a hard time with her son. I don't know how they fitted into my life, but she was a very nice lady and there was always something on her porch to eat or drink. It was a tiny porch, very white, with red stairs and pretty flowers growing there.

"I still don't understand why I was so depressed last week when I left you."

After a pause, waiting for her to continue, I said "Could you possibly have been let down after all the work to pass those exams to get into graduate school?"

She said, "No, it's because I saw something in the material, I think maybe in relation to my brother. I never before last week realized how big a portion of my life my brother occupied, or why it was so hard to separate from him. Now things are beginning to be proportionalized. I'm just beginning to get a finger on it. I've been reading a book, and there is a line in it saying, 'A man must live with himself and be comfortable with himself before all else.' I am trying to act with some decency toward my brother. People here think I'm sensible, but my family has only told me that I'm an idiot, how no-good I am. It just doesn't balance. Some people see me one way, and others see me another way." [That sounded like a lack of identity and stable self-image, which was certainly lacking in her 0–6.] She was then silent for a moment, and I took this opportunity to explain to her about childhood patterns, namely that everyone forms certain patterns of emotional relationships in their childhood to the people who are closest to them and who are responsible for them, and these patterns continue usually for life. If they are extreme one way or another, they may make emotional problems. She seemed to understand, but said, "But I'm so insecure."

I replied, "Well, I think I've just tried to explain that. It is a continuation of your emotional pattern toward your mother, father, and brother. If the original pattern of being the 'princess' in the whole family had continued, you might have had other emotional problems in your life, but not the same as these, because your pattern toward your mother is that she was a pillow, she was soft, she was somebody that was good, but every time she was good to you, you expected her to clobber you later. With your father, you got no security because he was never there, and when he *was* there, he so often beat you up. And with your brother, it was beat up or be beaten up. You used to pinch him until he was black and blue, and now he beats you up by withholding your inheritance and telling you what an awful person you are. So you have this pattern of feeling from your family toward you; what you need to do is contrast this with the present reality which is not so bad. I have a patient who is retarded, and that is a very difficult reality, and that will be difficult for her to face—how will she face it? But with you, you are healthy, strong, and have a superior intelligence, are nice-looking and have a great deal of intuition and understanding and experience. So you have to replace this childhood view which was taken over from your parents and your brother with a realistic view of how you are today."

She said, "Now I'm just beginning to see what it is that you are driving at. Maybe that is why I like Cinderella so much. In fact, I used to think I was an orphan."

[It seems to me that in this session the patient is herself making the connections, is understanding more clearly the emotional pattern of her childhood . . . but beyond that, she is making some emotional connections between this pattern and the realities of her present life; so my feeling was of some definite analytic, therapeutic movement. It would be my guess that the patient remembers the house from two doors down because she got so little tender care in her own home, and that was always vitiated by the expectation of scoldings, reprimands, and actual beatings—so this house remains in her memory because there she always found uniform interest and kindness.]

As is to be expected and is already evident from the very beginning, going back and forth from the childhood pattern to the present-day complaint in a deliberate goal-conscious way, in addition to free associating, is only effective under certain circumstances and in certain patients. I tried it in the next interview with Amy Colton and think that it certainly did no harm, but even did some good, although it was not really satisfyingly effective. That hour with her went as follows:

I said, "Would you like to go a little further with the childhood pattern in relation to your present complaint?"

She indicated that she had a letter that she wanted to show me later, but that she would like to start with what I suggested. I therefore asked her what her complaints were when she first came to me, one year earlier.

"I certainly remember," she said. "It was how to handle the death of my mother."

[Her mother had died five years before the patient came to see me, but she still could not bear the thought. This patient, you will recall, was over thirty years old.]

"Also," she said, "I could not handle the other great losses. My mother, the loss of my father, and the thought that I would lose my brother. At the time, I remember feeling that things were going so badly in relation to my brother that I would have to move away from him—I felt I had to move away from my brother but I could not do it alone, I could not do it without help. In addition to handling these losses, I felt that everything was ass-backwards. Things were emotional that should not have been emotional, and things were *not* emotional that should have been."

I said, "Can you give me an example?"

"Yes," she said, "getting through school. Before an examination I would confuse the great amount of energy that I put into studying with the relationships with people or with heightened sexual levels. I'm not expressing that clearly because I'm not clear on it myself. It's murky. I became scared of certain people; I was unclear in the estimation of myself. People told me occasionally that I demeaned myself. Also, I just had plain fear of standing up to my brother, even more than standing up to my father. Then I did not handle information, like Mother saying that if anybody knew me they would not love me. That is much better now, just knowing that I am not that crazy. Before coming to see you I was known as 'Crazy Amy,' the daughter of 'Crazy Gus,' that is, my father. Now I feel much more solid as a person and I also feel like a woman. I never felt that before—and never felt the child, the girl, all those things that go into making up a woman. Those are all the complaints I can remember having when I came to see you. I don't like to use the word 'complaints' now because everything is so much better."

"Well, then, let's just use the term 'problem' instead of complaints. What are the problems that you still have today that we hope to resolve?"

"I feel as though I am in the middle of something and am going toward something, but don't know what. Maybe I'm a little afraid. I approach all information as though I were defending my life with it, and there's more, but I can't define it verbally just now. I feel kind of numb; partly I'm trying to become whole, an adult, but what my secret definition of adult is, I would not now be sure. I think it's largely to be free of my brother.

"When I was nineteen years old, a girlfriend of mine told me that my brother was awful. I denied it and still find myself denying it. It makes me feel very bad about this letter, which is an effort to put Mother's estate back in court, out of my brother's hands. I can't define my present problems too well. There is this letter about the estate . . . I guess you would call it day-to-day problems."

"Yes," I said, "that sounds like a good term."

She said, "I brought this letter from the lawyer about my brother, but it is hard to accept that my brother is not really a good friend to me. All people have told me is so many lies; my parents told me that blood is thicker than water, that my brother is my friend, that my father loved me, and I still believe the words in spite of the beatings and the sarcasm. And I think my brother is trying to take my share of the estate, in fact, taking it all so that I don't have anything to live on and cannot pay your bills . . . I don't mean that there were not some tender moments also. I could put my head on my mother's lap after a beating . . . but she would say that she wished me the kind of awful daughter that I had been to her. I must have really put a monkey wrench into her life . . . I think she was a simple soul, frustrated by a complicated world. I say the words, but the words I say do not have the feeling to go with them. In fact, I felt that the only person who really understood me at all was a schizophrenic girl whom I knew in college, and I could understand her. My mother said that Father was jealous of my brother because Mother gave Brother so much attention, but Father was never jealous of me. My mother said that I was supposed to be responsible for my brother. He was two and a half years younger than I. Both of my parents told me that I was responsible for him. But if I was responsible for him and he has turned out so badly, how does that make me feel?"

"Do you mean guilty?" I asked.

"Yes," she replied, "that's certainly what I am saying. I do love my cousin Jerry. He is three or four years older than I am, and he has been very nice to me. He is the one who invited me back home and sent me the train tickets this past year."

The next session with Amy we worked out her dynamic diagnosis. Drawing it up, together with the patient, had a powerful impact for Amy.

Dynamic Diagnosis: Amy Colton

Childhood: (1) Rejection and deprivation. Father not there, Mother there but not giving gratification of the dependent love needs, or else giving love to patient only as bait and then taking it away. Mother a big hen, *smothering*, gave some love but with a hook in it. Whenever Mother gave love, patient was soon afterward beaten. (2) This caused insecurity and anxiety, which in turn caused excessive clinging to Mother (needs to be loved and to love), and: (3) Hostility and hate of younger brother from his birth because patient was pushed out of what little she had of Mother. (4) Physical abuse (beatings) mostly by Father from age ten to twenty-three until patient left home.

Current: Feelings of deprivation, inferiority and being unlovable, that if patient is loved, then she will be rejected, clobbered. This leads to (a) reactive flashes of superiority feelings, but mostly (b) hurt, pain and anxiety, fear, and strong fight-flight: (c) hostility, rage ("tons of rage"), flight from close relations with people.

Strengths: (1) Strong will and control in face of loneliness and suffering. (2) High intelligence. (3) Confidence that can handle even very bad life situations.

V. Herbert Baxter: Perfectionist

Herbert Baxter was one of those young men who came to the University of Chicago with every promise: he was handsome, an athlete, and he had a brilliant scholastic record. There was no question about his admission, and everybody expected great things of him, including his parents. During his freshman year he fulfilled that promise. He became captain of the baseball team and had a brilliant academic record and was universally popular. He took up with a girl who was beautiful, intelligent, and an heiress. Then, suddenly, he began to think of himself as a new Messiah, to dress that way and to speak that way, to lecture on street corners—and before anyone realized it he had to be committed to a mental hospital.

After nearly two years he came out of the hospital and resumed his studies at the University, but was not quite able to make it and broke down again. He returned to the hospital, which, it seems, tried to encourage his dependence upon the hospital. His parents were desperate and called me in consultation. In addition to everything else, while they were well-off financially, they could not afford the enormous expense of a private psychiatric hospital. It seemed to me that Herbert had enough strength of ego so that the emotional problems could be dealt with without institutionalization. After seeing him for a while myself in the office, since I had no hospital practice at the time, I referred him to a friend and colleague who was excellent professionally with these borderline young people. He handled Herbert extremely well, dealing with his dynamics in ways Herbert could accept; Herbert made slow but steady progress on the long road back. Eventually he graduated and got his degree, but remained rather shaky and had another breakdown after graduation which necessitated institutionalization for a few months. Then he emerged from this into an externally good adjustment, yet internally he remained so insecure that his parents and he himself were not sure when and if he would have another breakdown.

Immediately after the war he came for an interview with me because he had moved to this area to live with relatives and be away from his parents. I saw him with great interest, allowing over two hours for the interview. It went about as follows:

I asked him what his complaints were now and he said, "A strong tendency to withdraw. For example, I went to visit my parents and no sooner did I arrive than I went to bed and stayed there for the afternoon. I got up for dinner, which was very pleasant, but afterward I went back to bed and stayed there until midmorning of the next day. I have just moved into an apartment near my job, but I tend not to eat lunch with the others; I go to my apartment and go to bed instead. I *hate* myself for this withdrawal. This morning on the way to seeing you I had the fantasy that you would say to me, 'Herbert, you've had a hard life. Come up to this nice white bedroom and I will tuck you in and we will talk. And you rest and do nothing for a while.' I have trouble taking care of myself," he continued. "I can't automatically in the morning get up, get dressed, make my bed, and go to work; I used to be well organized, but now I am not. I am not trying to say, however, that I am a helpless invalid. I have made friends, given dinner parties, some of which I have cooked myself; I have managed to get things done that have to be done, but it's the extras. There is no reason when I come home to my apartment that I should not clean my room, make my bed, and so on, but I don't do it."

"Do you have any other complaints than this withdrawal?" I asked.

"Yes," he answered. "My other main complaint is that I am still so introspective. Only occasionally do I suddenly realize that I have lived a few hours without watching how I feel, missing my mother, and so on."

I said, "Do you mean your energies are turned into excessive observation of yourself internally and not turned out externally? That is, you think about how you feel and how you are doing rather than about your job and making the bed?"

"Yes," he said, "that's exactly it. Now it's worse because I am going to be interviewed today for another job. At present I am in a job I don't like . . . it is in the world of athletics. As you know, they thought

I should do something simple, unemotional, and unintellectual, but at least when I am in good shape I like the academic life and want to do some sort of teaching instead of this. I think in part coming to see you today is a desperate reaching out for help because my desperation is often too strong to cope with. That one time when you said there was suicidal risk and we must get me to a hospital I felt great relief because then I no longer had to kill myself." [Herbert at the time was twenty-five years old, still handsome, and I think few people would pick up from talking to him how desperate he was internally.]

In this interview I told Herbert I thought it would be beneficial to try to review his 0–6 now that we had a little distance from his acute emotional problems and his psychotic breaks. I proceeded as usual to ask first the *general* question, "What do you consider the main feature or features of your emotional life from birth to the age of about six or seven?"

He said, "First, a strong loving father, physically present. Secondly, a less purely good but more Godlike mother, not as warm as father, who had punitive but also rewarding sides to her. Third, an almost physical relationship to a brother, two years older. We tussled together like bear cubs. I called it friendly aggression. And then I have a younger brother, four years younger, and an eight-year-old sister. Since the younger brother and sister arrived, there has been nothing I have felt for them both except pure love. The only thing that marred a perfect 0–6 was an intense fear of punishment and rejection by Mother because she demanded perfect behavior, and when we were not perfect, she got very angry.

"My *first memory*, which I think I told you about once before, was of helping Mother hang up something and asking her, 'Mommy, am I a good boy?' Most of the time when I asked her she would say yes, and then I would be bathed in light and glory, but when she said no I would be devastated. Father loved me unconditionally, but for Mother I had to be perfect." At this point tears began to roll down his cheeks.

I asked, "Why exactly these tears?"

He replied, "I don't know whether they are because I am crying or whether it is just because I yawned. If they were tears of crying, then it is because I have made so little progress. I am twenty-five years old and not yet weaned from Mother or Mother figures." At this point he broke down and wept freely and became silent.

I offered him a box of Kleenex and the weeping gradually subsided. "I feel so awful," he said, "that I am twenty-five and not weaned from Mother."

I said, "Realistically, I don't think that is at all unusual. Many men are not weaned from their mothers until they are well into middle age. I think that is something you will accomplish, and there is no need to feel so bad about it now, but I think the reason you *do* feel this way is the sustained feeling of perfectionism which you have been describing. You want to be perfect; you have the idea that to be perfect you should be weaned from Mother at the age of twenty-five. If not, then you are not perfect and you feel anxious and frustrated in your pride, and you weep."

He said, "Yes, but I must work out a way to live."

I replied, "Exactly, that's just the point."

He said, "My 0–6 was perhaps too happy. Everyone was congratulating everyone else. Father and Mother were convinced that they were the greatest parents, and had the brightest children. It was too golden. Sooner or later it had to come crashing down."

I said, "Very good. Now I will ask you more or less the same question I did before, but in a slightly different form. Who was the main person for you during your earliest childhood?"

He replied, "I must say Mother. I was aware of Father's physical presence, but I think Mother dominated. They were almost equal in the very early years." He paused; he was obviously in distress. I looked at him quizzically but said nothing. He said, "I had a terrible thought." He fell silent again.

I encouraged him: "Don't be afraid; tell it."

He said, "If Mother had died before the end of my 0–6, I might have been less tortured since. It was after the middle of 0–6 (i.e., 5–6) that Mother emerged as the most influential parent, the stronger of the two. Mother controlled my entire life; she would not let me alone, so I became very dependent on her. All this is so difficult to say because when I broke down, I really needed her, and then Father was helpless and hopeless to help me, while Mother really helped out." I said nothing, but his statement was correct. "It's only another way of saying my present withdrawal is a loss of energy; that is, without Mother or a Mother-substitute there is no motivation for me to do anything. In college I was well motivated because I had this wonderful girl, and her energy helped me out; but I have never been able to do things on my own. Looking back with hindsight, Mother was too ferocious for my 0–6. I never could be good enough for her. She really demanded perfection in her children; we had to be perfect, or she would be angry. We had to be perfect to the outside world, rather than letting us develop ourselves. The attitude was never 'What has this kid in him intrinsically which can be brought out?' but only 'How can we mold him to be perfect and the image of ourselves?'"

"What do you mean," I asked, "by saying that your mother was ferocious?"

He said, "I mean loud, punitive, strong. Not a soft, feminine mothering influence. Father was that, much more than Mother. He was more tender than Mother. When I was young, Father was the more unconditionally loving. In Mother's eyes I could do no right, while in Father's eyes I could do no wrong. Of course, that's an overstatement in regard to Mother. But beginning at about age twelve I could no longer relate to Father; he never changed roles, he never quit treating me like a six-year-old, patting my hand and caressing my cheek instead of talking with me about things. Where I respect Father is in his ability to function well, to keep clean, to keep fit, to keep working."

"How do you mean?" I asked,

"I'm so depressed I don't see how other people keep going, even how you keep going. I see how Mother does, but she is compulsive, she does not *dare* to stop. When she drove me somewhere and waited in the car, she would always have work to do and would never just relax or read a book."

"Why do you hate yourself?" I asked.

"I hate myself because I can't even read; I would rather just rest. If I could only read, instead of lying down and resting. The other figure in my life during 0–6 was my older brother. In the early years he was just a good friend, except I felt I had to live up to him, and I didn't want to have to do that. He was more the perfect, obedient child than I was. In school he was the perfect one, while I was the cutup, the delinquent. But I really did not want to be perfect like him. I really do not know too much about him from 0–6, but it feels as though the sibling rivalry did not start until secondary school where we had grades and athletics and girls to compare. My younger brother—four years younger—and my baby sister were just pure love. There was no jealousy there that I could see. With my older brother during 0–6 I feel that we were chiefly only friends and playmates without competition; if anything, there was competition for our parents' affection. If there were, he would play for it by being the perfect good boy, and I would play for it by being the clown and making them laugh."

I said, "Very good; you've told me your very first memory already ("Mommy, am I a good boy?") but what *other early memories* do you have?"

He replied, "(2) I was in the bathroom with Father when he was shaving, and I was thinking how pleasant that was. (3) A third memory is that I was sleeping in a room with my older brother, Ben, making shadows on the wall with a flashlight, but it is the first memory that seems so crucial because that is what is active today—asking, 'Mommy, am I a good boy?' That memory seems to be the keystone of my life; am I perfect for my Mother, and also am I perfect for you, for my teachers, and so on? The rest are just lovely memories of nice times with the family. It was an insulated family."

"Are you implying," I said, "that this made the relationships within the family that much more intense and they were not diluted much?"

"That is exactly it," he said, "they were not diluted."

"Do you have any dreams," I asked, "during 0-6, especially any repetitive dreams?"

"There is only one *dream* I remember," he said; "that one was a dream of whether or not Mother was a witch in disguise." [Probably reflecting his fear, hostility, and guilt toward his mother.]

"What do you make of it all?" I asked. "Can you reduce the essential of the dynamics which you have seen from this review with me to a very few words?"

"Yes, I was trained to be perfect by external standards, for example, appearance, behavior, achievement—rather than being encouraged in my own intrinsic development. But how can one solve this?"

I said, "There are several ways it might be solved. The first one is to be perfect, not by the external standards but by encouraging your own internal development. Or we could make it even simpler and reduce it to two words: *reduce perfectionism.*"

"I see that," he said, "but it's hard because I was brought up by my parents to think I was a superstar. Can I write that down, these formulas we are discussing?"

"Of course," I said.

"I could not really let myself flow," he said, "because of the perfectionism."

"All right," I said, "that would say it in a few words. Perfectionism and superstardom versus your own intrinsic development, letting it flow."

"I think," he replied, "that hits parts of it very well," and he proceeded to write it down.

"It seems that you have so much perfectionism—although everybody likes to be as good as they can—but with you it is in such excess there is a feeling that if you do not live up to it, you will hate yourself." I continued: "That makes it an impossible task, because nobody is perfect. To take the old Navy phrase, 'You do the best you can with what you've got.' I can see why it would be extremely difficult for you to teach or do anything well if you are not simply teaching but in the back of your mind was always the feeling, 'I've got to be perfect, I've got to be a superstar . . . but if I'm not I will be rejected by Mother and punished and will be devastated.' If this is going on emotionally in your mind, how can you be free for what we call 'object interest' and 'task orientation'? If you could only abandon the perfectionism, then your mind would be free just to do the job, to do the best you could and to develop from within."

"Now let me write that down," he said, "because that sounds just right to me."

This is an excellent example of a psychotic break not because of severe trauma in 0–3, but because of the intensity of the neurotic pattern; also, it was possible to work with Herbert psychodynamically because he had a bascally healthy ego, character, and had many good relationships in his 0–6. These enabled him to develop a strong positive transference, and work with what was essentially the neurotic, not psychotic, problem of conflict with his mother and rivalry with his older brother.

Dynamic Diagnosis: Herbert Baxter

Childhood: Much loved but perfectionism to external standards imposed by dominating mother by giving much love for obeying; but when he could not achieve perfection, patient felt rejected and devastated and a sense of never developing from within. Rivalry with older brother and withdrawal from rivalry with Mother, who was extremely energetic, efficient worker.

Current: Must be *perfect* and outstanding, with severe *anxiety* about failing to be; this makes every activity strenuous emotionally, and responsibility causes intense fight-flight: *regressive tendencies* to escape by total *withdrawal,* causing failure and frustration; *rage,* mostly against self with suicidal trends plus rage toward Mother with guilt and masochism. Inability to be superior to older brother and to identify with Mother and her great energy, work, responsibility, leads to inferiority feelings.

Strengths: (1) Many good relationships in 0-6. (2) High abilities. (3) Open to reason. (4) Protected by own narcissism, derived from parental love and adoration.

VI. Sally Bates: The Perennial Child

Sally Bates was a rather small, extremely pretty girl, blonde with brown eyes. She had been seeing me on and off for over two years for depression and inability to "get anywhere" in her life. She was now just passing her middle twenties. As she entered them, she began dating a boy (Harry) who she believed would not make a good husband for her, but she felt that he was all she had. When Harry finally broke it off, she became extremely depressed and, even worse, withdrew almost completely from the world. It was as though her thrust toward life was sufficient for her to venture out into this unsatisfactory relationship with Harry, but it was not strong and steady enough to sustain a first frustration, and she withdrew almost totally into the bosom of her family.

Sally did get far enough into life to obtain a job . . . one which she hated, but which she nevertheless stuck with until she could pay off the employment agency fee. The physical and emotional drain on her was very considerable, but she did manage to stick it out. She felt that they were apt to fire her at any point. Therefore, in its way, these few months of work were a great step forward into life, with its frustrations and difficulties. I did a review of her 0-6, repeating what I had done in the first hour that we met; the present review went as follows:

"My parents have each other, but they have given up on me. I am not worth anything; I am not worth any of the thousands of dollars they have poured into me, for my education and doctors' bills since childhood, and which have done no good. I have nobody. Nobody, but my parents think I must adapt to that. They are ashamed of me. It is a lost cause. It is not the passivity but the nerves that are so bad . . . I'm not sure what it is that I am fighting. Is it leaving them, my parents? I have reached a point where I want to slit my wrists in a motel and get it over with . . . I don't want to live. I am at the point where I don't care, or rather, I care enough to want to get it over with. I don't think there is a heaven or hell. I suffer too much to make small talk. I am beyond that. I told them I didn't want to live. Father does not believe in psychiatry. He thinks I never should have seen you, but I think you have saved my life so far. My parents did try to help me get a job, but I've just got no one. You have got your wife. So it is as simple as that. I just don't want to live. I don't remember my 0–6, but you want me to. I don't remember it; I guess that means I hated it."

I said, "Well let's do it anyway. Let's make believe that we have met for the first time. Tell me who the main people were in your life from the time you were born until you were about age six or seven."

Sally: "Mother and Father. Period."

I said, "Any nurse, aunt, grandmother, anybody else at all?"

Sally: "No, no, no one at all except Mother and Father. That was it."

"Were they both together in your mind as a unit, or did you have a different relationship to your mother than to your father?"

Sally: "My mother cared more; my father liked me only if I were just so, if I looked right to his friends who were about forty or fifty years of age. They never leveled with me; they never told me their ages. But I know they were about forty when I was born. I visited my mother's home town last summer and Father said, 'That's the place where your mother used to work,' and Mother said 'Ssh, ssh,' and hushed him up. They never tell me anything. My mother had a nickname in those days; but if she meets anyone today who came from the same home town and calls her by her nickname, she ignores them. My only living relative on my father's side is his sister, who never married. Mother kept me away from her; I never met her, but she used to send me little gifts every birthday until this year. Now she too has given up on me, like everyone I've ever been in touch with. Father was away at business; but, apart from that, I was much closer to Mother. Father always had his own bathroom, the best shower bath, and so on. He always blamed Mother for spoiling me. My mother sacrificed herself for my father and for me."

"How?" I asked.

"Well, for example, just today I was in a big hurry to get over here to see you. I was so tense and something fell off the table and I screamed, and Mother said, 'Why do you torture me?' They have no idea how lonely I am and was. Even before the age of six I used to sit quiet while Father and Mother visited with their friends of their own generation. I was born on the near Northside and never lived anywhere else, but I wish I had lived where there were some relatives of my mother and father. But there is nothing here, absolutely nothing. Mother tells me what may have been true, namely that I had a happy normal childhood, but she did say I loved my bed. She would take me swimming. I was always sick; I was always happy, though, Mother says, until I went to the church nursery school. I was such an extension of my parents that I don't know whether that's true or not.

I said, "Apart from what your Mother says, what do you remember as your relationship to her?"

Sally: "I was probably very happy with her; she was my best friend; she was my only friend. I had nobody—no brothers or sisters. We had neighbors, a wealthy family, and sometimes I had a few children through them to play with, but I was so picked on. I couldn't do things in clay; I couldn't draw a straight line. Mother had done everything for me, I guess. In my present job it took me 40 times to learn to work a simple mimeograph machine. A mentally retarded person could do as well or better."

[This patient, when I first saw her, was in college with two years to go and was rapidly failing. It was possible, however, by support and encouragement and ego-strengthening to get her to finish, so she was *not* mentally retarded and had an I.Q. close to 120. She struck me in some ways (verbally) as quite intelligent, but in other ways (mechanically, as in bookkeeping, mathematics, and so on) she was without doubt extremely slow. She learned typing without too much difficulty. Of course, the possibility of an organic brain impairment occurred to me early in the game; but she had had repeated physical exams including neurological ones, and no neurologist had ever come up with any evidence whatever of organic pathology.]

Out loud I said, "How would you summarize your relationships to your mother during your 0-6.?"

Sally: "We were best friends, very close; the minute I would go away from Mother, it was hell. The kids picked on me, the teachers picked on me; it was hell, it was misery. Father blamed Mother for my difficulties and said I must learn to fight back. I couldn't do the gymnastic things; I couldn't do anything in the gym. I couldn't compete in sports."

"How would you summarize your relationship to your father?" I asked.

"I was very proud of Father and of Mother, and I told people how wonderful they were. Father was very strict and spanked me often, and then I wouldn't eat my food, but Father did not eat either. Father was not with me much; there were only the three of us, though; so we were probably together more than most fathers. There was something very weird on Father's side. Mother's side of the family was O.K., except that during my babyhood, my 0–6, Mother had ulcers for about three years and had to eat babyfood. Father has been self-centered and ashamed of me if I am not just so, but are children usually just so? Once Mother and I met him at a motel. I was so happy to see him that I crawled over the carpet to him. The carpet was dirty, and instead of picking me up, Father was disgusted and sent me back to Mother. I walked about a half year to one year late, but I crawled so fast no one could catch me. Once I stood up and walked, I was so proud that I did it in front of my grandmother to show off, and I never crawled again. I've done everything late; in my 0–6 I was a nothing, and I was sick all the time. I was always with adults. That was the only time I could get along, only with adults.

"Father had an old friend; he was married. They had no children. Sometimes they would come to visit us, and then they invited the three of us to come down and visit them in St. Louis. My parents said it would cost too much for all of us to go, but they would send me. I was then sixteen years old. When I arrived they thought they should get friends for me of my own age, but I was not interested. I just stayed with them and slept late. I went to dinner with them and went around and saw old homes, and so on. I had no interest in meeting young people. I was sixteen; but when I traveled down on the train, I met a man who thought I was twenty-one. I was not afraid in those days of being away from my parents, the way I am now. If there is anything in this hour, it is wildly repressed. I may be an old Victorian and not one of those whose parents are divorced and whose children run around. When I talked about going off with Harry, it was because it was different from my present life, but it was just talk. It is like something gripping me, something very Calvinistic; everything is repressed. Sex is repressed. That affair with Harry just about destroyed me, morally and psychologically. I was too repressed to talk about it with my parents; I was so repressed! But at twenty I could just jump into bed, and it was a sin, it was dumb. But then there was that little spark of life still in me. Jack was the first guy I was ever close to, but I was only close to him through letters, words on a piece of paper. I realized it would never work out with Jack, and I also knew that I would have been a terrible mother. Marriage would have been a disaster, Harry would have left me if we had ever been married. My parents are very repressed on sex; they put it down to a physical problem, at least Father does. Mother, I don't know."

Thus far it seems that important parts of this material are the extreme loneliness and withdrawal, extreme dependence upon her parents, especially her mother, and Sally's statement that when she was twenty she still had some spark of life in her, but that this she no longer has; and she attributes this problem to severe repression especially of sexuality. But I think that the implication is that sex is not the only problem; rather, it is a repression of all spontaneous, strong feelings toward other people, so that the only way Sally was able to relate at all was through sex. This was a powerful enough force to bring her into at least some slight intimacy with Jack—by letter—and then later with Harry, a relationship which was more intimate and serious. When Harry broke that off, it meant severing the last libidinal tie, always a serious situation. She retreated so far that she was almost completely cut off from other people. There was another girl whom she sometimes saw and went out with; otherwise, in truth, Sally was only with her parents and never ventured forth into life. The reason for this situation was not clear from the 0-6; it seemed to be some combination of some spoiling with illnesses from early childhood, a great deal of overprotection and restrictiveness, and a great deal of restrictive repressions, with some rejection (as when she crawled to her father and he repulsed her) and no pattern of association with peers, or association only connected with fear. So her spontaneity as a young child was seriously hampered if not discouraged. I think the concept of a thrust to life is a very important one; her thrust toward life was weak, and when it was frustrated by her being rejected by Harry, she really gave up on living—which was in part rationalized in that she honestly, sincerely believed that she was totally inadequate, both in personal relationships and in taking responsibility; that she was so inadequate a person that no one could possibly be interested in her.

I think her suicidal talk was serious, that there was a very real tendency to give up on life and make the ultimate withdrawal; but what

I depended on to prevent this was Sally's capacity for transference. I thought she had in the course of our sessions developed a very strong dependent attachment to me, and with this leverage I hoped and expected to pry her away from danger. She did not reveal in her 0–6 a very important trend, namely an intense rage. It was dangerous but in a way healthy, because it was something of a defense and a spark of life. It showed that she was not taking her suffering lying down, but was angry about it and had at least a bit of fight left in her. This made a not uncommon analytic problem of reducing the hostility which antagonized people and contained a suicidal threat and kept her masochistic; the question was of how to reduce that and keep a real fighting *spirit*, without too much hostility in it to herself and others, that is.

Also, the countertransference in a case like this, with a person who has almost no human contacts whatever, is extremely important in the whole process. Fortunately, I liked Sally very much and I believe this gave her a lot of sustainment. When she ran herself down and told me she was worthless, a nothing, I sometimes would attack her statement head-on with a little acerbity, and say, "I will not have you run yourself down this way, that is not true." And I would list her good points for her honestly, while at the same time agreeing that the problem was a difficult one for her.

Her very *first memory*, between the ages of two or three, seems to tell the story. In it, Sally is sick; she forgets what the illness was, but she is alone in her room, looking through the window, watching other children at play. There are a number of different interrelationships here with her parents, but they all seem to tend toward the same result. First, there is an overclose relationship to her mother, and also the fact that her mother took over everything that Sally tried to do—if she tried to help in the kitchen, the mother took over and did things so much more efficiently and rapidly that Sally thought there was no use doing anything at all, and she withdrew. Two, there was the lack of full approval from her father. Sally tries to be "just so," even to this day, dressing very nicely, appearing very pretty, and yet she feels she is not getting love and approval. There was also the very strict, puritanical training, which put her at odds with her natural impulses to such a degree that she had given up there also. Her pleasant manner belied the rage that lay beneath the surface and made her depreciate herself, made her parents miserable, made her suicidal, and antagonized people she would like to be close to. Thus far, the flight part of the fight-flight reaction had resulted only in psychological withdrawal; but if it became strong enough to fuse with the rage against herself, then the suicidal threat would become serious. But perhaps the rage could be turned into a "fighting spirit" and serve to bring about improvement in independence and capacity for more enjoyment of life. When her parents went away for two weeks on a vacation, Sally barely survived. She told me that upon their return she finally realized how totally dependent on them she was.

Dynamic Diagnosis: Sally Bates

Childhood: Overattached by excessive dependent love needs to Mother; some rejection by Father; overly restricted and repressed, with no encouragement of independence.

Current: Still overattached to Mother, overly dependent; loneliness, causing frustration and fight-flight: withdrawal from peers to Mother; repression of sex and other drives to life and to independence, causing increased frustration and barely repressed hostility as *rage,* with suicidal tendencies and further withdrawal.

Strengths: Capacity for transference to analyst (following pattern to Mother) and willingness to be supported by him in her efforts toward independence.

VII. Oliver Dixon: Success at a Price

Here is an example of one of those relatively unusual, very repressed patients from whom I was unable to elicit much of the unconscious childhood pattern in the first interview.

Oliver Dixon, a successful professional man, came because of a marital problem. He could not recall any first memories before the age of six, nor could he recall any dreams in childhood or since. He could not portray in any detail his emotional interactions with the individual members of his family. About all he could say was that he thought all the emotional interrelations in his family from 0-6 were rather detached, cold, and distant. Because of that, he said, he grew up expecting nothing from anyone. From an early age he had a paper route, did baby-sitting, cut lawns, and so on, to earn what money he wanted; he continued this pattern, working nights, to put himself through college and professional school, and had done well in his chosen field, reaching prominence and financial success through long hours of work. What dynamics led to his reacting to the early distance and coldness of his family by this successful independence and drive instead of depression and withdrawal were not apparent; one could guess that one element in his marital problem was a lack in himself of capacity for giving and receiving closeness and warmth because of its lack in his childhood relationships, and this turned out to be correct. All that could be readily seen in this patient in the first interviews was his own statement of the overall of his 0–6: deprivation in childhood in the form of coldness and distance, reacted against by repressing his needs and being unusually independent and hard-working, thereby achieving a success which brought him esteem and recognition if not direct love. But this statement was unsupported by such unconscious material as first memories and dreams. The outlook for the analysis was very favorable from the standpoint of ego strength, but care would have to be taken to watch closely for any possible weakening of this by the mobilization of repressed dependent love needs which might tempt him to relinquish his excessive independent responsible effort or to escape from it temporarily by addiction to cigarettes or alcohol. One goal of his therapy would be to alleviate his excessive drive to work in order to lessen the chances of addiction and of psychosomatic symptoms such as ulcers, high blood pressure, or other effects of unrelieved effort inadequately balanced by sleep and recreation. Another goal would be to soften this drive without diminishing it too far and to ease his feelings, probably mostly through the transference, so that he could give and accept a little more closeness and warmth. In this case, then, the central dynamics could not be clearly discerned in the first interview or so, because first memories and dreams could not be obtained to confirm or deny the patient's overall statement about his 0–6. Because of this lack, the analyst could not "feel his way" (as Freud put it) into the patient's unconscious emotional life. Nevertheless, the attempt did yield at least a hypothesis of clinical use.

Dynamic Diagnosis: Oliver Dixon

Childhood—0–6: (1) Next to youngest of six. Family cold, distant (but saved by some emotional support from an aunt), leading to insecurity. (2) Premature independence and responsibility which won approval. Hostility repressed.

Current: Excessive drive to achievement and independence to win love and security. (2) Frustration of dependent love needs leading to fight-flight: repressed hostility and anger, turned onto self as masochism by driving self to exhaustion, plus excessive cigarette smoking jeopardizing his health. Difficulty in giving warmth and affection leading to marital problem. Distance from people. Flight from personal relations into work.

Strengths: (1) Drive to independence. (2) Superior physical vitality. (3) Is hard worker. (4) Outstanding success in his field, which wins love in the form of recognition and financial income.

VIII. Pat Ralston: Orphan of the Storm

As a rough guide, with exceptions such as Herbert Baxter (see above, p. 170), we can use "0 to 6" for neurosis and "0 to 3" for psychosis. The reason is probably very simple, namely, that before age three the small child's ego, without fully developed speech for conscious thinking and for expression of feelings, is much less well developed, much less strong, has much less effective reality testing, and is much more at the mercy of its feelings, and much more prone to distortions of reality. In the next patient the major trauma began at about age three and one-half, and in a way continued thereafter. I only wish that I were a skilled short-story writer or novelist and could convey the *feeling* of this patient's unconscious. The details of the interview, designed to reveal the early life childhood patterns, were as follows:

Her name was Pat Ralston. She was a little above average height, well set up, intelligent, attractive, brunette, forty years old, married, with four nearly grown children. She came to me with a symptom of acute anxiety, so severe that at times she was totally unable to be alone and could not let her husband out of her sight. She was also subjected to frequent rages at him, for which there seemed to be only very slight excuse. After explaining that this was a review of the emotional patterns of her early life, I said, "Make believe that you have never seen me in your life before and just let me ask you these questions naively, and you answer them in the same manner; I will ask you two main questions—what do you consider were the main features of your emotional life from your birth up to the age of five or six, and who were the main people for you emotionally in those early years?"

I should not have indicated the second question at this point, for she neglected the first and plunged into the second:

"My father and mother, and possibly my maternal grandparents; my sister Marge, three years younger than I, was also important, and also a cousin named Lucy. Lucy and I were born within a week of each other. In fact, our mothers were in the hospital within the same time and when we were babies, she and I even looked a little bit alike. We do not today. Another important person was my godmother. She was my mother's best friend, and her name was Doris. She liked me very much, and at that time she had no children of her own. She told me many more stories than Mother did. Doris died about three years ago, and I never wrote to her because I did not know what to write. She denied to everyone, even to herself, the fact that she was dying until the very end. I had good relationships with her all of my life, but she and her husband moved to Atlanta, so I didn't see them very much later on. My mother used to fight with Doris quite a lot, and I did not want to get into it. Once I went to Atlanta to visit Doris, and my mother was angry with me for going. Mother and Doris were very close ever since they were young. Doris had a fantastic sense of humor and was sophisticated. It seemed as though Doris could not have any children and adopted a daughter; after adopting her, she had two children of her own. Doris never got along with the adopted daughter; she got along with her own two sons quite well. They were blonde and the adopted daughter—Louise—was dark. Louise never did anything right in Doris' eyes. Doris' husband, Dave, usually took Louise's side. Doris wanted Louise to be sophisticated like herself, but Louise was a little bit crude, although nice. Louise married and had children, and said that she was sick of hearing Doris say, 'Why are you not more like Pat?' But when I was in the hospital, my mother did not visit me nearly so much as she visited Louise. I liked Doris and her husband a lot, and was sorry when they moved away from California."

[It seemed to me that this material thus far was characterized by ambivalence toward the Mother figures. There was some complaint about her own mother, that she did not visit Pat as much as she did her friend's daughter, Louise. Also, deprivation was evident, in that Pat liked her godmother Doris and Doris' husband Dave, but then they moved away from California to Atlanta and became inaccessible, and Pat's mother was angry with Pat for going to see them.]

I tried to ask as few questions as possible in getting the early child-

hood pattern, but I did not want her to get too far afield from focusing
on the important people in her life during this early period. So I said,
"Of all these people, let's take them in order of importance. Who are
the most important for you?"

Pat said, "Mother and Father."

"Which of these two was the more important?"

"I can't really answer that," she replied, "because Father died when I
was three and a half."

"All right," I said, "then is it that after four your mother was more
important because your father was not around? If so, who was the most
important person—father or mother—*before* you were four, before
father died?"

Pat said, "I have a suspicion that it was Father. I remember him as
very kind, secure, someone who would do anything for me. (1) I remember sitting in his lap and playing; I remember his carrying me
home after a party." And then Pat said, with a slight giggle, "(2) I
remember that I wet my pants. (3) I also remember going sledding
with him. I was afraid of going on a very steep hill, and he said 'No
problem, I will go with you.' And he did, but we turned over at the
very end of the slide; it was sort of like a bobsled, and the end went
over my ankle and hurt me somewhat. Then we were at the beach one
day and a big aquaplane landed, and I was afraid. (4) I remember
when they came home from the hospital with my sister, who was just
born, and I was three years old. My father brought me a teddy bear and
I kept it for years and years. It did not disappear until I was married.
My younger brother, Mike, cut the ears off it, and I was simply furious
at him and made him sew them back on, even though by then it was a
ragged old thing with almost all the hair off it. I know when people
are dead they get glorified, but I never heard anything bad about my
father. Except possibly once my mother said, 'Father sulks.' Just
before Father died in the auto accident he said, 'At the end of each day
look at the sun and think of me, and I will do the same thing and think
of you.'" At this point the patient wept. She was in obvious psychic
pain. She excused herself to go to the powder room but returned well
composed in a few moments.

"After Father died I used to think Father was somewhere in heaven
and that I still should look into the sun at the end of every day and
think of him." With this, more tears flowed down her cheeks.

"Anything else about your Father?" I asked.

"Well," she said, "a few little things. I remember on my third birthday I walked into the bedroom and they said to me 'Happy Birthday,' and I did not know what to say when somebody said that to me, so I said 'Happy Birthday' to them, and they laughed. I don't remember what Mother said about Father getting angry and sulking; I remember him as quiet with a good sense of humor, and he would kid a lot. He would sit and think a lot too. I think he was a philosophical type of person. In general, I remember Father would pay a lot of attention to me, that I was important to him, and he would not ignore me."

[All of the above, including the patient's emphasis on the fact that Father paid attention to her and she was important to him and he did not ignore her fitted in with what we already knew, namely her sense of deprivation after his death.]

"I had a dream the night before last. [It occurred to me that she was now again getting away from concentrating on the 0–6, but it was nearly the end of the hour and I thought it best to let her tell the dream and see what her unconscious was saying about all this.] In the dream," said Pat, "something was wrong with my throat, and I went to see a doctor, and I fell in love with him. He was nice. He said I needed an operation and I must have anesthesia. As you know, I am deathly afraid of anesthesia. So in the dream I said no, I was allergic to it. The doctor then said, 'We must test you for it.' Then I was leaving, and the doctor was at the window and I loved him. Then a gang came and the doctor came out and they shot him and I tried to help him, and I said, 'Don't die,' but the doctor said, 'I must'; he was between life and death . . . not really alive but not dead. He was suffering terribly. He said to me, 'Kick me in the head.' I said that I couldn't do that. He said, 'If you were suffering, wouldn't you want me to help you?' so I did kick him in the head, and he died. But it was not a nightmare; I loved the feeling of loving him, and in the dream after he had died, someone said I had on the most beautiful pair of shoes, and I took them off and said, 'You wear them,' but they did not fit her, and she could not wear them. It sounds strange, but this dream was not a nightmare but more sad. The feeling of love I had for the doctor stayed on all through the next day and night. Sometimes I would have a dream during childhood which was so strong that it would stay with me. Usually it was of a helpless child that I wanted to protect in the dream. Does this dream mean that I am psychotic? Is it a schizophrenic dream?" she asked.

I replied, "Just the opposite, It shows great progress." [Of course I was speaking the absolute truth.] I said, "Most of your dreams have been of terrible blood and thunder, violence with lots of people getting killed. This is the first dream you've ever reported to me in which the feeling is one of love and in which you like that feeling. This dream is the opposite of a schizophrenic dream. A schizophrenic person withdraws into his own fantasies and tends to be withdrawn in his feelings toward other people and life, whereas in your dream you not only have people in general but a specific person; although there is still hostility in it, yet there is also love. I think this is progress, and the opposite of what you suggest." [I did not attempt to interpret this dream, or point out what appeared to be transference in it, but only responded with a few remarks to the patient's questions. In the first place, our time was up and in the second place, I did not want to get off into an interpretation of the dream until we had finished doing our review of the emotional relationships of her early childhood. I thought the meaning of the dream had to be gone into very carefully when we had plenty of time. The reason was that Pat had defended herself strongly against the transference to me; the previous year she had found excuse after excuse for not coming to the hour . . . she had a cold, a sore throat, sinusitis, or was busy, there was a party, or she had to shop . . . she defended herself against coming at all. This dream was a good statement of ambivalent feelings, but nevertheless of some attachment and not pure hostility and dependence. The other material had been anger for feelings of deprivation, and I thought that the dream showed her desire to protect the helpless child, the helpless child being herself; she felt she did not get help from others and was therefore trying to give it to herself.]

The next meeting with Pat, a week later, was complicated by the fact that it was only two days before she was leaving on vacation with her husband, and two of her children. It is better to go into these early patterns when things are relatively calm in the patient's current life, and when she is not under pressure to talk of immediate things. However, she did very well I thought, and said the following, "What I told you about Louise last time was probably not important because that was after I was more grown-up and out of early childhood, but that dream of the sore throat really did come true. Three days later I awoke with a bad sore throat."

I said, "Do you think that is something mystical or supernatural, or could it be, for one thing, that when you are asleep and your mind is not occupied with all the demands and responsibilities of the day that it perceives some bodily sensations which you do not perceive during the day?"

She replied, "Maybe it's the same as my menstrual period; the few days before my period I almost always dream about blood in some way, even if it's only a passing thought. For example, maybe somebody spilled a little catsup on the floor in the dream and I simply think, 'That looks like blood,' or else I will dream that somebody sticks their finger and loses a drop or two of blood."

I said, "That might be the same thing, and it is very interesting, but could it be that you are resisting telling me about your patterns of earliest childhood?"

Pat replied, "I don't like to talk about it; I don't like to tell you. Do you want every detail of every relationship?"

"No," I said; "what I asked you initially for was the *main features* of the relationships. Do you think you have told me the main features of your relationship with your father?"

"There must be more," she said. "I used to try to pump Mother for information about Father, but she would not tell me. Later I asked her which husband she preferred—Father or Bill or Keith. Mother said, 'What kind of a question is that?' But one time she did say it was my father that she preferred, and I asked her why, and she said it was because he was so 'humane.' But Mother said that when she and he fought, she wanted to get out the anger and get over and done with it, but Father would just be silent and not talk for days. An aunt told me that Father once bought me a hobby horse and that he was so delighted with it that I was afraid to get on it. My aunt, in telling the story, made it very funny. My mother used to read to my sister Marge and me, so it must have been when I was near four years of age that she read *Winnie the Pooh* and *Snow White* and a terrible book about a spider, and a scary book of poems about a boy named Peter and what happens if you suck you thumb or play with matches and so on, and one about a boy who did not eat. I did not eat as a child, at about the time when my sister Marge was born. She had a nurse, and the nurse would force-feed me in her room. She would hold me in her lap and hold my arms and my nose and force food down my throat. I don't remember Mother and Father doing that themselves."

[Here again is the pattern: the ambivalence toward her mother and in a way, toward Mother figures and possibly a trace toward her father. Her mother read to her, but it was mostly scary stories. Mother, if she did not order it, condoned the force-feeding by the nurse, but now the patient was going on about that era in her life before she was three and one-half years old and said the following:]

"Before Father died I had some strange illnesses; something about my kidney. I had a terrible pain in the pit of my stomach. The treatment was to lie down in the middle of the day with a hot water bag on my stomach. It was very uncomfortable, and I became constipated. One day Mother came home and said to me, 'I have a present for you.' I was all excited and happy that she was bringing me a present, but when she opened the box it turned out to be a glass potty, so she could see whether I did anything without lifting me off the potty."

[I think this memory is absolutely typical of her relationship to her mother—her consuming wish for attention; but when she got it, it was always in some way frustrating, hostile, or disappointing, or frightening—somewhat as for Amy Colton, p. 161]

"After my father died, my mother went out a lot and she had a maid who would come in and spend a lot of time with me. The maid would read, play the piano, take us (Marge and me) with her to the hairdresser, shopping, and so on. But I think I told you all that, and I don't want to repeat it now."

"O.K.," I said, "but let us try to organize what you have told. Are you saying that the relationship with your father was that basically he was warm and loving to you, only good?"

"Yes," Pat responded, "only good. The only bad memory is that after Father died I missed him terribly. I couldn't tell anyone how much . . . I could not tell Mother because I did not want her to be sad, I did not want to remind her of his loss. One day I was thinking of my father and I was crying. Mother asked, 'What is the matter?' and I did not want to tell her and remind her of Father. All I could think of was to tell her I was scared of a witch."

I asked, "Was your mother very upset by the death of your father?"

Pat replied, "I don't know. I remember the day we got the news that he had died in the auto accident. Grandma would always call out when she came to see us and extend her arms to us, but this time when she came she did not notice us . . . she was just so serious. In fact, no one ever told me that my father was dead but I knew anyway. Of course, I did not know what it meant. After that came a terrible period. We stayed with all kinds of people and in all kinds of strange places. For a while we stayed with a family that was O.K. But then I stayed in an orphanage. They did not take care of the children; they were dirty. A lot of them in diapers were not changed. I had no friend there. I was so homesick for Mother, I can't tell you. The only one I could talk to was an old woman, a cook. I told her she must swear to me that she would get my mother and maybe she did get her, because later Mother came and we moved into town. We slept downstairs and my sister Marge, still a little baby, was upstairs. I screamed that she must bring Marge downstairs with us, but my mother got angry at me and said, 'I will not wake her. If I do, she will never go to sleep again.' When my sister and I awoke at night, scared, Mother would never let us get into bed with her. I remember once Mother was going downstairs and slipped, and she began to laugh hysterically. I though she was crying but later found out she was laughing. Also, she once had a sort of girdle or corset and was half way out of it and had her hands up in the air. My father's brother's wife was trying to help her get into it or out of it, and my mother again laughed hysterically and I thought she was crying.

"At the marriage ceremony to Keith, her third husband, Mother laughed again hysterically, but not loud . . . she managed to suppress it. But I cried during the whole wedding and had to be taken out, and I cried during the whole day. I cried at the luncheon at the hotel and at the champagne party. I cried so because I did not like Keith, and I did not want Mother to marry him."

"But before your father died," I asked, "did you have any difficulty with your mother?"

"I can't be sure," said Pat; "I think it was mostly a pleasant relationship, but after Father died I had this thing with Mother. I clung to her so; I thought she was so beautiful. Then one or two years after my father died Mother married a Canadian named William and was in Canada for nearly five years. But somehow, William changed tremendously. He said he was no longer interested in life or marriage, so they agreed on a divorce. . . . William was very nice; he would send beautiful dolls to Marge and me. At any rate, Mother was in Canada for five years and I thought when she came back we would all be happy living together—Mother, sister, and I—but instead of that, of our having a home together, along came Keith into the picture, just about a half year later. With this I went into a state of shock; I got high. After waiting five years for her, and then she came back to marry him! While she was away we lived with her mother and father, our grandparents. But nothing was organized. I thought we had such happy plans for the three of us to live somewhere else. After Father died I clung so to Mother and thought her so beautiful . . . but you already know the rest. You know that Keith was awful and that he completely ignored my sister Marge and me. It was as though we didn't exist, yet my mother had to act in a way to please him. He was not a bit attractive, but there must have been something about him . . . maybe it was his money . . . he never had trouble getting girls, so he always had a lot of girls all his life. Eventually my mother got a divorce.

"Now Dave, the husband of Doris, my godmother who died a few years ago, is showing some interest in my mother. He is really very nice, and I would like to have him for a father."

[I think this is a rather significant comment, for Pat is a charming, intelligent, responsible woman almost forty years old, with a husband and nearly grown children, but she really is thinking sincerely in terms of wishing she had a mother and a father. This is something in her 0–6 that was not provided her, and as a result she is in a constant state of frustration, deprivation, and rage. This, I think, expresses her main dynamics and is very intelligible on the basis of her early history, the childhood pattern of her early life. It has been so severe and resistant to analytic treatment because it is really a trauma of just before age four, rather than any time after six or seven when she was a little further developed as a personality and had a stronger ego.]

At this point in the interview, she again broke off and said, "But I want to tell you about my rheumatic fever when I was about six years old. It was a terrible experience. I had just been swimming and the water was very cold. I ran back to the cottage and suddenly I got a terrible pain in my knees, as though lightning had struck. I had to squat down; I couldn't get up. Then it struck my elbow, and then both my knees and elbows were in splints. Then I had my tonsils removed; I had to keep warm; I was not allowed to walk. Sometimes I think that this was what gave me the phobia which keeps me from going to bed when I am sick. I was all alone in that room, and no one was around. Then came the operation to take out the tonsils. Mother said she would hold me; they gave me ether, but the cone caught in the eyelash of my right eye and I couldn't close my eye and I screamed, and Mother couldn't stand it and left. But after it was over, Mother brought me *Snow White* and some little things and was nice to me. I liked some of the nurses; they were nice, but there were no other children in the hospital. I must have been there about two weeks. I am still afraid to go to bed when I am sick because I am afraid of being helpless and not able to walk; so if I don't get in a nightgown and go to bed, I stay propped up with some pillows and I don't feel so frightened, or so sick . . . ."

[How frequently patients report memories of illnesses or operations that bring some attention—probably expressing mostly hostility, guilt, anxiety, but relief of deprivation by attention; probably containing the rebuke to the depriving mother: "I have to have a serious illness or operation to get any love or attention from you."]

That ended our interview, and the patient was to leave in a couple of days for a two-week vacation. I felt that the whole story of the formation of the childhood patterns which so influenced her present life and her anxiety and a certain shyness with people had not been explored in an entirely adequate way, but still I thought that the main points had not been missed. I could readily identify with it and feel with it, and only hope that the bare statement of the factual material from these hours will convey some of this feeling to the reader.

When she left, Pat remarked that on the vacation they would be stopping to see relatives of her husband, and she feared it would not be much of a vacation because there would not be sufficient privacy between her husband and herself. At bottom, I have an idea (but not enough material to support it) that this was an expression of her life-long feeling since losing her father, and her mother as well—the feeling she had had when she clung to her mother and felt her so beautiful but at the same time had repressed rage against her mother. So I think her feeling that she and her husband would not have sufficient privacy and intimacy was probably still a reflection of what she wanted from her mother and of the frustrations of separation from her mother. I can only hope that we had worked through her anger because of this sufficiently for her to follow that transference dream in which the love of the doctor outweighed the nightmare quality of his being shot and killed. I hoped she would not be that angry with her husband on the vacation.

We can now attempt briefly to summarize Pat's 0–6 and the pattern formed therein that persisted through her life. For me, as for many others, the most enchanting age of childhood is about three and one-half, that blossoming out of babyhood into early childhood with beginning speech. Pat was a very attractive matron nearing forty, and in her I could see the little girl of three and a half. She must have been delightful and adorable. But at this age she lost her warm, devoted father, who (she said) cared about her and valued her and never ignored her, and would do anything for her. She felt important with him. Losing him and his indispensable love she turned her intense needs toward her mother, but apparently her mother was never so devoted to her as her father was. In fact, her mother—faced with finding livelihood and a new husband—was now downright rejecting, leaving little Pat in an orphanage, and then being in Canada for five years, leaving Pat and her sister Marge behind. Pat's longings all attached to her mother since her father was no longer present, although she still looked at the setting sun and thought of him now and wept. As she wept, she told me about him. She was sustained by her fantasies of her mother's returning from Canada, at first with kindly William who sent her gifts of pretty dolls, but then, after the divorce, of fantasies of living happily with Mother and Marge. But then, again, her mother married, this time to Keith, who totally ignored and rejected the two lost little girls. Small wonder that Pat later developed a degree of paranoid jealousy!

Now Pat was sent away to distant boarding schools, and when she wrote to her mother, Mother ignored her pleas for attention and help. Outwardly Pat took the rejection stoically, but she was not entirely unconscious of her rage against her mother. Thus the emotional pattern became set, and the intense longing for her mother and the reality of the neglect and rejection and the violence of suppressed rage were set, the rage against her mother that she never dared hint at for fear of losing her mother entirely. With this warped pattern she flowered into womanhood.

She married a kind, devoted man who loved her, but shortly after the ceremony she accused him of paying attention to other women or making it clear that he wanted to. In her own words to me (the analyst) she said once she was married, "the wall was down." That is, put the other way around, the pattern erupted. She could not get all her continuing demands of childhood for her mother satisfied by her husband, and she now felt secure enough in the marriage to relax her controls on her rage at her mother. Only now her rage was directed toward her husband without danger of completely losing her mother, which would have been the case if the anger came out directly toward her mother. In analytic treatment her rage slowly diminished, and she gradually became a good wife and mother. Her best relationship was, as might be expected, with her first child, a son. That is to be expected because her best relationship in early life was toward her father, a male. Nevertheless, the inner feelings of lack of intimacy and closeness and the sense of not getting sufficient love and attention and of not being valued sufficiently (everything she had had from her father and lost) lingered on, and working it through was a long haul. Unfortunately, the entire pattern of intense desire, frustration, and rage began repeating itself toward her long-suffering husband.

After three years, she was much more relaxed and could converse more freely, and began to come out of her shell, even though her mother continued to show gross preference toward Pat's half-siblings, the children of Keith. One of her half-sisters whom Pat liked very much came to visit Pat for a week. Her mother, now single again since her divorce from Keith, was on a trip to Hawaii. She wrote cards and letters to the half-sister, Ruth, but sent nothing to Pat, yet Pat continued consciously to love her mother and (as I agreed) had no reason to tell her of being so angry at her. She still hoped for a much improved relationship with her, and later she did discuss with her mother her repressed anger, which helped the relationship. Pat's identification with Louise and Marge had formed a pattern of good relations with her peers.

There are many other details of Pat's dynamics, of course; for example, her identification with her mother, who depreciated her and kept her waiting, and now this is what Pat tends to do to others. She has low opinions of others, and is usually late. I mentioned above how she found excuses to cancel appointments with me, her analyst, and usually did so at the last moment. But here we have been interested not in every detail but in the main features, the central macroscopic emotional pattern, the major central pattern that determined her main interplay of feelings with other persons, the course of her life, and the emotional atmosphere in which she lived, and which we have seen so tragically blocked her from accepting the very love and closeness she craved more than anything else in the world.

I have never been entirely satisfied with Pat's dynamic diagnosis, which came out as follows:

Dynamic Diagnosis: Pat Ralston

Childhood: Loss of Father intensifies dependent love needs toward Mother, frustrated by Mother's distance geographically and emotionally, and Mother's open preference for patient's half-siblings.

Current: Excessive dependent love needs and needs to be valued (plus inferiority feelings because of deprivation), feeling frustrated leads to fight-flight; leads to repressed anger, mobilized by any closeness (with guilt plus masochism) leads to (a) emotional distance plus some resentment of independence and responsibility partly because of identification with Mother, and (b) fear of being left alone, i.e., fight-flight leads to constant hostility, withdrawal, and anxiety.

Strengths: (1) Good relations with Father until age three and a half, some good relations to Mother, and good relations with Sister and girl cousin give her: (2) capacity for emotional honesty; (3) devotion to her children; (4) quiet determination. (5) Deprivation makes her appealing, attractive. (6) Protected by strength of her defense and efforts at independence and accomplishment.

IX. Jenny Wales: The Working Parents

As I have repeatedly written and demonstrated, it is usually possible (and my estimate is in 85 percent of patients seen) to get the major issues of the dynamics in the very first interview. Here is an example; I consider it rather average—certainly not the most difficult one I have encountered, yet not the easiest.

Jenny Wales had just come to town because her husband had been transferred by the company for whom he worked. She did not yet know what she was going to do, meaning outside of the home, but her major problem she told me was that she felt she might "mess up" her daughter because of traits within herself. Jenny was thirty-five years old, her husband was about the same age, and they had one child, Rita. I asked her to go ahead and tell me more about her situation.

She said, "I'm afraid I will mess up my daughter by my own traits, but I can't help it. I get angry, and then I can't control my anger, and I withdraw. I know I should have had some psychotherapy before this, but we were only temporarily situated because of my husband's job. Therefore I waited until we got back to Chicago.

"The problem with my daughter is not new; I had that problem before she was born. Now I am close to her, and it comes out with her because I think it is really a problem with closeness. I feel it especially when my daughter is demanding. I guess I want to be the infant myself, and this makes me angry and disgusted with myself."

"How do you get along with your husband," I asked, "if closeness is a problem?"

"Pretty well," she replied, "but we have a nonaggression pact between us. My husband is from a family in which his father and mother fought a lot, so he doesn't like that; but we have a pretty good relationship in spite of that—maybe even too nice. My husband told me last night that he is opposed to my starting psychotherapy; he is afraid it will disrupt our relationship. We lived together for several years, but when I became pregnant we got married. That was three years ago, so my daughter is now just three. At that time, I had seen a psychiatrist a few times, and we had just been talking about my getting out of the relationship with my husband."

I asked, "How far back does your problem go?"

She said, "I try not to think of these things. I graduated from college without any idea of what I wanted to do. I applied for one job and they gave me a mini-questionnaire. One of the questions was 'Is Life Worth Living?' and I said, 'No.'"

"If you have a problem with closeness," I asked, "how do you get on with people—friends, acquaintances?"

She replied, "Very good but superficial. I like to feel liked, but feel like I am fooling people and have done so all my life."

"What came of your treatment with the analyst you saw before?"

She said, "I was with him for two and a half years, sitting twice a week, but he thought I should come more often. But first I couldn't afford it, and then I would go blank. It was hard for me to free associate. There was a great deal of silence."

I said, "Let us start at the very beginning, and I will ask you a few questions. Who were the most important people in your life, from the time you were born until you were six or seven years old?"

She said, "I was the youngest of three. I had a brother eight years older and a sister six and a half years older."

"How are they settled in life?" I asked.

"They both seem to be settled. My brother has a very good job, and both he and my sister are married and have children."

"But who among these people," I asked again, "was the most important emotionally for you up to the age of six or seven?"

"My mother and father . . . I guess I lump them together. They were very close to each other. My father was away for two years and there must have been other people around. My mother had a job and worked all that time, but I have no memory of other people. I do remember one . . . a black lady who did cleaning, and she must have taken care of me. I really do not remember my brother and sister at all until I was twelve years old. I slept in the same room as my sister, and I have a vague memory of joking with her about something under the bed, but I don't remember any personal contact with her."

I said, "Looking back, to before you were six years old, do you remember any bits or fragments?"

"No," she said, but after a pause she said, "Oh, yes, when I was just about six I remember the family was going to a show of some kind, and I had severe tonsillitis and could not go, but I only remember my mother and father and not my brother and sister. I remember nothing at all before the age of six." She was silent for a moment. "Oh, yes, I do remember one incident at three. My father used to leave early in the morning before it was light. I remember we used to watch him drive the car away in the dark. Father would send us packages, candy, and so forth. Then I remember that once we were opening one of these packages and either my sister or myself told my mother that my brother had said 'darn,' and that we thought it was just awful. Then Mother got a job nights and slept in the daytime . . . this was while Father was away. But I still have no memory of who took care of me."

I asked, "About 'darn' being such an awful word to say—was the atmosphere of your family so strict?"

"No," she said, "I don't think so. When we told Mother, she replied, 'So what?' On the other hand, yes, we were strict. The only sign of any emotions in the family was between Father and Sister. I remember once when we were a little older he and Sister were having an argument and Sister said 'Oh, shit,' and to me that seemed something absolutely catastrophic. There was a right and a wrong way to do things, and I was very careful always to do things right."

I said, "You said the main people in childhood were Mother and Father. Was it one more than the other?"

She said, "I don't know; I can only say I must have spent more time with Mother because Father was out so much, but I have no real feeling about it. There was a story in the family that when I was in kindergarten, Mother told me not to take anything out of the icebox, and I phoned her to ask if I could share a strawberry with my little friend, Chester. When I was just starting grade school, I would get home and of course Mother would not be there, and I would phone her and ask her what I should do. Also, I remember there was a window by way of which I could get on the roof, and I used to do this, and the neighbors would phone Mother and tell her, but she never did anything about it."

I asked, "Do you think that there was a lack of closeness?"

She said, "You mean toward Mother?"

I said, "Yes, or to any member of the family."

She replied, "I think so. I feel paradoxical about it. I always lumped Father and Mother together. I think Mother can't feel close; I believe she is threatened by any close relationship. They certainly cared about me and what happened to me, but I guess I would have to say there was something lacking. Father, as I grew up, I came to like as a person, but I do not like Mother. Mother had a reputation with my friends of being straitlaced, cold, and military. I recognize it now, but that does not change my resentment. These things now seem to repeat toward my daughter."

Our time was now running out, even though I always allow an hour and a half or two hours for an initial interview. I asked Jenny, "Did you have a dream last night?" That was the night preceding her coming to see me, and these dreams usually have a transference meaning that can be very illuminating as to what the patient is feeling and is liable to do in the future in therapy in relation to the analyst.

"Yes," she said, "my daughter woke me at five in the morning and I went back to sleep. I dreamed that I was coming here but that something was preventing it, so that I would have to be late. I think it was because I could not find the way, and I think there was somebody else in the car."

[In reality, the patient arrived precisely on time.]

I said, "What do you think of this element of the dream, being prevented from getting here?"

She said, "The whole thing makes me very anxious. I don't know *why* I do not want to know, but I feel there is something in me that I don't want to know. I've had a book on psychoanalysis for two years and can hardly read it; in fact, I can hardly read anything. It makes me very anxious and I try to avoid anxiety. Maybe that is why I feel I am phony, that I am getting through life by imitating what I should be doing. Sometimes I feel I could be a better person, but at other times I feel I am fatally flawed. I told my husband recently that I was afraid I would condemn my daughter to a life of depression such as I have."

I now thought I had some clue as to the major features of Jenny's dynamics, and I would see how well she could follow them, so I tried a formulation in the form of questions. I said, "If I understand you correctly, there seem to be two elements in your emotional relationship to your mother. First, that she is cold and distant. Secondly, that she is straitlaced, militaristic, and strict. What do you think of that?"

She was silent for a bit, thinking. Then she said, "I think that is right, and I think my living with my husband without being married to him was perhaps a reaction to that, a defiance. My father was able to say 'I don't approve, but you are my daughter.' But my mother acted as though it were a catastrophe. After that she did bizarre things, such as sending me some meaningless object that was supposed to be a present.

"As a child, I had a fantasy that my mother would sneak up and stab me in the back. In therapy, I thought that was how I saw my mother's hostility to me."

I said, "Yes, but might it not be a projection of your own hostility to your mother?"

She said, "You might be right, and now I feel I am enacting the same thing to my daughter."

"Yes," I said. "So do we not already see some picture of your dynamics in reaction to the two characteristics you described in your mother—her coldness and distance and her militarism, and her strait-laced and strict attitudes?" I went on to say, "Perhaps your anxiety which is so troublesome and which you defend yourself against is in part from your repressed hostility, and also it seems to me that you are trying to fight off an identification with your mother, especially in regard to your daughter . . . you do not want to rear your daughter the way your mother treated you?"

She was silent a moment, and I said, "Do you follow what I just said, or is it just words?"

She replied, "I think I follow what you are saying. What bothers me the most in what you say is this irrational anger. For example, just recently my husband shut the door so the cat could not get out and the dog could not get in; the cat defecated and the dog scattered the garbage, and I was so furious with the dog I hit him, and my daughter saw it and I am afraid she may have identified with the dog. It's amazing; of course, the situation was annoying. To be annoyed would have been normal. But to be so furious is not reasonable, nor to lose control of my anger and hit a poor dog."

[We already have a clue to at least some of the important parts of Jenny's dynamics. The only close relationship, and that was not very close, and the determining relationship, was with her mother. The mother was cold and distant; secondly, she was very straitlaced, militaristic, and strict. The patient's reaction to this was apparently repressed rebellion and rage; but also the usual unavoidable identification with her mother which was not egosyntonic, which she could not stand, and which she was fighting against. Jenny resisted this identification with her mother, who was away working most of the time, to Jenny's neglect. Jenny wanted to do something outside the home, but did not want to reject and deprive her daughter as she herself had been deprived by *her* mother. The hostile rage reaction kept her constantly angry beneath the surface; some of this came out against her daughter, and she was on constant guard against its coming out elsewhere, defending against it in part by withdrawing. She therefore felt she was phony and not genuine in some way, not really herself.]

Jenny apparently reacted in a very positive way to this interview and felt encouraged. I was also, although we did not discuss this; but I felt that if somebody as repressed as she was could bring out the major features of her pathodynamics in one interview and had the capacity for this much insight, even though the pattern went back almost to birth, she had a good enough ego to hope for considerable growth out of the pattern. The change was reasonably good that she would benefit greatly from treatment.

A comment is in order here about Jenny's two and a half years in analysis, going twice a week, before the birth of her daughter. As usual, I inquired about this in a sympathetic fashion, trying to learn in as short a time as possible what the bases of her symptoms were; but all I could get her to relate was that it did not go well, that she was unable to associate freely, that it was mostly long silences, and that the analyst's solution to this was for Jenny to come more often. Now one cannot assume naively that what a patient says about the analytic experience is the precise truth, and probably a great deal more went on than Jenny was able in her interview with me to comprehend and formulate. Nevertheless, there is a certain fact here which I think is extremely important, and that is a negative one: namely, no effort was evident to elucidate the main features of her pathodynamics, the main traumatic situations of childhood and how these affected her present problems. Since that time, I have had many experiences just like this; and even allowing for the fact that much had gone on which the patient could not relate in a first interview, I still think the least she should have got out of the analysis was what I try to get in the first interview, namely the ability to formulate and *write down* what the main traumatic features of childhood were and what her reactions were to them, and how this pattern was underlying her present symptoms. That, in my experience, should be done in the first hour or first few hours, so that the patient has a clear, conscious knowledge of what it is she is trying to solve and why she is trying to solve it by the psychoanalytic process. In fact, because this tool of getting a childhood pattern and seeing its effect in the patient's life is such a powerful one but is not used with full effectiveness, this present book is written. If she does not get the early childhood traumatic situations and the patterns of reaction they form and the present dynamics underlying the symptoms, it seems to me that the patient has a quite confused idea of the whole process and is never entirely clear as to what she is trying to solve or outgrow.

One more point in relation to Jenny's case: her dream, the transference dream which she had the night before coming to see me, was so clear in its manifest content that I ventured to ask her why she thought she had this great anxiety and resistance to coming; and when she repeated that there was something in her she did not want to know, I asked her if this could be her rebellion against her mother and perhaps her feeling that something was lacking in her mother's emotional giving to her, with the resulting anger. Although I initiated this bit of discussion, she immediately caught on to the idea that she was already repeating to me the pattern toward her mother—a feeling that she was not loved sufficiently; that she was doing what I had said, feeling rebellion and hostility and also straight-out anxiety from fear of what her mother would think and do.

Then, when the interview was just about over, she said there was one important problem she had not mentioned, which was that she felt horribly inferior as a woman. Moreover, she thought this was just sociological, because women have an inferior position in society. I said, "That may be, but I certainly cannot agree with it as the entire answer, if only because not all women feel that way. It seems to me we already have some idea of the childhood pattern shaping your problem; there must be something in your childhood pattern. Was Brother preferred to you, or did Mother prefer Father to you, or was there something else that could have caused this inferior feeling for being a woman?"

She said, "No, it wasn't that, but suddenly I see that it was because Mother herself felt so inferior as a woman."

I said, "Are you telling me then that your inferiority as a woman is part of your identification with your mother, which we have already discussed?"

She replied, "That seems to be it. I think that must be where it comes from."

I include this because I believe it is very important to note that Jenny was already thinking in terms of childhood patterns that were repeating themselves in her current life, in this case coming right out in the transference. Thus, in one interview, this patient showed clearly both the object relations of childhood, her feelings particularly toward her mother and how her mother treated her, and also her identification with her mother. (This rapid grasp was probably a result of her previous analysis, although she seemed not to realize it.) Thus, we knew why we were recommending psychoanalysis as the preferred method of treatment, and what we intended to accomplish by it. Also we discussed whether she should see a male or a female analyst. It seemed to me that she should go ahead and see a male analyst, since she seemed to have a much better relationship with her father than her mother, and work in that atmosphere of the transference to her father on her major dynamics, and then end up eventually with a woman analyst if the pattern toward her mother was not sufficiently worked through.

At the very end of her interview, Jenny again mentioned her husband's opposition to her going into treatment. In reply I said, as quietly, rapidly and gently as possible, "You remember your dream that something interfered with your coming here today—perhaps it is not just your husband's opposition but also your anxiety. As to his fear that the analysis will have a bad effect on the marriage and possibly result in his losing you, you remember your dynamics: your mother's coldness and distance, the something lacking; the puritanical strictness and the military control; and your reactions to that which we have just discussed, of feeling that you are phony because you are not spontaneous but must always do the right thing in order to be liked; your lack of closeness and your repressed anger that goes out of control, even to your daughter, which is your chief complaint; and your resisting the identification with your mother—then it is a little hard to see how, if the treatment is successful, if your hostilities are reduced and your capacity for closeness increases and you feel easier about yourself, how this is going to have any deleterious effect on the marriage. If it makes you a better mother, it is hard to see how it could fail to make you a better wife. Please tell me if I am wrong about this."

She said, "No I don't think you are wrong; I see your point."
The above review of Jenny's 0-6 led to the following dynamic diagnosis:

Dynamic Diagnosis: Jenny Wales

Childhood: (1) Mother major figure, cold, distant, puritanically strict, military control. Relations with Father better, but Father away mostly.

Current: (2) Always does what is right, but only because supposed to and hence feels "phony," lacks ability to be close: rebellion; all leads to fight-flight: much hostility defended against partly by withdrawal, but some identification with Mother which patient fights against. Hostility causes guilt and anxiety, and some comes out to daughter with much guilt and fear of damaging daughter.

Strengths: (1) Some good relations with Father and Sister. (2) Drive to protect her child and love her and raise her well. (3) Youth, vitality. (4) Identification with Father makes her a hard worker.

X. Claudia Atkins: The Victorian

Claudia Atkins was a slight, intelligent brunette. She had come to me nearly ten years previously when I had first started seeing private patients. She came largely because the Chicago Institute for Psychoanalysis was a new facility, and, like many others, she was interested in knowing what it was all about. In addition, she had one psychosomatic complaint, namely, headaches. Seeing her almost ten years later, I learned the headaches had continued, that nothing had helped. In her period of analysis she had found reasons for the headaches, and she did have fewer bad ones; but they had become a pattern of her life, and she controlled them as best she could with painkillers. Now she was seeing me at my suggestion for a review of her early years. I told her I would ask her two questions about them; first, a general one; "What do you consider the main emotional features of your life from birth to age six or seven?"

She said, "Do you want to know what I remember, which is bits and pieces, or what I have deduced from how my father and mother are?"

I said, "Both, but let us start with what you actually remember."

Claudia replied, "Brother teased me and was always bigger and smarter and better able to do things than I was. My younger sister was not born until I was five years old. My mother was always telling me to wear rubbers and I refused, but then it would in fact rain. Mother was very bossy; things had to be done her way. It was set up for me to be with a maid, Mary, and I was mostly with her. I accepted the walks and the nap with her.

"When I was three or four I was sent to nursery school and I was always resentful, especially the second year. Mother was pregnant with my sister that year and could not drive, and the school picked me up and delivered me. I remember Father did not talk much and he snarled and came home with headaches from being nervous, tired, and under stress. He was with a large corporation and took his job very seriously. As I said, the next child—my sister—was born when I was five, but I don't think I had anything to do with her. Along with her, the new baby, came a nurse. We lived well in those days; we had a maid and a gardener also. My parents always thought it was good to work—good for them and good for others. My mother was brought up in a house with lots of servants, but now she does all her own housework, works harder now than she did when she was thirty. I always admired her; everyone did. She never did anything wrong, and that was a great burden to live under. I thought that Father was the villain in my life with his snarling; that's what I thought when I saw you years ago. But now I think it was Mother, because her way of belittling was more subtle than Father's. Her way of undermining my confidence. There was no way to build confidence in my family. If you did well in school, athletics, and so on, it was only what was expected of you, and there was no room at all for failure, anxiety, fear, or shyness. All those were unwanted feelings.

"When I was five we got a summer house that we used to go to for three months in the summer. We would pack up, cover all the furniture with white covers.

"That year I went to nursery school and I liked it, although I had a horrible first day. I did not know my way, I was lost and wet my pants, and Mother spanked me for it with a hairbrush. A poor little kid, lost and not knowing what door to go in, but I couldn't tell Mother that I was lost or scared because I was trained to be only brave and strong."

She seemed to run out at this point, and I said, "Now my second question about your 0–6 is the more specific one; who do you consider to be the important person or persons emotionally for you from birth to the age of six or seven?"

She said, "Mother, Father, and Brother. Must I pick one? If so, I guess it was Mother. I have enjoyed all my time with my children, but Mother said she only liked children when they were grown-up. Mother did not like us; Brother teased me, and Father snarled at me. Mother did not like babies; she was busy with her activities, mostly volunteer. There were special events like trips or expeditions to the zoo, but during day-to-day living she showed no interest in us. She would come up and tuck us in, but only *after* we were in bed. She would hear us say our prayers. Mother did everything well and still does; I can't imagine Mother failing at anything. Once a child was hurt, and she took him to the hospital and took me along, and that is the only time I remember being with Mother when she was engaged in any of her activities.

"Sundays we would rake leaves and take Sunday walks. Mother was so important, not because of what she did but because she was not there. I wonder what my daughter would say about me? Would she say I am a great competitive threat? That's how I felt about my mother."

"Meaning what?" I asked.

"Mother did everything so well that I had to also, and that reinforced the idea that failure, fright, and anxiety simply were not acceptable. They were recognized, but they were not permitted. Mother was a shy, awkward teenager, but she learned to cope with it by doing everything so well. It is hard for me to separate past and present, because the same feelings go on. I know she disapproves of my husband, but she does not have to say so for me to get the picture. I sit and read a book and think, 'Should I go on reading or should I get dinner ready?' Mother never had that conflict. She would do what she was supposed to do first; she would get the dinner and then after that she would read. Yet, she was more shy as a teenager than I ever was; how did she get to be so perfect?"

I said, "I don't want to get off the track, but maybe she had an aunt or grandparent or somebody in her family who gave her the support."

"Yes," said Claudia, "I think it was her sisters."

"But let us go on," I said, "What was the emotional interchange between you and your mother?"

"Emotions were simply not allowed. Mother was never really happy or angry. Occasionally she was cross, that is, only a mild emotion. Emotions she considered to be vulgar. I never saw her hug or kiss Father. It's hard for me to remember what we were forbidden to remember . . . there were a couple neighbors who became very excited over something and hugged and kissed each other. Mother and Father thought that was vulgar. Mother, of course, cannot understand psychiatry and that people would talk about their feelings."

I said, "Can you say what your forbidden feelings to your mother were?"

"Well, when I was seeing you analytically I talked a lot about Brother and Father, but now I think it's Mother. I must have longed to be with her, but she had no interest in us, simply did not like children. I remember my nurse Mary taking me out, feeding me, but I don't remember Mother doing any of that. There was a nurse in a white uniform from my birth until I was two, and then there was Mary. I am scrounging around now for feelings about Mother; I am thinking into my teens and trying to get back to 0–6, but I am just drawing a blank."

I said, "All right, then tell me about your teens."

"I guess it began to dawn on me," said Claudia, "that Mother said she did not like babies or children at all until they were teen-age. Then she tried to tell me about menstruation, but never succeeded. There was never any cuddling in the family. I saw her when she was dressed up, and she was dressed up, and we were not dressed for cuddling. What would she think if she heard this conversation? She could not conceive that she had failed in anything. Why am I so shy socially when I have done so well? When I am here with you it is hard not to free associate. To this day, when Mother and Father come to visit us Mother takes over. She is the first one up in the morning, she makes the breakfast, she arranges the visits with friends, everything. On one single occasion Mother and I went out to lunch and she was out of money and I paid. That was one of those exceedingly rare times that I have ever seen her plans go awry. It is hard for me to talk about my feelings toward Mother; they included admiration and competitiveness. It was hard for her to recognize that I have weaknesses and failings and want to be loved unconditionally. At the same time, everybody says how wonderful she is, and of course that is good for me to hear. Mother looks ten years younger than her age, but Father is getting old, yet he can still make me angry.

"When I was fourteen or fifteen, Mother insisted that I give a party, but I was afraid to because I was sure it would fail, and I wanted to avoid giving it at all. But I gave it, and it went well. I have always had the fear in talking at a party or with just anyone that the conversation will die. At the party I sat myself between the two talkingest girls I knew."

At this point I asked Claudia, "Who was of next importance to you, after Mother?"

"It should be Father," said Claudia, "But I think it was Brother. He was the apple of my parent's eye . . . smarter, more athletic, and I was always trying to keep up with him, to run as fast and play games as well, to be as amusing, to be as much approved of. Father and Mother always thought it was stupid not to do things perfectly, and Brother was a tease and reinforced that. I lay in bed awake at night while Mother took Brother to an early movie because I was not old enough, and I thought that was unfair. Once, Brother stuffed grass down my neck. Oddly, I have made a better life and marriage, and children, than my Brother or next youngest sister. Brother is on his second marriage; but still, when I write to him, I want his approval. I did not know that Sister was alive until I was ten and she was five and I could play with her. Now she and I are very close, even though she lives on the East Coast. Her marriage is very shaky. She is very sexy and wants sex, but her husband is not interested. He just wants to sit and read a book and sip a little bourbon. He is very nice, and I wish she would learn to leave him alone."

"Anything else about your brother?" I asked.

"No," she said, "only the feeling that he is the one I must catch up with. In fact, about the only thing that he does well is play games. Father was the obvious baddie in my life; he never approved of anything. He made me feel stupid and still does; he makes everyone feel stupid. But he can turn on the charm at parties. In day-to-day living he is just disapproving; he lets you know you are stupid; you can't do anything right and you will never learn to.

"My son had an injury on his bike, and Father could only be angry that he had damaged the bike. I wrote Father, asking why he was so concerned about the bike when the child was injured and he said, 'I only know about giving financial security and not about the emotions,' as though the emotions were some newfangled idea. Now he is old and I am no longer afraid of him; I just don't like him. He lets Mother decide what clothes he should wear, what parties they should go to. I don't remember Father doing anything at all for us as kids.

The family walk on Sundays was Mother's idea. Once we had a family picnic. I don't like to be with Father now; he doesn't talk at all, and I don't talk very well, so there is just silence."

I asked, "Do you recall any childhood dreams, especially repetitive ones.?"

Claudia said, "At the time of a kidnapping that made the newspapers I frequently dreamt of the devil coming in the window for me. Also, I dreamt of running away from something, but I could not run. Also I dreamt of flying, only five or six feet off the ground and it was a great effort to do it. Then in college I had dreams, repetitive ones, that it was time for an exam and I did not study for it, or it was time for graduation and I did not have enough credits. I no longer dreamed of the devil nor do I now, but I still have the dream of flying and of running in slow motion, and am afraid that I will be caught."

I said nothing, but it seemed evident that these dreams of failure in spite of great effort and of being caught really were part of her feeling disapproval that she is not living up to the impossible standards of perfection set for her by her parents, and somebody will find out what her guilty feelings are and catch up with her deficiencies.

As I thought this to myself, she said, "This morning I dreamt of being buried in sand. When I saw you analytically I used to dream of old and new houses. I tried to get away from the old patterns into new ones. I still have not gotten away from my feeling that I am not loved, that no one approves, that I don't do anything right."

These associations seemed to confirm my impression of the meaning of these repetitive dreams she had just told. More deeply, the new house expressed the wish for new, more unconditionally loving parents. "All this," went on Claudia, "is at such variance with the real picture; I have a nice husband, nice children, life is easy now, but I feel it should be hard. I always have these nagging thoughts, that I should clean up the house, I should give parties, I should do more, I should be more like Mother."

I said, "All children have to have somebody to identify with, and this sounds like some degree of identification with your mother. It also sounds as though there is something here that you did not mention, probably because it was among the forbidden emotions, even though we went into it in great detail when you saw me years ago, and that is hostility and anger."

Claudia said, "That's right . . . anger was of course forbidden. Sex and anger and headaches have never entered my mind in this hour talking to you. We know I have sex, anger, and headaches in my life, but anger was never allowed. That's what the vulgar neighbors had. Sex became all right when I realized that the climax was not thunder and lightning but only a nice feeling. I thought it was not as perfect as it should be, and it bothered me. My sister is crippled emotionally and anxious, depressed . . . her hands shake, she vomits, and her marriage does not help. My husband is not sympathetic and understanding, but he lets me do what I want and he does not criticize me. I have had no headaches at all for the past ten days, which is unheard of for me . . . I certainly never could do that years back. I wonder if that could be a reaction to the prospect of seeing you today? Because it was just ten days ago that we made the appointment."

I said, "Can you summarize what we have covered?" and we arrived at the following:

"1. Lack of approval, so that whatever I did was wrong.
2. But it was really strong disapproval, that I was stupid; my husband's feelings toward me are only a lack of approval, but my parents' feeling was active, strong disapproval."

We could therefore list the main features:

"1. Disapproval, plus
2. Competition with Mother and Brother. That I can see, because competition was the one thing that was allowed—you were allowed to be competitive.
3. Disapproval of feelings causes strong repression.
4. No love—I received none and there was rejection; I was brought up by people other than my parents.
5. The anger, almost totally repressed, simply not allowed, which leads me to remark that I remember Mary, the good maid, but there were other maids who were bad.
6. I was trained to be perfect but cannot be perfect."

Apparently, as usual, this interview had great impact and Claudia said, "This sounds like a sad story . . . is there anybody that has a happy childhood, does it exist?"

In retrospect, it was evident that the period of analysis with me, although it had made some attempt to analyze her feelings and the resistance (from the repression), had not fully succeeded in doing so. Feelings remained forbidden, and that prohibition upon feeling had not been sufficiently worked through in the analysis, so that she had never become close enough to her feelings to achieve a change in them. Partly beyond this, however, she could not bear the guilt connected with the intensity of her anger at her parents. But now, later, one single interview with a careful, meticulous questioning about her 0–6 was able to give her the insight into the dynamics, including the strong resistance. I knew after this hour that, if she should return for more analytic work, we both had a good grasp on what was going on and could work through these resistances and deal with her feelings quite openly; she could bring them out and become close to them and change and outgrow those which still caused headaches and other problems. But I also knew there was very little chance that she would accept this opportunity and put in further work on it, especially as she now lived outside Chicago in the western suburbs, at a considerable distance.

In making these notes, it is hard not to think how much better I would have handled Claudia's emotional problems when she first came to see me if I had been acquainted with this way of taking an intensive childhood history, getting it in perspective myself, and giving one to the patient on just what were the problems involved. Of course, it may be that she would have been unable to give such a history and that the resistances would have been so strong that I could not have understood the dynamics well at that time, whereas only *after* that period (of two or three years of analysis) would she have been able to bring this out as clearly as she did now. In any event, I record this so that other beginners in the field may learn from my experience and become more effective analysts much sooner in their careers. My own early patients, I think, were helped considerably and turned out relatively well, considering that they came to a rank beginner, but how much better they would have turned out if I had had this knowledge.

Dynamic Diagnosis: Claudia Atkins

Childhood: "Mother did not like us as small children and showed no interest in us. She only liked children when grown-up. Brother teased me and was bigger and could do everything better. Father growled at me. Mother did everything so well I had to try to also, but in vain. Failure, fright, and anxiety were not permitted, and certainly not sex or anger. Emotions were simply not allowed. I must have longed to be with Mother but she had no interest, did not like children; my nurse did everything for me. I felt toward Mother admiration and competitiveness. Brother was preferred by Mother and Father, and I tried to keep up with him. Father always disapproving, made me feel stupid; we could never talk."

Current: (1) Feels unloved, disapproved of, does nothing right, inferior, but must unceasingly strive for perfection and beating out those whom she sees as competitors. (2) Competition with Mother and Brother. (3) Severe repression of all feeling, especially anger and sex. (4) Trained to be perfect but cannot be.

Strengths: Mostly from identification with Mother, she possesses superior intelligence, determination, perseverence, fighting spirit.

XI. Jerry Bingham: Insecurity

Jerry Bingham was a rather tall, slender man in his mid-forties, who held an engineering job in a large company. He had no serious complaints but thought analysis could "help me improve myself and live better." He had been in analytic work for four or five years, on and off, when the following review of his 0–6 was done. At this time it was over half a year since he had left treatment, and apparently had been doing well. I asked him to come in for a review of the 0–6, to see if we could tie things together a little better than before.

As usual, I asked, "What do you consider the main feature or features of your life from birth to the age of about six?"

He replied almost immediately, "Intensity." Then he hesitated, and from this point on he spoke with some difficulty, stopping often to think.

I asked, "What do you mean by intensity?"

He replied, "The specifics are hard to remember . . . maybe going back to kindergarten. It seemed there were a number of people over me—Father, who had intensity—I used to ride on his shoulders. He was big, he was full of undefined love that persists to this day. Mother I hardly remember. She was remote. There was a nurse in the way, between us; the nurse was huge physically. She was kind and good-humored; she was uncontrollable, but not unreasonable.

"I had three older sisters, but one was so much older that I saw nothing of her—she was gone out of the home. The second oldest, Alice, was a threat to me and I was frightened of her, but she had a lot of love too. But it was sort of like being in a terrorist organization;

if I did not do as she told me, I would be killed. Those were her words. She used to beat me up. When I was about eight years old I fell in with a gang of neighborhood kids, and we stole something from the house next door, and I lied at first to my parents and said I had not taken it. I had unsettled feelings about what was right; I knew that incident was wrong, but I felt I had to do it because I was with the crowd.

"When I was in the third grade I hid from my father under the bed so as not to have to go to a spelling class for fear I would fail that class. I don't remember much about the summers. I do remember fireflies and a love of the outdoors. I have just vague feelings about a place we went to at the shore. To my sisters, I was a spoiled brat, and they called me that.

"I remember my giving a lecture at about age eight and deciding I wanted to be a minister. I had been influenced by a religious man who read the Bible to me, and I thought that was great. Father built a lectern for me, and I gave a lecture or else read from the Bible and then made some remarks. My sisters laughed at me.

"I remember riding on a pony's back. As a baby, I was in a carriage and I remember being walked around the hill where we lived, and I remember the sweetness of a family who lived nearby—they were very rarified, very aristocratic, and super-refined. Then there was another family—they were all very big. There was one boy about my age, but he was very big. Then I remember once I was in the bathtub and defecated, and that was terrible. Until the second grade I had very poor control of my bowels. Some of the children did not have control after they were in the second grade, and I was very proud of myself because I did.

"When I was about one year old I had some sort of stomach disorder and I was supposed to eat only protein, and so I was on a very specialized diet—lamb chops, bacon, and orange gelatin. Usually I had to eat in the kitchen, but it was fairly warm and all right because of a large nurse I had.

"I remember a birthday party at about the age of six." At this point I asked him if he knew anything he would consider outstanding as a feature of his childhood. He replied, "I don't know; everything was sort of so big and hard to control. The dog was big . . . there were all sorts of things that I could not control. I was ashamed that I could not control my bowels, but on the other hand I was sort of a focus of attention. My sisters were jealous and angry because I got bigger Christmas presents than they did, with dolls and teddy bears. I remember feeling the need for possessions, like Christmas presents."

Having received some impressions from this, I now asked Jerry, "Whom do you consider the most important people in your life from birth to about six?"

He replied immediately, "My nurse. I remember one time I was in bed and my mother was talking to the nurse in French, so I could not understand, and she said 'hopital,' and I said 'You mean you are going to take me to the hospital'; this made me very angry that they were trying to talk without me understanding. Once the nurse slapped me so hard for a well-defined reason; I had walked down the street when I had been told not to. I think I was trying to decide who was the authority in the family, the nurse or Mother.

"I used to listen to the Victrola and get great pleasure from that. I remember being at home with my toys, which I loved, especially the blocks and teddy bears with whom I had a fantasy relationship. There was no one to play with."

I said, "You have told me the nurse was your most important relationship, but what *was* that relationship?"

He said, "Mother was out and the nurse was there. Also, she did much of the cooking so she was not involved in my play, so she was always there at mealtime and bedtime. She was kind and had a sense of humor, and I liked her. She stayed in touch with our family until about ten years ago when she died. I spent a lot of my time in the kitchen.

"I remember being scared by a kidnapping that was in the newspaper. My sisters and I slept in the same room, but there was no problem."

I asked Jerry, "Who was the second most important person, next to your nurse?"

He said, "That's funny, I can't answer that. There are different areas of importance. In terms of bigness and authority, it was Father, but I respected Mother. Later on, from six to twelve, when I shifted from the nurse to Mother, I had more to do with Mother, and there was a kind of affection. Probably I was close to the nurse when I was a baby and involved in baby things, and then later with Mother because she was there at school things when I began to go to school.

"Once Mother said to me, 'Will you stay with me if I leave your father?' But in those days, only the most reprehensible people got divorced. Really, Father and Mother's relationship was well developed and warm. Later on, they got involved with four couples who dominated their social life. I was conscious of Father and Mother being away on holidays, and I got so that I wanted them to be away. They wanted to have children to show them off, but not to be involved with their day-to-day lives and care."

I asked, "But was the relationship to your mother the second most important?"

Jerry replied, "I don't know. She was leaving all the time. I do remember her being, in my estimate, beautiful and imperious, dominating, with both of the servants. Also, it seems funny, I had a feeling that she was not competent to deal with the day-to-day needs of children. Later on, when I was about twelve, my sisters and I were sitting at the dinner table one night, and we all opposed my mother in something; we came together, coalesced, and with that Mother's authority disintegrated. As I see it now, in retrospect, my second oldest sister, Alice, was at a bad point in life—she was rebelling hard and was especially hard-pressed by Mary, the next youngest, who was brighter than Alice. Mother did not know how to handle this situation; Father reacted with undisciplined emotion. One time he even struck Alice at the dinner table. I did not feel strongly on one side or the other; I only wanted refuge from the chaos.

"One time Alice was to drive me somewhere; we were sitting in the car and had not yet left the house. Suddenly she hit me with her fist. She was in the driver's seat, and I was next to her. She swung out her hand and hit me with the back of it; then I pummeled her with both fists. That was really triggered by months and months of my holding back, and Mother had even said that she would not be surprised if I did hit Alice; I made her face black and blue. After that, she let me alone, but then we never had much of a relationship again.

"In my 0–6 I just don't remember Mother. Probably I sensed her as the ultimate authority, but she was like God—not actually in evidence. What angered me was her patronizing. She would pay attention to the problem but not to the person."

This much of our interview took an hour and a quarter, and I could continue no longer. We made another appointment to resume. In the second session I asked Jerry for his earliest memories.

He said, "My first memory is that I was in a wicker baby carriage in the sun, or, anyway, on the porch; I was put out afternoons, sun or not. The idea was really fresh air.

"My second memory is about age three, eating in the kitchen, sitting in a youth chair, and I remember a curved silver spoon. Then the third memory at age five is a very strong one, of being in a bathtub with a strange nurse and defecating in the tub and being horribly ashamed of it. And the fourth memory, when I was two or three, of riding on Father's shoulders; but there were pictures of that, and I am not sure if I am remembering it or projecting back from looking at the pictures.

"Fifth memory: I was sitting on a chair when a Russian came to play chess with Father and I was supposed to be in bed.

"Sixth memory: I was in the nursery, playing with pastel-colored blocks, set up like soldiers; you would push one and they would all fall down.

"The seventh memory is really no memory, because I have no memory of playing with other children, not until much later. At about age five I was playing with my sister. It was then things began to happen when we went away for the summer. I remember being on a steamboat. I was seasick at night, and my cousin took me for a walk on the deck. I guess I was pretty little, still not six, because I slept at the foot of my sister's bed.

"The relations to my sisters, Alice and Mary, are hard to pin down. I know we went to the shore, but I don't remember anything except the waves, and I was frightened of them. There must have been some music in the picture, because I learned a song, and I sang it at a country fair and got a prize for it. We stayed in a log cabin and I can still remember the smell of the pitch, and I remember it with great pleasure.

"Then there are isolated spots, but I cannot pin my age down. For example, people moved nearby. They were Father's friends and they were very fancy, and we had to get all dressed up when we went to visit them.

"I remember our photos being taken when I was about four. Oh yes, I remember a tricycle—that was important, around the garage and in the driveway. I loved my tricycle, and it was a big one. It was important because it was *my* possession. I can't remember anything else I did except lie on the floor and listen to classical records. My mother's relatives and their children, my cousins, were all understandable to me, but my father's relatives were all rather mysterious. I associated the classical records with them. When the one cousin, considerably older, got married I was upset."

"Why would that have been?" I asked.

"I don't know for sure," he replied, "but I may have been in love with the girl he married, who was a friend of my sister. I was probably about twelve at the time."

I asked, "Do you get any impression from what you have been saying?"

He said, "The essence of my feelings is that from 0 to 6 was a vacant life. What in the world *was* I doing for those six years? My feelings when I think of it now were of being suppressed—everyone and everything was bigger than I; the house, the hill behind the house, the dog, the neighbors, they were all bigger. I was physically a runt. All of us, that is, my sisters and I, were small. Father and Mother were big; they were not small. I don't know if it was because we were undernourished or what. I was small until my teens, and then I grew a lot; I had a sense of having felt small, and alone."

"What," I asked, "were your chief complaints five years ago when you came to see me?"

He said, "It was a specific problem about one of my cousins, and I came to see you to see what you thought and get an opinion as to what I should do. And then my wife was much in favor of my coming to see you, but put no pressure on me. I came with much concern that seeing a psychiatrist might be an admission of weakness, despite the fact that I knew Alice was by then a very real problem. And you told me that only certain things could be done, but it never crystallized in my mind as an objective. The analytic work turned out to be a positive thing in my life. I had just started working in a new job, we were about to have another child, and it was spring. The stock market was going up, and my stocks were going up too, and I thought I had some financial strength. There were no real complaints; it was more a question of how to live better with my wife, even though we had no marital difficulties. But my wife blamed me for quite a lot of things and I could see my own inadequacies. I had just a few things that might be called symptoms—that is, masturbation and drinking more than I do now. It was not a matter of having disastrous symptoms, but that maybe the analytic work would help me improve myself."

I asked, "And how about the chief complaints today?" He said, "The analytic work helped enormously in improving many things, particularly the recognition of my own anger. It made the bad parts of my life, both at home and work, much less bad, and I did not seem to be able to communicate my thoughts at all; that would drive my wife simply mad. You once told me that you would not be doing anything for me that maturity could not do, but your help would just hurry up the maturing process; yet I feel it was absolutely crucial. I might have gone on without any maturity at all, and that would have been disastrous, particularly in the area of my being able to handle my own anger, the palpitations I would have when speaking before any group of people, my mind just going blank. That has become so much better that I really have no more anxiety about it; now, if I have anything to say, I can say it before anybody.

"But there is one symptom left—a sense of failure, which I fight against. Also, a feeling of being put down. These feelings are much more manageable now, though, and I think that is because of the analysis and not just from experience. Also, there is still some feeling of not being able to *do* anything, like the present feeling of being trapped. I simply don't have enough money and can't please my wife. For example, I can't repair the driveway and keep up with our next-door neighbors. You know that is in large part because my stocks dropped until they became almost valueless. But what makes me feel good is that what we have done together has 'stuck' very well over the six months' interval since I've seen you last. It helped at the international meetings that I attended; that there was a much more positive experience than it would have been. And it helped in a series of engineering presentations that I made, especially in the face of several letters from customers complaining about me. It has also helped me in dealing with my parents, and in general in human relations with others."

This was of course very gratifying to hear from Jerry, especially as I had considered this an extremely difficult problem—not because it was so much a matter of helping Jerry resolve a conflict as it was helping him supply something that had been missing in his 0-6, namely the human contact and warmth and support (and, in a way, the authority, which was conveyed analytically by not exerting any authority but by reasoning out situations together as they arose, thereby providing him at the age of forty with a "corrective emotional experience" [Alexander and French, 1946], something that was apparently totally lacking in his first six years). It was a way of building in a friendly, understanding, supportive superego. This was by way of contrast to the uncertainty about authority, lack of warmth and support, and a big depreciation by his sisters in childhood, directly by their laughter and Alice's beating him up, and indirectly by his parents' general neglect and their treating him as the 'little one,' of no importance.

Dynamic Diagnosis: Jerry Bingham

Childhood: Mother remote, hardly remembered. A big, pleasant nurse between Mother and patient. Second of three older sisters intimidated patient, beat him up, threatened him with death. Uncertain whether Mother or nurse was the authority. Mother and Father not involved with their children. Mother beautiful, dominating, patronizing, incompetent with children. Conflict between Mother and next two older sisters from which patient sought refuge. Essence of feelings from 0–6: a vacant life, feelings suppressed, being small and alone, everything and everyone big and hard to control.

Current: Feelings of immaturity, inferiority, smallness, ineffectiveness leading to flight as shyness, withdrawal from people; and to fight as masochistically not working with full efficiency, with poorly controlled anger, palpitations, inability to communicate thoughts, mind going blank; and combined with flight turned on self as sense of failure, being depreciated and trapped.

Strengths: Fine mind with deep interest in profession. Courage in facing own unconscious. Strong therapeutic urge to improve self and do well for wife and children and in profession.

References

Alexander, F., and French, T. (1946): *Psychoanalytic Therapy.* New York: Ronald Press.

13
THE AGE OF 6–16

The circumstances of W. Somerset Maugham's early life, as recorded in the excellent biography by his nephew, Robin Maugham (*Somerset and all the Maughams*, New York: The New American Library, 1966), reveal with unusual vividness the operation of trauma during 6 to 16. Robin's Uncle Willie, as he calls him, was born in Paris, where his father was a lawyer to the British Consulate. Both parents were English, but Willie grew up speaking only French. His three older brothers were away at school most of the time, and Willie had his mother, an eminent beauty, to himself. There was deep love between them. Until his death at age ninety-one, Willie kept a picture of her on his bedside table. He often said, "I shall never get over it," meaning her death, and apparently he never did. When Willie was eight years old he lost his young, beautiful, loving mother by consumption, and shortly thereafter, when he was nine, his father by cancer of the stomach. Bereft of his parents, he was taken to England to the guardianship of Henry Macdonald Maugham, the strict, parsimonious, bootlicking, snobbish Vicar of Whitstable, by his mother's nurse, his one remaining link with his mother's love. But the Vicar told him the day they arrived that the nurse must go back because he could not afford to support her. Willie was now in a foreign land, with a foreign tongue that he could not speak, and was sent to a boarding school where he was treated with cruelty by both students and masters, as related in his masterpiece *Of Human Bondage*. Besides everything else, he had a stammer so severe that at times he could not say a word for moments. He was utterly miserable, most of the time in mental agony. But he survived because of a certain strength and stubbornness.

His trauma from 6 to 16 did not cause him to break down but affected his entire life with depression, withdrawal, and cynicism; but he transformed it, through arduous work, into the literary productions which brought him fame and wealth. The reason for his strength seems to lie in the good, loving relation with his mother from 0 to 6. The point his story makes so clearly is this: because of his good 0 to 6 he had the strength to survive the severe trauma of his 6 to 16; but the trauma of 6 to 16 caused pathology, serious emotional problems, and suffering for the rest of his long life.

From the biography it is not certain that his 0 to 6 was all loving, because his next older brother committed suicide at 35. His treatment in childhood seems to have affected his attitudes and feelings toward women and made him hostile to women. His brief marriage ended in his being divorced by his popular wife, Syrie. It is conceivable but unlikely that his lifelong emotional warpings, which he transformed into literary masterpieces, originated entirely in the terrible trauma of his 6 to 16. But the point remains: whatever may have been wrong in his 0 to 6, there was enough love in it to see him through his 6 to 16 without a breakdown.*

Biographers of the future, if they wish to explain the personalities and accomplishments of their subjects, will have to do assiduous research into their earliest lives, 0 to 3, 0 to 6, and 6 to 16.

Freud observed correctly that 0–6 is the period of greatest emotional vulnerability, but this does not mean that *only* during 0–6 can development be interfered with, or that after age six the personality is so fixed that no damaging influences can have any deleterious effects.

If he looks for it, I think every clinician will see plenty of material on traumatic effects during the ages of about 6–16. Of course, these are somewhat different from the effects during 0–6. For from 0–6 experiences operate upon a cleaner slate—the *tabula rasa*. Some conditioning may take place in utero, but this is probably minimal compared to the amount of conditioning that takes place from birth to age six or seven. As a general principle, the younger the child the greater the emotional effects of life experiences, but by age five to seven there is a certain amount of crystallization of the personality. Experiences after age six (for convenience let us say 6–16) operate upon a mind and set of attitudes and feelings which have already been formed, to a certain extent, by the child's earlier experiences. Put another way, how a child is formed or affected or molded by his experiences during 6–16 is determined very largely by how his personality was shaped before the age of six. This general principle, of course, is true for a lifetime.

*For other excellent Maugham material, see:
Cordell, R. (1961): *Somerset Maugham*. Bloomington, Indiana: Indiana University Press.
Pfeiffer, K. (1959): *W. Somerset Maugham*. New York: W. W. Norton.

One learns emotionally during all of one's life, and one is subject to potentially traumatic experiences all of one's life; but how one reacts to these experiences is a function very largely of what his personality was before the traumatic experience. How a person reacts to unusual degrees of failure, pressure, or to any marked change in his life is determined by the kind of person he was—that is, by the dynamics he brings to the situation. Trauma in later life is not something that exists by itself alone; it is a matter of the external life experience operating upon the emotional dynamics of the individual, particularly upon his specific emotional vulnerabilities. Put the other way around, his specific emotional vulnerabilities are one of the heavily weighed determinants of what, in his experience, is reacted to as a trauma. Therefore, trauma for one person may not be a trauma for another (Saul, 1971, Chap. 10). One person can become extremely upset over something which another person reacts to but little. Sometimes innocent remarks cause intense reaction, and all we know is that "a nerve has been touched."

Here, however, we are concerned only with the influences during the years 6–16 in producing emotional problems and psychopathology. Instead of one case, given in detail, here are the highlights of three cases:

I. Nell

The first case is Nell, a tall and capable brunette, married with three children, who complained of a sense of impending disaster. She had a comfortably secure emotional and physical 0–6. When Nell was six, however, her mother developed a serious illness, and she died when Nell was about fourteen. The family burden fell upon the father, who was not earning much money and was trying to put some aside for the college education of Nell's three older brothers. He had almost nothing left over emotionally to give the children, particularly to Nell, the youngest. Her life during these years was one of emotional deprivation in a family that was struggling to survive financially and emotionally. When she was in her mid-thirties, when I saw her, the effects of all this were evident: she was a good person, basically stable, but under a great deal of tension. She had gotten little in the way of love and support in her life, but her personality makeup was readily intelligible in terms of her 0–6 and her 6–16 after the illness and death of her mother, making her feel she must not complain but must carry on without emotional support. Nevertheless, underneath this was a great deal of resentment at the deprivation, and the resentment built up and took form mostly in anxieties, particularly the anticipation of catastrophe. She was energetic and vivacious and not overtly depressed, but she had a depressive outlook in the sense of always expecting the worst. Thus, she continued almost unaltered the same orientation and outlook and basic feelings that she had during the years 6–16: courage in the face of deprivation, but underlying resentment generating anxiety and anticipation of catastrophe. If she had been subjected to this kind of deprivation from birth, she would undoubtedly have been a much more disturbed individual. The effects were less because she had a basically good 0–6, but they were strong because of her traumatic experience from 6–16. Her mother's love from 0–6 gave Nell the inner support (the good superego) which enabled her to survive the illness and death of her mother and her years from 6–16. But 6–16 left its mold upon the permanent dynamics of her personality.

One often sees the effects of experiences during 6–16 in families in which no great misfortune, like Nell's, or physical illness has occurred. This is because there are many parents who react warmly to babies but lose interest in children after age six. In other families, as soon as a child develops enough of an ego to respond to discretion or control, the parents exaggerate enormously in their own minds those things of which the child is now capable. They expect no self-discipline from a baby or toddler; but as soon as the child is out of this stage, they think he is ready for all the self-control of a well-disciplined adult. This leads the parents to give the child less than it needs and to expect much more from the child than the child is capable of. Of course, some parents do not like young children and only establish rapport with their own youngsters when they are older, not until adolescence.

II. Gloria

For example, Gloria's parents gave her a secure loving environment until she was seven years old. At that time, they sent her to a school some distance away, requiring her to travel alone, making two changes of trains. This was more than Gloria could handle emotionally. She did manage in reality to do it, but with such fear that she wept for hours after going to bed every night. Also, the parents seemed to lose interest in her as soon as she was able to take care of herself to this extent, without realizing the price she paid for it. The parents were so taken up in their own interests that they began to think they could now let Gloria simply take care of herself; the rapport between the parents and Gloria dwindled to very little. As an adult, the same pattern continued: Gloria drove herself to do all sorts of things—either to contribute to the community or for self-cultivation—reflecting the parents' training from 6–16, but she was resentful underneath because of this. As a result she was anxious. Also, an important part of her problem was her failure to have close rapport first with her friends and then, after marriage, with her husband, therefore creating a marital problem. Again, what was good in her 0–6 kept her from being much more upset than she would have been because of the pressures during her 6–16. The healthy dynamics formed during 0–6 gave a good core to her personality so that the traumatic effects from 6–16 were less than they would otherwise have been.

III. Joy

Joy was a girl with more mixed pathological dynamics. She was a middle child who had had much love during her 0–6, but from six on she was raised to be the perfect little girl—perfectly dressed, perfectly behaved, perfect in her accomplishments in school as well as in extracurricular activities. A problem arose, however, at about age ten or eleven when her younger sister and older brother outdid her, especially in accomplishments and popularity. This she could not stand, and she reacted to it from age twelve mostly with withdrawal. If there were any sort of competition, she might even at the last minute do something to necessitate her withdrawal from the activity. As a trivial example, she damaged the strings of her racquet to avoid playing in a competition tennis match. This soon led to her becoming depressed, and it was with these symptoms she entered adult life. Thus 6–16 seems also to be a formative period, although it has marked differences from 0–6.

In the same way, conception to age six contains in itself different formative periods. Formative really means "conditioning," which is a form of learning. The effects on the fetus are different from the effects on the baby, and the effects on the newborn are different from those on the toddler (Mahler, 1965, 1968), and so on throughout life.

In summary, then, we have been discussing not the effects of brief, transient individual traumatic experiences; these experiences are traumatic mostly because they impinge upon specific emotional vulnerabilities. We are discussing the traumatic effects of *longstanding influences*, such as the emotional relationships to the parents, siblings, and substitutes that occur from 0–6 and, although differently, from 6–16—and there are still different effects which occur at later age periods.

People are vulnerable all their lives, but they are never so vulnerable as from conception to age about six, and it is mostly then that the personality is formed. By age six, a certain amount of crystallization of personality has taken place; one can see in the six-year-old the rudiments of an already formed personality; even at age three some of this is evident. The individual remains vulnerable and malleable all the rest of his life, but much less so. Perhaps a dividing line would be when continuous memory and full speech and the ability to read develop, for these capabilities enormously strengthen the ego by providing language for more conscious thought, feeling, and reason. It is especially worth the therapist's paying attention, in addition to 0–6, to ages 0–3 and 6–16. In observing effects during the latter stage, however, one must always bear in mind how it is affected by the earlier dynamics already formed from 0–6.

In reactive cases, that is, in those in which the emotional upset of the patient is basically in reaction to external pressures and relatively appropriate to them, whether or not to try to get the childhood emotional pattern in the first interview varies from patient to patient. If the reaction to the external events seems excessive relative to the pressure, then usually it is important to get the childhood pattern in the first interview, because without it one does not know the emotional vulnerabilities and one cannot understand what is going on. This would be exemplified by Pat Ralston, who, after marrying a very nice man with whom she was in love, became acutely anxious and developed a certain amount of paranoid jealousy toward him. This reaction was quite unintelligible until one found out from her childhood pattern the degree of rejection and deprivation to which she had been subjected. She had kept it repressed all these years, as well as the anger she felt in reaction to it. Once she was married, she felt secure but also close to another human being—closer than she had hitherto permitted herself to be; with this closeness, the whole reaction of the frustrated dependent love needs and the rage was suddenly mobilized. Without knowledge of that background one could not understand, I believe, why she would react in such a fashion to something that the rest of her personality very much desired, namely, marriage to a man of her choice.

But another patient, Maria Brown, at age thirty-five, through no fault or behavior of her own, was suddenly under such pressures in life, including pressure from her own father, that one could expect even the strongest person to be upset by them. In such a case it is usually more important to give emotional support and practical guidance so far as the analyst's knowledge and experience enable him to do so, until these external pressures are alleviated. For detailed reactive cases, see *Emotional Maturity* (Saul, 1971).

IV. Karen: Postadolescent Drifting

The following notes are on a patient seen in my earlier psychoanalytic days, before I had learned a little bit better how to obtain a clear picture of 0-6. My later technique of asking two basic questions in order to elicit the childhood dynamics was not available. I doubt that this made a great difference in Karen's case, however. The main issue was her strong resistance, which I did not understand sufficiently to hold her in treatment long enough to do a reasonably thorough job and to get a satisfying, permanent result. As I have noted before (Saul 1972), it is usually possible in 85 or 90 percent of analytic patients, to reach the major dynamics in the first interview or two. Karen is an illustration of the 10 or 15 percent in which this is not achieved.

Karen was an attractive, well-built, apparently physically healthy and wholesome girl about twenty-four years old. Her chief complaint was dissatisfaction with her job; she did not know what to do. She was born and brought up in a middle western town of moderate size, and she had been thinking for a long time about getting away from home to attend a northeastern college. At age eighteen she finally made the break. It was her first venture away from home and the first time she had been required to take care of the minutiae of existence—laundry, bank account, and so on—but she managed these details very well and liked doing it. Her room in the dormitory was the first time she had a room of her own, and she liked it. She liked it still better when the dorm became coed and there was a lot of life around with "all those high-powered people." Karen found it all very exciting, but she never quite knew what she wanted from life—so she selected American literature. But this did not help her find her way. She did not want to do graduate academic work; she did not want to marry because, she said, marriage was "not enough." Karen was looking for something so absorbing that she would not be conscious of time passing. When she came to see me it was two years after her college graduation; she still did not know what to do with her life. She was working as a secretary, but that was a stop-gap job.

Usually a careful history of the patient from 0–6 reveals at least a clue as to what is causing the current problem. Nothing in Karen's history, however, stood out with any degree of certainty. She said that her 0–6 was happy. Her sister was three years older, and the family was quite close. Her father and mother both made the family their profession. The children spent plenty of time outdoors playing ball and going to ball games with their father; there was a lot of music with their mother. They chatted a lot at meals. The parents were interested in politics, and Karen grew up in that atmosphere and felt at ease. In fact, when the newspaper arrived, she was the first one of the family to read it.

When Karen was a little older, she was still not settled. When she was between the ages of eight and fourteen, her father had a series of different jobs and this was unsettling. Yet so far as I could see, it occurred somewhat too late in her life to form a deep, persisting pattern, and I could not find any direct pattern in her family relative to hers. Of course, she might have been identifying with her father because of his numerous job changes, prompting her to have a series of jobs too, but I could not believe that the motivation for this instability was so late a childhood identification with her father. Apparently her father was not much appreciated by her mother's family until the girls grew up and distinguished themselves academically. Her father never complained, and finally settled in a job he liked as the manager of a small business.

Karen's earliest memories were: (1) She was standing on a sidewalk and looking up at her maternal grandmother; a little after that came the second memory. (2) At age two she was being lifted up onto a counter at a political rally, and there was a lot of laughter. (3) Still at an early age (a little more than two) Karen was in her crib, and her mother was feeding her pudding. (4) She was sitting on a couch with her mother, who was reading to her.

What I got out of this series of memories was obvious, namely that they were all in relationship to Mother figures, either her own or her maternal grandmother, and she was getting some attention from them. This was of course not pathological, but it might possibly have indicated that the attachment to her mother was so strong that it accounted for all the early memories, and those memories were probably remembered because they signified something in the patient's current dynamics. In other words, she may have remembered the closeness to her mother and her mother's reading to her or feeding her pudding because at the present moment, as a young adult, she still had strong longings for this kind of care and attention from her mother or from Mother figures. It is also probably significant that she had no great urge to marry, and there is no male in her early memories. Concerning marriage, Karen still wanted a home, but she felt strongly that it would simply not be enough. Only since college, she indicated, had she felt strongly about wanting a home, but she had not yet met the right man. That was part of her dissatisfaction with her job, which involved long hours and work over the weekends so that she had no time to move about, meet people, and, hopefully, meet the right man. All this was elicited in our first interview; while I had that hint about her possible too-strong attachment to her mother and the absence of her father or any male in her memories, still it was not solid enough for me to feel secure in understanding Karen's present dissatisfaction with her work and life, including the other problem, her failure so far to be interested in a man or get one interested enough in her to contemplate marriage.

At the second hour a week later, Karen said, "I just don't know what to do with my life; I am really miserable. I have constant anxiety thinking about what to do the following week—whether to quit my job and look for something else, or what. Friday I nearly collapsed. I was glad to have the food shopping to do so that I would not have to think about the coming week."

I asked, "Why have you been so miserable?"

She replied, "Because I simply do not like the kind of work I do, nor do I like that kind of people. There is simply nothing productive or worthwhile about it; it is not rewarding. It is seven days a week, and it never ends. The people are so lower middle class and they are all dissatisfied, not interested in anything."

I asked whether it was any better when she was in college, and she said, "Well, in a way it wasn't. I need some*body*, not some*thing*, to motivate me. In college I was remote from the faculty; I was simply being lectured *at* with a lot of other students; there was no personal relationship with the faculty. I was looking for a model in an older person. The only one with any personal relationship at all was the dormitory couple, with a young child of their own. I only sat in lecture halls."

"Didn't you make any friends among the boys living in the coed dorms?" I asked.

"The guys," said Karen, "were pretty much like guys everywhere: very much full of energy, insecure, striving to excel. I have kept up with a few of them and some girls I knew then, but they are all at a considerable distance, either in the South or the East, not near Chicago. In other words, I had a few friends but no special friends. There were some girls that I still write to and visit occasionally; the boys were just friends. I did not have any sexual relationships, and still haven't. One boy married one of my close girlfriends. The only boy I had some interest in did not have that much interest in me and that ended. I went with another boy for two or three months, and he was a rising star. I also had a girlfriend who was the daughter of an eminent professor at the school. I had gone with one boy, William, who was not particularly nice to me. He made me feel bad about myself. He was always chastising me for not being interested in schoolwork, not knowing where I was going. He let me know that I did not amount to much. He told me he could not go out with me because he had just bought three new records—in other words, having three new records was more important to William than going out with me! One summer we drove back from my hometown to college, and on the way we fought and broke up.

"I returned that time to college in the middle of a stressful situation. The girl in the next room was a violent personality. When I knocked on her door to greet her in a friendly way, she simply slammed the door in my face. She mounted campaigns to get me out of the dorm. We were getting into exam time, and I was harassed by her friends. Then I got sick and a new boy whom I was seeing a bit started going out with my friend, the professor's daughter. He said I was getting too possessive. He used that girl simply to get a good connection with her father, and then he dropped her too. But through her he met other leading professors and got grants and fellowships. I must admit that he was good at getting along in life. My roommate during freshman year was good at taking care of her own interest, regardless of other people. She had her whole life planned; she took only those courses that she had knowledge of beforehand, to be sure of passing. Now she has graduated from law school.

"I did make a few close friends, but they are only at great distances from Chicago, and we write seldom. Since coming here I've made no close friends at all. Two people at work invited me home to meet their families, but it is no more intimate than that. I can see what is going on in your mind," Karen added. "You want me to go out, meet a fellow, and get married."

"No," I answered, "that's not true. I have no goals for you nor advice. I only would like to see you achieve what you yourself want. You seem to me to be a very normal, healthy, bright, and attractive girl, and you tell me that what *you* want is to meet and marry a man, but I think there must be something in you which resists the development of such a relationship leading to marriage. It is our job to find out together what that resistance might be and to understand it. Why should you have to find a career first and then marry? Especially when you feel so lonely and isolated? Why can't you first find close friends, then maybe marry and finally see how you feel about a career, establishing one at your leisure? Why does it have to be career first and then marriage, instead of marriage first?"

At out third meeting Karen again complained bitterly about how unhappy she was, that she hated her job and that she did not want to be here seeing me. I asked her if she meant by this a suicidal tendency. After some hesitation she answered, "Well, possibly some."

I said, "Let's be frank about it; our goal is to understand everything. Let's face whatever we find."

I tried taking a little more history, but got nowhere. I was left, then, with the only clue being really those first early memories, which were so consistently ones of being given care and attention by her mother; no other person appeared in the memories except her maternal grandmother.

I do not like to ask a patient who is first seen to begin free associating before I understand the dynamics reasonably well; for, once the free associating begins and the analyst makes interpretations, the material is apt to get clouded, and it is more difficult to get the perspective to see the dynamics. It was with reluctance that I switched from the history taking (because it had failed to yield her dynamics with any certainty) and asked Karen simply to pour out whatever was on her mind. It then came out that she had written away for another job at some distance from Chicago. She had written to a business concern that she had heard about over a year before. Karen no longer liked to wake up in the morning; she woke up, especially on Saturdays, and just simply went to pieces—she wept.

"I am not a very nice person," she told me. "I get angry."

"Go ahead," I said, "pour it out."

"Perhaps I should just give it all up, just quit," she said.

"Tell me more, Karen," I said.

"Well, I telephone my mother, I telephone my sister, and then I blow up at them and hang up on them."

I began to have a slight idea as to what must be going on, and I asked Karen if she were not looking for other jobs also instead of just trying to get this one job with the business concern she had heard about a year previously. "I guess I have just collapsed," she said. "I just weep; I hate my job because it has no beauty, there is no closeness with other people, there is no interest, there is no conversation."

It was near the end of the hour. I would have felt more secure with another hour of associations, but I thought I had sufficient clues as to where the material was heading; and because she resisted coming to see me so strongly, wanting to quit, it seemed safer to hazard a tentative interpretation at this point. This was the end of our third interview.

So I said, "It seems to me, Karen, that you want a job that has beauty, closeness, pleasantness, interest, etc., but you are hung up on finding it because of at least one thing, and every job I ask you about you show a lack of interest in or find fault with it. It sounds as though you may not really want *any* job, do not want that adult effort and responsibility; or else you want this ideal job but are waiting for somebody to serve it to you on a platter, and I wonder if that is not along the lines of your first memories and your description of your home and your mother, who showed all this solicitude and gave you anything you wanted? Now you are a big girl, you are twenty-four, you are two years out of college and an adult, you are on your own, which you yourself have indicated is what you want—you want to be independent. But that means you cannot wait for somebody to *give* you what you want as somebody lifted you onto the counter and as mother fed you the pudding. You have to make the effort and take the initiative to step out and get it for yourself. We've already discussed many ways in which you could do that, but you have found fault with all of them. But I think the real fault is that down underneath you are a little bit spoiled, and you would like it given to you as it has always been, by your mother, rather than stepping out and getting it for yourself. Don't think I'm unsympathetic; I am very sympathetic, but I think you are caught in your own fight-flight reaction. There is a strong tendency to just give up your present job rather than first look for something else, and this leads to your weeping. Also the weeping, as you saw, is an expression of the fight reaction of rage; you have strong tendencies to be angry and withdraw and not go out in the world and use the fighting spirit of responsibility and effort to find the kind of job you would like.

"This is all right. I feel sorry it's such a struggle for you, but this is how one grows up also. One matures by learning to do these things for oneself—in other words, to take responsibility for oneself independently; and I think if you understand these dynamics, you will certainly succeed in doing things for yourself because you are young, strong, and intelligent, a graduate of a good university, and if anyone can do it, you can. There is nothing wrong with the instrument."

This she digested between our interview and the following one, seeming to understand it reasonably well. From this point on it was perfectly feasible to have her free associating, because now I had in mind some skeleton, however vague, for a small part of her major dynamics and its significance. She proceeded to become more active, meet more people, even started dating, and found a job at the University of Chicago. It was not an ideal job but was a great improvement over her poorly paid, boring typing position. She began to get over the flight part of her reaction, her weeping, repression, and withdrawal, and also the fight part, her need to telephone her mother and sister and then blow up at them.

In a way, this was a typical adolescent or rather postadolescent conflict—an adolescent conflict that one often sees, not in the midst of adolescence but after it. It is part of the transition to adult life from dependence to independence, and into the capacity for responsibility for one's own self—into responsible independence and productivity, into the ability to carry a job. It also illustrates the fact that if one is more or less stuck diagnostically, and if one inquires carefully, either openly or by subtle indirect tactful methods into the status of the hostility and the whole fight-flight reaction, this procedure usually leads to what at least some of the major dynamics might be; for the fight-flight response results from the major frustrations that are part of these dynamics, which are in turn causing the patient his unhappiness.

The third point that Karen illustrates is the common problem of "finding oneself"; in other words, in finding one's own identity. The identity crisis is usually caused by a childhood pattern that has not been outgrown, and is resolved only by understanding and outgrowing this childhood pattern. Everyone's identity is intimately bound up in his or her independent responsibilities, whether for job or profession or for home, husband, and children.

It must be added, however, that Karen's resistance to analytic treatment continued, and as soon as she was more comfortable, had a better job and a few boys to date, she broke it off. I thought she was probably unanalyzable, at least by me, and that this might be because of a transference to me of her pattern toward her father, who was so conspicuously absent in Karen's early memories. Therefore I suggested to her that she try a period of work with a woman analyst. But she rejected this idea, and I had to go along with her urge to break off seeing me. We liked each other, and parted with friendly feelings, but I did not hear from her after I left Chicago.

Of course, if the analyst does not know his patient's unconscious well, he does not know the outcome of therapy with any certainty. I have presented Karen as an illustration of my own failure to reach her basic dynamics and the subsequent failure of therapy because she broke it off. But sometimes an emotional shift occurs of which both patient and analyst might be unaware. It is possible that the transference, even in these few weeks, provided Karen with a degree of permissiveness and a current pathway to a good relationship with a man. Perhaps the seeds of the insights fell on therapeutically fertile soil, so that Karen benefited from her brief experience, which is not an unusual occurrence in an analytic practice. This is speculation, however, because all attempts to reach Karen in later years for a follow-up have failed.

V. Martha Mason: Courage Conquers All

The pathodynamics of most patients are such as to require long, arduous work to correct them. But occasionally a patient responds so well to the analytic approach that it seems that Freud lived and developed his technique to treat that patient alone! I would like to end this clinical section of the book with an example of just such a gratifying outcome.

Success in discerning the main emotional pattern from birth to the age of six or seven depends in part upon the frame of mind of the patient at the time. For example, a charming young girl of twenty who was so anxious that she was unable to be alone, even in her own home, came to see me. Her mother was taking Martha, the patient, for analysis five days a week at a distance of about one hour's drive each way. The mother had a job herself, which she enjoyed and which helped out the family finances. Although the family was fairly comfortable, the extra income was welcome. The point is that it was a great sacrifice for the mother and difficult for Martha to make the long trip each morning for an hour with the analyst. I phoned the analyst. With some embarrassment, I yielded to the wishes of all involved and accepted Martha as a patient myself. As tactfully as I could, I let Martha know I thought it would be worth a trial of only one day a week. The prospect of this alone was therapeutic for both the patient and her mother, because of their being spared a long trip every morning in the week.

Being unable to obtain a clear-cut childhood emotional pattern in the first hours, I was forced to deal with the material as it came up. Martha was good at recognizing her underlying feelings; she quickly saw the connection between her anxieties and her anger, and this fact alone reduced the anxieties dramatically. She improved steadily and rapidly, and was altogether a most gratifying patient. After about nine or ten months she was able to go out alone and had obtained a good job in a paramedical position. She enjoyed her work and got along well with her colleagues. By now, then, things were under good enough control and her anxiety was sufficiently reduced that I again decided to devote an hour to get her childhood pattern. This time, when Martha's anxiety was much reduced, the following came out:

"Now I recognize what I never saw before, which is that I am pretty angry at my mother because she is so bossy. Also, I am angry at my father because sometimes I think he does not treat my mother very well. Nevertheless, I have a good relationship with Father. The anger at my mother now, today, and not when I was little, is mostly because I wanted to go to a college where Charles was. Charles is my boyfriend and has been for the past four years, since I was sixteen; we have slept together since then, but Mother insisted that I go to a different college, which took me away from Charles. I think that has something to do with my breakdown at college and my coming home. Thinking about when I was quite small, before six years old, I have a sort of vague feeling that I always thought I was not wanted by my mother. Both parents had an attitude of 'We can't wait till you kids are out of here and Father retires. We will not be taking care of your grandchildren.' Father says that and so does Mother, but my feeling is that he does not mean it very seriously, nor does she; I can understand that."

From this point on, when she realized her attitudes and patterns toward her parents, her progress accelerated even more. About three weeks later she said, "I am now well enough to be secure and see my own dynamics. I think I could not face them before. My parents, but especially Mother, are so controlling, they try to run me. For example, I think of buying a present for my sister who is five years younger than I am. That present would be for her birthday. I have it pretty well figured out, and then my mother comes in and tells me what to get—it must not be too small, it must not be too large, etc., etc.— and tries to tell me exactly what to do and how to do it . . . that is something I cannot stand. Father, as I've told you, is always talking rejection; he says that he and Mother no longer want to work, they will leave some money but not much for me and my sister because they want to keep it to retire and travel and want to just 'dump' us girls."

I said, "Is there anything further that irritates you beyond this control and talk of rejection?"

"Yes," Martha said, "there is a third important factor, and that is the gross preference for my younger sister. She is so immature—my parents say they will not leave me any money, but they will leave some for her. If my sister dirties her clothes, she just leaves them for my mother to wash. I don't dirty my clothes; I know how to care for them, and when I *do* dirty them, I wash them out myself—but then my mother says, '*You girls* don't know how to care for your clothes, or know how to wash them.' In other words, she lumps me with my sister although this is not correct at all; but if there is a complaint about me, she complains to me but does not include my sister."

Martha continued to improve, and her boyfriend, Charles, who had stood by her during the difficult period of her anxieties, became still closer when she was well. They got an apartment together and were so happy that they hesitated to change anything by getting married. But chiefly they did not want to marry for purely financial reasons, until they both finished their education. Eventually, however, they did marry.

It is pleasant to have such a satisfactory outcome . . . in less than two years Martha went from being totally paralyzed by her anxiety, afraid to walk on the street alone, afraid to be anywhere alone, even in her own home, to obtaining a good job in which she worked well, was responsible, and enjoyed the relationships with her colleagues and friends. When I last heard, she was still very happy in her marriage.

Dynamic Diagnosis: Martha Mason

Childhood: (1) Father and Mother (especially Mother) controlling and always trying to run patient. (2) Father and Mother rejecting; they talk of "dumping" the girls and using their money to retire; patient feels unwanted. (3) Father and Mother show gross preference for Sister. This leads to hostility toward Mother (because of sibling jealousy and because she is "bossy") and some hostility toward Father, but basically patient's relations with Father are O.K.

Current: Insecure dependent love needs with Mother (and some with Father) leading to anger (the fight), rebellion (by sex), and independence leading to anxiety (the flight) as phobias.

Strengths: Identification with strong parents, basically loved during 0–6, high intelligence, drive to independence, attractiveness, and monogamous trends.

*   *   *   *   *

Martha Mason's Own Story

Martha wanted to write about her experience in therapy, for, as she put it:

"It was an experience to look back and try to remember how I felt before seeing you. I have become happy and when you are happy you do not think about the past so much. But when I made the effort to remember and even wrote some of it down, it all began to come back . . . it was so weird then. I think it would have helped me personally at the beginning of my therapy with you if I had been able to read some other patient's account of his or her treatment, telling how he or she came through it all; I always felt a certain confidence that *I* would come through. Nevertheless, I felt so weird in those days that it would have been reassuring to read what some other patient had written. And writing about oneself is therapeutic, at least it has been for me."

This, then, is Martha's own account of her therapy, which she sent to me before I left Chicago:

"When I first visited Dr. Saul my situation was absolutely desperate, and my life was ruled by anxiety, fear and depression. Unable to continue a normal life through participation in either college life or the working world, I had totally dropped out of everything to become a recluse at age twenty, living at home with my parents. I had been venturing out only for my daily trips to my psychoanalyst, Dr. Banholtz. He practiced nearly one hour's drive from my home, so my mother had to drive me there; it took from nine to twelve o'clock every morning of the week. Anxiety prevented my going alone.

"In response to my frequent skepticism about the effectiveness of his treatment, Dr. Banholtz assured me time and again that 'psychoanalysis takes a long time . . . .' Nevertheless, my only response to his treatment over the months was a continued worsening of my symptoms. I began to strongly dislike my sessions with him when I was asked to free-associate. To me it was boring, monotonous, unproductive, and Dr. Banholtz had no positive influence on me at all.

"By this time I was totally discouraged and frustrated by the seeming unavailabiity of any effective treatment. (I had seen three or four psychiatrists on a weekly basis before this.) Then I began seeing Dr. Saul. My attitude was far from optimistic as I told him my symptoms:

"I was literally paralyzed by anxiety and the many fears accompanying it—afraid of driving, being alone, attending classes, often deeply depressed, even suicidal, and in an almost constant state of emotional agony. I doubt that it is possible for a healthy individual to understand the extent of my suffering; I wonder at it myself.

"Still, I could sense that my relationship with Dr. Saul was going to be a good one—so unlike the cold, unresponsive nihilism of my former psychoanalyst. For Dr. Saul exhibited such a positive attitude, such warmth and kindness, that it began to refurbish my hopes of overcoming my problems and gave me a desire to put forth the effort needed.

"As it turned out, a *great* deal of effort was needed. I began facing my problems in a totally honest way with difficulty; it was hard to overcome strongly ingrained phobias, but I went out to do those things that I had first feared. That helped me begin to deal with my problems, and it was Dr. Saul's positive influence that precipitated it. What helped most was the feeling I got that he genuinely *liked* me, and would like me regardless of whether I made mistakes or did things that others considered wrong. (I had grown up with a mother who was also very warm, but could be judgmental at times.) In addition, Dr. Saul assured me that he was always available to me, I could telephone him any time if I needed help and support. I don't think the stabilizing effect this had on me can be overemphasized, particularly at first when I was forcing myself to go out of the house and do things that had formerly made me fearful. And I was careful not to abuse the privilege of calling Dr. Saul; just knowing that I could do so helped a lot.

"Then too, Dr. Saul was so reasonable, so rational, so realistic. He seemed to have a knack for taking the upside-down way I looked at things and turning it right-side up. He extracted clear and meaningful explanations for my jumbled emotions, and I felt he had a great deal of wisdom to offer. One of the first things he did which turned things around was to tell me that he thought my problem was simply an ordinary everyday, garden-variety anxiety and he believed that with help in understanding it I could resolve it well and rapidly with only one meeting a week. My mother worked and using up all her mornings was hard on her, as well as reducing the family income. I soon realized I was building up a huge burden of guilt to Mother and the whole family for requiring this sacrifice and my guilt dissolved with the sudden drop in these demands.

"With renewed hope in the possibility of attaining health I began to investigate my own anxiety. Before Dr. Saul suggested this approach I had never really fully realized that there was a cause and effect relationship between my emotional reactions to things that happened to me and subsequent anxiety attacks. With his help I first began to discover what was causing my anxiety, and once I had something tangible to deal with I could begin to work it out for myself. It made me feel so good just to know there were clearly definable problems that were contributing to my anxiety; this made therapy much more constructive than it had been in the past—while I was in 'psychoanalysis' I felt like I was up against a wall of anxiety but had no idea what any of the components were, so I had no way to deal with them.

"At each session with Dr. Saul I began telling him about the anxiety that I had experienced during the preceding week, and he would immediately say, 'What happened right before that?' or 'What was going on at the time?' This channeled a great deal of the energy that I would have spent merely bemoaning my anxiety into a constructive effort to analyze and correct. In fact, one of the major complaints of all those close to me during the height of my illness was that I had a 'bad attitude.' Then the criticism merely angered me because I felt no one understood my feelings, yet I was too depressed to correct the situation, and no one offered me viable suggestions. I can remember the helpless and angry feeling I would get when Mother would say, 'Your major problem is that you have a bad attitude—you have to work to correct that.' My unspoken reaction was: 'That's *not* the major problem. My attitude is bad because I'm always in pain and anxious, and I'm never without suffering. I am trying but it takes all my effort just to keep from being suicidal and I don't know what else to do! And you don't know what it feels like!'

"Coupled with this reaction was a very deep feeling of guilt because I knew that my parents and my boyfriend were giving very deeply of themselves to help me in every way that they could, and they were being unselfish and patient. Expressions of annoyance far more severe and frequent than the ones I heard from them would have been justified, I felt.

"Dr. Saul broke this angry-helpless-guilty cycle by a program of constructive probing for the reasons for my anxious reactions; I began searching for the *why* to all my fears and anxieties.

"I remember during one of our initial sessions Dr. Saul asked me a question to which he obviously attached some significance. It was, 'What is the first memory of your early childhood?' My reaction was surprise and fascination at the question, but astonishingly a very clear memory came to me almost instantly. I remembered being an infant so young that I was in a crib and wearing those little Dr. Dentin sleeper pajamas; it was in the neighbor's house across the street from my home. Evidently my mother and father had been out and the neighbor was caring for me, but my mother had come back and was putting my pajama suit on me to take me home. The most striking part of my memory was Mother buttoning the pajamas at the neck and that gave me a horribly uncomfortable feeling of being choked. I remember feeling frustrated and wishing that there was some way to tell her that I felt uncomfortable. But I was too young to talk or reach up and unbutton the pajamas for myself—there was no way to get my feelings across. Later on, Dr. Saul helped me see that this frustration played a large part in my problems.

"This memory was just one of the things that helped me begin to realize what a large part of my problems was related to the incorrect way I handled the guilt and anger cycle in which I was caught. We discovered the cycle was closely related to a feeling revealed by another event of my earliest childhood:

"Sometime between the ages of 2 and 2½ my parents went on a two-week vacation and left me with my maternal grandparents for one week and the paternal grandparents for the second week. I recall flashes of a very cold and lonely, 'I've been deserted' feeling; my grandparents have since told me that I cried a great deal of the time I was with them. Mother has often commented on my reaction when she returned: she said I acted stunned, as if I absolutely could not believe that my parents had returned at all. She says I clung to her, repeatedly saying, 'This is my mother,' as if I could not believe she was back.

"Although this experience took place so many years ago it became clear to me that it showed there were some residual effects from the anger and fear I felt at that time. One of the strongest symptoms of my current problems was a fear of being alone, and this fear had cropped up at various times during my pre-adolescent childhood as well. I have numerous memories of being left alone in the car when Mother went into a store to shop and at times I would actually panic for fear that she had deserted me and would never come back. These were traumatic emotional experiences and occurred despite the fact that I simultaneously knew Mother loved me and in reality would never leave me like that. Mother was an extremely warm and loving person, but the fears existed despite my knowledge they were irrational.

"The guilt-anxiety cycle generated a lot of anger in me; anger because I felt rejected and yet prevented from freely expressing it because I felt it would be unjustified to express it against such an obviously warm and caring mother. How could I possibly express anger toward a mother who had practically given up her whole life to drive me to my former therapist every day and cared for me in my illness? I was caught in the bondage of pent-up anger compounded by guilt for even feeling any anger. And the guilt prevented me from cleansing myself of anger through open expression, or from dealing with it in any manner. In fact at the time, I wasn't even willing to admit that I was angry! And so the acute anxiety . . . .

"My sensitivity toward feeling 'unloved' was further complicated by a rivalry with my younger sister. Once again guilt was added to my sense of anger, for I realized Sister was really a wonderful person and good to me. How could I justify anger toward her? Still, at many times during our teenage years we found ourselves competing with one another; I could not rid myself of the feeling, probably unjustified, that Mother and Father favored her. In angry reaction to the cocky, rebellious, know-it-all intellectualism that I exhibited at age sixteen, my mother once commented, 'You may be smart, and you think you are so great, but you are not nearly as kind and lovely and helpful as Leslie (my sister).' That one remark hurt me deeply, hitting a sore spot that had probably existed since my sister's birth. My mother, in fact, recalls all the attention-getting calisthenics (headstands, cartwheels, dances) that I performed in her room when she was breast-feeding Leslie. I guess I just felt that love and attention given *to* baby sister equaled love and attention taken *from* me.

"In addition to this jealousy of my sister I had further difficulties because Mother tended to be very dominant, even 'bossy.' To this I was over-sensitive and felt helpless and frustrated because I wanted to rebel against Mother, yet felt guilt about doing so. And it became a vicious cycle: the more I reacted with anxiety about this situation, the more I regressed into a childlike need of Mother. So any efforts toward achieving my greatly-needed independence were thwarted by my reactions, which included fear of being left alone. I wanted independence yet could not achieve it.

"One incident I can remember illustrates the kind of dominance Mother showed toward me. We were out shopping together and bought a plant which we later decided to return. While Mother was in another section of the store I took the plant back and said I would meet Mother at a designated place. After waiting in line to explain my reason for returning the plant to a clerk, just when the clerk and I were working out an arrangement my Mother arrived and quickly took charge. She began making all the explanations, she wanted to work out the arrangements. I deeply resented this intrusion since I felt perfectly capable and was doing a good job of it myself. I considered it to be an overt statement by Mother that she felt me incapable of handling even little things on my own. This was a typical example of what seemed to happen whenever I was with her.

"In examining the particular things I was afraid of in my current life, the dynamics of these early resentments became more clear. I feared driving—why? It seems to be a particularly strong expression of any child's independence from his or her parents to want to drive and get around by himself. But I feared stopping the car at red lights; this seemed symbolic of my fear and dislike of the restriction and control by my parents that I was trying to resist. I feared sitting in my college classes, and finally left school altogether. Just like the red light, I looked upon this as a forced control, a restriction, for I *had to* stay in the classroom until the class was over. It was reminiscent of the uncomfortably-tight button on my pajamas when I was very young.

"Once I understood that these factors were the cause of my anxiety, prohibiting me from living a normal, productive life, it became much easier to deal with the real causes of my fears. As a result I began going for walks alone, starting with short distances, and looking for jobs. When I made those first efforts in these areas I began to break out of the cycle of fear that had imprisoned me for nearly two years.

"Some physical discoveries were made about me by my internist, whom Dr. Saul thought I should see for a thorough physical examination. It turned out that I had diabetic tendencies, and am currently overtly diabetic, but once brought under control it became a lot easier for me to make the transition into an active, happy, functioning life. The physical problems had aggravated and worked with my emotional problems to cause my withdrawal from everyday living. But when the diabetes was diagnosed and treatment effected, it was a 'shot in the arm' for me and my efforts to dig out of the bondage of emotional illness.

"It has been months since I have felt the need for an appointment with Dr. Saul; the change in my life has been nothing short of radical. I am happy, content, married, working full time, active in church and social activities. The change in me has been from a suffering invalid to a healthy, productive and fulfilled person, and I am thankful to have had the opportunity to participate in therapy that was so meaningful, so workable, and which played such a large part in bringing me back to health."

References

Mahler, M. (1965): On the significance of the normal separation-individuation phase, in *Drives, Affects, Behavior*, vol. 2, ed. M. Schur. New York: International Universities Press, pp. 161–169.

———— (1968): On human symbiosis and the vicissitudes of individuation, *Annual Progress in Child Psychiatry*, pp. 109–129.

Saul, L. (1971): *Emotional Maturity*, Third Edition. Philadelphia: Lippincott.

———— (1972): *Psychodynamically Based Psychotherapy*. New York: Science House.

SECTION III:
SOME IMPLICATIONS
OF CHILDHOOD
EMOTIONAL PATTERNS

14
SEQUESTRATION

A concise written formulation of a patient's basic pattern, even if not entirely complete or even not entirely accurate in every detail, is still a potent tool for therapy in many ways.

Soon after an intensive, comprehensive review of the childhood pattern, bits and pieces of it usually emerge with special emphasis and clarity in the following meetings. And such a review helps the patient gain a perspective on his problem, a certain distance from it. This process has been called "sequestration," in analogy to the detachment and walling off of infected bone in osteomyelitis (Alexander, 1961, pp. 253–256).

To illustrate, Hortense Thompson (p. 101) as a result of relative neglect in her 0–3 and of growing up later in the position of "only the little sister," who could not join the family talk at the dinner table and could never be expected to accomplish anything "significant" or "worthwhile," as her parents already had and as her four-year-older brother was expected to do, continued this feeling of inadequacy in adult life. It inhibited everything she tried to do. I tried to convince her of the reality—that there was nothing wrong with her intellect or her body. She was in fact superior in looks, youth, attractiveness, brains, and vitality and could do anything—there was indeed nothing wrong with the instrument. Meanwhile, her associations were all complaints that finishing graduate school was too much. I pointed out her unconscious transference tendency to manipulate me into the same attitudes that her parents and brother had, namely, to get me to say, "You are right, it is too much for you, *we* can do it but you are only the little sister and cannot." I could also point out to her accurately and truthfully, "there is nothing the matter with *you*. You have all that it takes. Only *you* are interfered with by this fragment of childhood pattern, which is like a foreign body, like a splinter in a sound, strong muscle that causes pain and inhibits its use. There, sequestrated, is the childhood problem that is inhibiting you. You have what it takes and in superior degree—it is this foreign body, this bit of your childhood dynamics, which we must soften up and reduce."

References

Alexander, F. (1961): *Scope of Psychoanalysis.* New York: Basic Books, pp. 253–256.

15
TERMINATION

If the analyst is able to summarize in words what he and the patient agree upon as the main pathodynamic pattern and further to condense this to a diagnosis, then toward the end of an analysis both can see what remains to be worked through. This provides at least some end point, rather than only the general feeling that the law of diminishing returns is setting in.

Rachel Roswell seemed quite happy and satisfied with her analysis and was making perceptible progress on her own. But occasionally she would phone me with some problem and come in, and after two or three interviews she would feel she had finished and should stop. This she and I both agreed was a manifestation in the transference to me of the childhood pattern toward her mother. She missed me, wanted me, but then as soon as we were in touch by visits or phone, Rachel felt I was controlling her life and that she must break off and do it on her own. She soon saw that this pattern toward her needed-but-controlling mother lurked in the transference. This was the real reason for her behavior—the time she must take for analysis, the interruptions, and money all played a part, but were mostly rationalizations. The other residue was a lack of a satisfying identity with an absent, disinterested father; a distant, overcontrolling mother; and brothers who displaced her and were favored by her mother. Thus, we could define what needed working through and proceed with the job systematically.

Pat Ralston reached a greatly improved relationship with her husband, but still seemed wary of me. Here, too, the pattern of fear of frankness and of opening up her feelings including the deep resentment she had felt all her life toward her mother continued beneath the surface in the transference to me. Defining it sharply helped us focus on the remaining dynamics that required working through, and speeded up this process. These are examples of what is true for almost every patient.

Dynamic diagnoses are not always easy to formulate accurately and sometimes take many days, even weeks, and many revisions. But they can be an indispensible tool of therapy. For *every* analytic hour reflects one or another bit or facet of this nuclear interplay of emotional forces and reactions. Hence, it is so useful, even indispensable, to have a condensed formulation in mind, but always to be open to revising it in the light of new material and insights as they arise.

As remarked previously, keeping the detailed notes of the interviews in which dynamic diagnoses were obtained and re-reading them from time to time can be a valuable therapeutic aid. No one has a flawless memory, able to retain every detail, and re-reading these notes occasionally sometimes recalls to the analyst those details which are important for effecting the best possible therapy.

Another important advantage of precisely formulating the childhood emotional pattern and its distillation into the formula of a dynamic diagnosis is that these formulations provide a guide to recognizing and understanding the transference. As always, the analyst must shun preconceived ideas as to the transference and must read it as it is. Nevertheless, he must be aware of certain probabilities and possibilities, and be certain not to miss these if they are present. A patient told of being punished as a child for revealing a secret. With this material prominent in his 0–6, the analyst must be alert to his possible fear of associating freely, i.e., of telling secrets to the analyst.

Usually I make these formulations of the summaries of 0–6 and the highly condensed abstracts, the dynamic diagnoses, in the evening when I have the leisure to concentrate uninterruptedly. But then I go over them in minute detail with the patient, every thought and every word chosen to express them succinctly. And the patient usually suggests emendations that sharpen the formulation of the childhood pattern and its effects on the present-day patterns of his life. Developing these highly condensed formulations of the early childhood pattern and of the essentials of the current dynamics is not easy, but requires considerable concentrated mental effort.

As already stated, the emotional impact of this process can be powerful. For example, when Amy Colton (see p. 161) came to the session after our formulating her dynamic diagnosis, her first words were, "Put back in 'deprivation' and 'rage.' I resisted using them last week, but that was because it took some time for it to sink in. I have been weeping and having cramps in my stomach ever since. I'm still very upset. This is going to be a Kleenex hour. I can't quite understand it all, but I think partly it shattered my myth of my happy childhood—even though we've been seeing for a whole year how it really was. But it never struck me as *un*happy until we made that little card!" Amy quieted down during this hour, in which I let her talk without interruption, but at the end of it I pointed out that she was in reality a good and, in many ways, a superior person, with relative youth, strength, a fine mind, an unusual imagination, basic good health, reasonably good looks and personality. The card represented not "herself" but a foreign body in her personality like a splinter in her finger. The card stated the problem that needed to be solved, reduced, outgrown, gotten rid of so far as possible. This she could see, and she thereby gained a sharper perspective on herself and her problem, and was able to work more smoothly and effectively in her analytic therapy.

Working out the dynamic diagnosis can be helpful even if it is not entirely complete or correct, and even if the emphasis is somewhat wrong. For it provides at least a skeletal outline of the main issues. It can be taken as a model to be worked from and also with; naturally, as each hour's work of the analysis proceeds, much is learned that can modify the childhood pattern which analyst and patient have in mind. Hence, having this skeleton as a model to start with, both analyst and patient have at least a concept of the main interplay of forces in the patient and can modify the formulation as both learn more. This is the usual method of science: accumulating enough facts to make a workable theory and then further testing the theory with more facts, modifying the theory to fit the whole picture. An example of this is Hortense Thompson. (p. 000) In her case, my first dynamic diagnosis was somewhat incomplete in the matter of *emphasis*.

What emerged so clearly over a number of months of analysis was the symbolic scene of the family together. In this scene, Hortense's parents and older brother engaged in discussion of the events of the day. Hortense was only the little sister, and if she said anything it seemed to be of no significance, and she was more or less silenced by her parents. Then, either for speaking up and interrupting them or because of her anger for being silenced, she would be sent to her room. It was this that gave her a sense of not being valued and also a sense of futility in trying to contribute anything significant. It never worked; all she got was criticism or rejection. Either directly or indirectly she got angry and then was banished because of her anger. This played a considerable role in her whole personality and expectations toward people, always expecting to fail, not to be accepted, not to be valued; and it also played a specific part in her inability to write. She was afraid that anything she said or wrote would be of no value and she would get only criticism for it. Hence her inhibition in speaking and writing.

My mistake in this first formulation lay in not giving sufficient emphasis to the first two or three years of Hortense's life. During this time, her 0–3, her father was away practically all the time; she saw almost nothing of him. But also, her mother was helping out by holding down a job, so Hortense also saw very little of her either. Therefore, the feeling of neglect and rejection and not being valued dated back from birth to age three, and it was into this soil (of rejection, isolation, and early feelings of not being valued) that the trauma of being excluded from family conversation later fell. She already had this vulnerability in her makeup by the age of three. When she was excluded from the family discussions, something of an overreaction occurred, because the early groundwork had been laid when the parents were away working during earlier years. She was not secure enough in the love of her parents during the neglect of her 0–3 to be able to tolerate this exclusion later on.

As this material emerged clearly and definitely in her analysis, it was not necessary to rewrite completely her dynamic diagnosis, but only to modify it, making it more accurate and complete.

In another case, tensions in the home did not appear in the early material of the patient because he was reacting so strongly to pressures outside his home. A review of this patient's 0–6 after some months of analysis, when he was less upset by external pressures, brought out the intrafamily pressures. It was this combination of pressures within the family and outside it that created more strain than his immature ego could handle and caused the regression by extreme withdrawal.

Sometimes a patient does not feel the impact of a review of his 0–6 at the time it is done, although most patients do; but he *does* feel it when the analyst during a later hour reads back the review and dynamic diagnosis to the patient.

Familiarity with the patient's childhood pattern and dynamic diagnosis introduces nothing entirely new to the problem of terminating treatment, but it can make the decision a little more rational and precise, in this way:

The analyst must ask himself, and discuss with the patient, whether the pathological elements in all of the childhood relationships have been adequately worked through, and whether their results in the patient's current motivations as finally formulated in the dynamic diagnosis are sufficiently on their way to resolution. Doing this systematically for each relationship and each part of the current dynamics usually makes the criteria for termination a little more concrete and accurate, and provides a rational guide for the decision— certainly a rational, systematic guide that goes far deeper than relief of symptoms or a sense of slowed-down analytic progress.

It is extremely difficult for an analyst to be able to hold in therapy a person with no good relationship during 0–6.

Terry Weston teetered in uncertainty against a strong resistance at the beginning of treatment and continued, I think, only because of a relatively good relationship with her father during 0–6. Wilma Blake's early relations were disturbed enough to result in psychotic breaks with institutionalization, yet there was enough good in her human relations in her earliest childhood for her to continue in analytic therapy and work through her powerful resistances against it. She finally stabilized in a relatively happy marriage.

As Freud said, the patient soon slips the analyst into the place of some kindly childhood image and then can analyse with him. But if a person has no such good image, then, however keen and alert the analyst, there is no way to get the analysis started, for there is no positive transference to carry the patient through the resistance.

16
SELF-ANALYSIS

Can a person help himself by analyzing himself? Apparently Freud did so to some extent (Jones, 1952), relieving himself of a phobia. The difficulty of analyzing oneself lies in two areas: insight is the indispensable first step, but is not the last step; although it reveals the emotional problem, it does not solve it. Resolution is accomplished in therapy primarily through the use of the "transference," i.e., the working out of the childhood pattern as it emerges toward the analyst in the office as a laboratory sample of the patient's human relationships. In self-analysis there is no transference to "carry" the process.

However, progress in insight and in the resolution of problems takes place mostly after an analysis; and if the analysis was well done, the progress continues for life. In other words, the analysis has provided the insight and initiated a process of outgrowing the childhood pattern that continues through insightful practice in living for all the rest of one's days. Much of the "cure" takes both insight and practice in living. If a person is well aware of his tendency to be overly dependent, he can work on it consciously and reduce it as he sees it appear in many aspects of his daily life. The same is true for other trends, such as hostility, vanity, overcompetitiveness.

It is therefore possible that a person with adequate psychological capacity, if he knows what to look for, can discern his own childhood pattern and the difficulties it is causing in his current life. Or he can learn it from a skilled therapist who is able to see his pattern in only a few interviews, so that thereafter the individual has sufficient insight into the *essentials* of his problem to make progress with them on his own. If so, occasional visits to the therapist may keep him on the right track. Thus, a thorough understanding and appreciation of childhood emotional problems can help certain persons, once they have adequate insight, to make considerable analytic progress on their own—through living—with a minimum of therapeutic help.

References

Jones, E. (1952): *The Life and Work of Sigmund Freud.* New York: Basic Books.

17
MARRIAGE

As we have said before, each person tends to repeat toward other persons in some form and degree the patterns into which he was molded by the pressures upon him as a child, by those persons most important for him emotionally, from birth to about six years old. The tendency to repeat these patterns occurs regardless of age or sex. Men thrown together and women thrown together tend to repeat them toward each other. Marriage is a special case of this repetition by two adults toward each other of patterns formed in childhood.

The first special feature is the intimacy. While an adult relationship is relatively loose and distant, the ego (the mature standards, sense, and judgment) can control the interplay of feelings between them, keeping a certain calm and harmony. But with continuing closeness, the old childhood patterns, however repressed, gradually, sooner or later, emerge toward each other. This is the interpersonal (to use Harry Stack Sullivan's term) pattern of childhood, revivified in an adult edition by a continuing degree of closeness unknown since early life (Mullahy, 1970).

The small child is physically far too weak to stand up to adults and older siblings, and often resorts to other methods of resistance and hostility, such as refusal to eat or other passive or secret disobedience. The husband usually has at least two advantages over his wife: first is physical strength. For example, a patient told me that for years her husband's favorite pastime was raping her. The husband's other big advantage, at least traditionally and before women's liberation, was breadwinning—that is, his job, which took him physically and psychologically out of the house all day, diverted him from marital problems and gave him a sense of prestige and financial security.

The wife's special advantage is more subtle. It lies in the tendency of every man who is anywhere near normal to react eventually to every woman as though she were his mother; this is usually part of his deepest childhood pattern. Perhaps this is why (from my experience) it seems that those marriages work the best which are matriarchies—marriages in which the most powerful man in the big bad world, once he crosses the threshold into his own home, accedes to his wife as mistress of the home.

The above is an effort to deduce from a knowledge of childhood patterns some fundamental generalizations about marriage; exception can be found wherever the neurosis, i.e., the excessive predominance of a disordered childhood pattern, is extreme.

The obviously complicating feature in the relationship of two people in marriage is sexual intercourse. To have this at all, the man must have an erection, and that is something beyond conscious control. Powerful as the sex drive is, it is also sensitive in the extreme to the emotional state. Some degree of impotence in men and some amount of frigidity in women is said to occur in nearly half of the adult population. This is not too surprising if one considers that the early training of children is generally inhibitory of sex play, and conveys the idea that sex is wrong, at least until marriage. Also, since the sexual feelings follow the strongest emotional attachments, they are usually toward family members and therefore incestuous, and subject to the usual taboos. One husband, a big, strong and attractive man, was only potent when in a certain internal state of mind, in which case, without warning, he would rush across the room and practically rape his wife. When in bed or in a tender relationship he was impotent. As she described it, he made hate not love.

Another husband had no problem with potency, but derived no satisfaction from coitus unless his wife had an orgasm, which she could do only with difficulty, especially when she felt obligated by her husband's attitude.

Of course, women have problems also. One couple were very harmonious, but as time passed the wife lost sex interest in her husband. She had no complaints about him, but simply no longer desired him physically and even resented his making her have an orgasm. Yet she met another man with whom she had an orgasm if he only put his arms around her.

Thus even the physical need for coitus is sensitive to the childhood patterns and can complicate their interaction between husband and wife. There is no need here to discuss its role in homosexuality. (Saul and Beck, 1961).

Just how sensitive the physiological sexual functioning is, the analyst frequently sees:

A couple about twenty years old "go steady" for two years, often sleeping together and having satisfying coitus. Then they marry, and the wife complains that almost immediately after the ceremony her husband becomes extremely dependent upon her and shows almost no affection or sexual interest, so that she is starving physically and emotionally.

In a marriage the most fateful expression of the childhood pattern is in the adult parent toward the children, whether expressed directly toward the children or indirectly by its effects on the marriage, or in providing the children a figure with whom to identify. For this childhood pattern is what makes the parent a good one, who can facilitate the child's development to healthy maturity; or it can inhibit and warp the child's development to form neurosis, psychosis, perversion, addiction, and criminality. Thus, it is this pattern that makes the kind of world in which each generation must live, and determines humanity's misery and the ultimate question of whether or not *homo sapiens* will survive.

References

Mullahy, P. (1970): *Psychoanalysis and Interpersonal Psychiatry: The Contributions of Harry Stack Sullivan.* New York: Science House.

Saul, L., and Beck, A. (1961): Psychodynamics of male homosexuality, *Intl. J. Psycho-Analysis* 42: Parts I–II.

18
RESPONSIBILITY

Blessed is he who has found his work; let him ask no other blessedness.

Thomas Carlyle

I

Reactive cases aside (i.e., relatively healthy persons who break down under unusual and excessive environmental pressures, as in war, for example), the degree to which the childhood pattern dominates a person's life determines the degree of his neurosis. For that is what neurosis is—the excessive predominance in adult life of childhood patterns of feeling, thinking, and behavior. If they are so strong as to swamp the ego, the person is to that degree psychotic. If the hostile elements predominate and are acted out, then to that extent he is criminal.

The concept of regression appears throughout Freud's writings and he devotes a chapter of his *Introductory Lectures* (1916) to a lucid explication of it. Hence we know what the regression is *to*, namely, a previous stage or pattern in the emotional development. But Freud devoted less attention to what the regression is *from*, beyond the concept of the "genital level" and "object interest" as the mature stages of the development of the libido. It seems to this author that in the analyst's actual clinical experience, in his daily *observation* of his patients rather than in theoretical concepts, the regression is largely from the patient's *independence* and *responsibility* for himself and those dependent upon him, usually his spouse and children, and others involved in his occupation and his society. A student who is supported emotionally and financially by his parents may only have the responsibility of learning and of passing his examinations— Eisenhower had the responsibility of destroying the German armies. Thus, the degree and kind of independence and responsibility vary widely, but the *capacity to carry it*—the energy, judgment, and sense of commitment, interest, and obligation—all these forces of ego, id, and superego must be there and constitute, in this author's opinion, one of the essentials of emotional maturity (Saul, 1971, Chaps. 1, 2, 3).

Proper, adequate maturing (without which a satisfying adult life is impossible) involves sufficient "outgrowing" of these emotional patterns of childhood: the too strong dependent love needs, identifications, narcissism, inferiority feelings, competitiveness, and too-ready distortion of reality by one's wishes, in favor of relative, realistic independence and responsibility for self, intimates, and society (Saul, 1971, pp. 23–46).

A review of the literature, which covers those references included in this chapter's bibliography, shows that responsibility (for self, others, and work) has received little direct, explicit attention as a part of psychodynamics and as a fundamental in the capacities of the individual for mature function.

II

First, let us consider the nature of responsibility in terms of its "historics," and then something of its dynamics. Responsibility as seen in the history of every individual is about the same in almost all species, and certainly in all mammals, including man. It is therefore a basic biological force, motivation, or capacity. Ontogenetically, the unborn child seems incapable of any responsibility whatever. Only after birth does it become able even to breathe for itself and, soon after, to take in liquid food. Even when these functions—the respiratory and the gastrointestinal—are well established, the amount of responsibility it can take for itself is negligible or nonexistent. Someone else, its mother or substitute, must take all other responsibility for it—food, air, warmth, shelter, protection, everything upon which life depends—or the infant will not survive at all for more than a few days. Responsibility for the young, then, appears during pregnancy and at birth as a function so demanding and burdensome that the mother may need to share it with others. It has been shared traditionally with the father, whose work provides the home and food for mother and child, and often also shared with persons who help in the direct care of the child, e.g., grandparent, older child, relative, friend, or paid helper. The infant gradually develops the ability to crawl and then walk, which means that it can take some responsibility for moving by itself, and need no longer be completely dependent on being carried by someone responsible for it. In time, it becomes able to feed itself and to dress itself, relieving others of that responsibility also. Later it becomes capable of taking some responsibility for something outside of itself, such as helping set or clear the table at mealtime. In time, too, it becomes able to take care of itself not only within the home but outside it, and can go to and from school and run simple errands. It becomes able to earn some money by delivering newspapers or other simple, socially useful work. It becomes able to take responsibility for doing its schoolwork and for getting along with people outside the family. A difficult responsibility in adolescence is handling relationships to the opposite sex, and then come the two great decision-making responsibilities of postadolescent or early adult life: choice of career and earning a living, and choice of mate and rearing young. Thus the parasitic fetus and utterly helpless infant, for whose existence every responsibility *must be taken* by its parents or substitutes, develops into an adult responsible for himself or herself and also for his or her own spouse, children, and society. It seems to me that just as Freud was able to describe the maturation of personality very largely in terms of the libidinal development, so this maturation of personality also can be described in terms of the development of responsibility (Benedek, 1950, 1959).

Perhaps responsibility can be thought of as a manifestation of libido, that is, of "object interest." But responsibility—whatever its sources—is of such enormous importance in the development of personality and in its disorders that it demands specific recognition and study for itself. The sense of responsibility, the capacity for it, and the willingness to undertake it are the results of long development and are strongly influenced by how the child is reared and by the dynamics of his emotional relations with family members or substitutes. Like all human functions, it can be either inhibited or exaggerated by emotional forces and unconscious patterns.

III

Following these remarks on the *history* of responsibility in the *individual*, we consider its *most common dynamics*. These are seen in almost every patient and are its relations with regression: (1) relinquishing responsibility usually causes feelings of inferiority, narcissism, and the fight-flight reaction; and (2) carrying responsibility but protesting against it arouses the fight-flight reaction. Whatever the details of the psychology of regression, its central effect is usually the tendency to relinquish responsibility. Withdrawal is usually a withdrawal from personal relations and from responsibility for self and others (Saul, 1971).

Occasionally, however, a person plunges *into* responsibilities as a withdrawal from close human relations, e.g., Oliver Dixon, p. 183. A withdrawal that involves failure to carry the responsibilities that others carry or that persons in one's childhood carried usually makes the patient feel like a child again, with others having to take responsibility to some extent for him, a situation that creates feelings of inferiority which hurt his self-esteem. This, in turn, often generates overcompensatory overestimation of the self, an intensified secondary narcissism (Freud, 1914). The underlying hurt narcissism makes anger, guilt, and anxiety. However, if the person does not escape responsibility but accepts and discharges it, yet the responsibility is demanding beyond his emotional means and contrary to strong regressive forces, then he also becomes angry and hostile, because he is forcing himself to do more than he can adapt to emotionally. Whatever the frustration, the reaction to it is regularly the fight-flight response, resulting in rage and regression with all their consequences.

The basic instinctual conflict here is between the progressive trends to responsibility, independence, and maturity and the regressive trends to earlier passive-receptive-dependent childhood patterns. Responsibility enters into all or almost all dynamics. Its impairment is seen in problems ranging from simple schizophrenia with its almost total withdrawal from responsibility, through the neuroses, addictions, and perversions, and in many neurotic and psychotic and criminal personalities.

The *sources* of the *capacity* for responsibility lie, it seems, in all three groupings of the personality functions: In part it stems from the id, being an important element, as we have said, in the whole process of maturing in every human, and seen throughout the animal kingdom. In part it is motivated by the superego, as an ideal and a sense of duty learned from authority figures, especially identification with those who were responsible for one in childhood (Freud, 1940b). In part, it seems to be an ego function, connected with awareness, consciousness, and recognition of the "reality principle," and also with "psychic energy." The connections with intelligence, physical vitality, fixation, regression, hostility and maturity, thought, and so on require detailed study.

Of course, there is a *specificity* to responsibility. A person may take responsibility for some things and do them easily, but not for other things. One woman is rapidly exhausted by her children but can enjoy and work well in a job. Another is the opposite, enjoying the demands of her children but unable to take any responsibility outside of the home.

Responsibility is generally of vital importance in the relatively healthy as well as in persons with more or less serious emotional problems. It is often important, as we have stressed, in arousing the fight-flight reaction, and therefore for all forms of regression and escape, and for all forms of hostility. It is an important element in emotional balance, how much one receives versus how much he expends—the "give-get" balance.

Needless to say, responsibility enters into all dynamics, not only the two major ones which we have mentioned; these "give-get" dynamics of protest and anger from taking too much responsibility versus hurt pride and self-esteem because of regression from responsibility seem to be universal basic dynamics. In fact, maturity can almost be defined in a single word, and that word is "responsibility." To be an adult, a mature adult, means to be responsible for one's own self and others, and contains that other essential of maturity, the feeling that to be adult is to be alone, but that being alone means very closely to be alone in one's ultimate decisions. One is alone in having to take eventually and essentially the full responsibility for what one decides, does, and does not do. To be an adult is very largely to be alone and to be responsible; the reward is invaluable, for the reward is feeling able to carry the responsibility for one's own life and those dependent upon one, with a sense of freedom and security.

IV

With some oversimplification, the genetic-dynamics of the inhibition of responsibility can be reduced to three groups: (1) those persons in whom responsibilty is blocked by childhood patterns; (2) those who are in rebellion because of having been forced prematurely into excessive responsibility; and (3) those with miscellaneous dynamics of all sorts, including exaggerated oedipal or sibling rivalry and any disordered childhood pattern that makes one want to give up and quit trying.

Exemplifying the first group is a young woman in her early thirties, a college graduate, who is unable to marry or hold a job (see Sally Bates p. 177). Her first memory is of being confined to her room with some illness and looking out a window at some children playing. This memory epitomizes her whole life. She was an only child, born to parents almost forty years old, and she had repeated illnesses throughout childhood. The parents, understandably, became extremely overprotective and restricted her activities. At the slightest inclemancy of weather they would not let her out at all. Her mother had little patience. When the girl tried to take simple responsibility in the house, for example, peeling potatoes, her mother took over and discharged every task so rapidly and efficiently that the child eventually gave up trying. As a young adult she disliked responsibilities of any kind and felt incapable of carrying them. She had several jobs, but they were too much for her emotionally; she retreated to her home, where everything was provided by her parents. She came for help because of feeling inferior and frustrated. It soon became evident that now she bitterly resented the overprotection and indulgence, but could not achieve a reasonable degree of independence and capacity for responsibilities without analytic help.

Exemplifying the second group is the boy, oldest of six children, who was forced from before the age of six to help materially in the care of his younger siblings and, when older, was in addition pushed to earn money by baby-sitting and delivering newspapers, and, later, by odd jobs and grass-cutting. This premature, unceremonious forcing into responsibilities at the cost of his own needs for play and his jealousy and resentment of the younger children left him with a hatred of responsibilities and a withdrawal from them when he entered his mid-twenties. He came for help because of incipient alcoholism, depression, and anxiety about his future.

One illustration of the third group was the son of an immigrant family. He had a three-years-younger sister over whom he was preferred. His mother doted on him, overprotected him, and did everything for him, while at the same time making clear that he was far better in her eyes than his father, who was hard-working and financially successful, but still retained his foreign accent. The mother made clear in her attitudes that the son was the family champion and would achieve limitless fame and fortune far beyond his father. Overprotected, the son grew up with a distaste for responsibility but an intense narcissistically competitive drive for success. He drove himself in his work in order to achieve the narcissistic satisfaction of surpassing his father, now experienced by him as a need to surpass every competitor. At the same time, he could not relax, because that meant being like his younger sister, i.e., a nobody in his mother's eyes. As he neared thirty the strain became too great, and he came for analytic help out of fear of losing his sanity.

V

Mentioned above are certain individual motivations that are fundamental, e.g., the child's dependence upon the mother and its needs for love. This fundamental force is reviewed in detail in *Dependence in Man* (Parens and Saul, 1972). Hostility and aggression are currently attracting more studies (Brenner, 1971; Carthy and Ebling, 1964; Chagnon, 1968; Erikson, 1965; Storr, 1968; Hartmann et al., 1949; Saul, 1976). Responsibility ranks, I believe, with these other fundamental forces and capacities of the mind.

Historically, the American frontier required of each individual that he assume responsibility for what had to be done for himself, his family, and his community; who did not work, did not eat. Thus, the colonies quickly developed the moral and ethical ideal of the self-reliant, responsible personality in opposition to the old European feudal ideal of an aristocracy.

Thomas Jefferson is a fascinating study of superior maturity and capacity for responsibility in conflict with regressive desires to abandon everything and withdraw to Monticello.

The deep interest, enormous capacity for hard work, and consequent great productivity of outstanding creators contrasts with the extreme passivity of some passive-dependent-receptive, irresponsible borderline schizoid patients. With our psychoanalytic observations on the neuroses, this contrast strongly suggests, as mentioned above, that the capacity for and enjoyment of responsibility is part of the libidinal development to object interest and is subject to the same vicissitudes as Freud described (1940).

Bill Williams was fixated, by overindulgence, in an excessively strong passive-dependent attachment to his mother. Life outside the home was a struggle for him, despite his superior mind and athletic prowess. In engineering school he became irritable, antisocial, downright mean to his beautiful, intelligent, and hard-working young wife. He began to neglect his studies. Bill had a nightmare one night that his wife left him. A few nights later he dreamed that he was in the Army but escaping. To this he associated the engineering school. Thus, he revealed his wish to shuffle off the responsibilities of wife and training for an independent career and his rage at carrying these responsibilities.

A patient with dynamics complementary to those of Bill Williams is Linda Bassett. As a child, her mother socialized her not by winning her with loving gradualness but with a rather dogmatic, dictatorial attitude. This caused a sense of being dominated and of interference with Linda's autonomy and identity. She grew up to be attractive and intellectually superior. She found identity as a wife and mother of three children. However, the old childhood feeling of impaired identity persisted, and she felt that she could not fulfill herself in the marriage alone, but only if she made some sort of success on her own independently in the big world. This feeling spurred her to take on broad and weighty responsibilities, first for local groups and then, because of her successes through intelligence, sense of responsibility, and hard work, for a large national organization.

Thus, Bill Williams' dynamics of fight-flight caused intense rage against his necessary responsibilities of young adulthood and also caused regressive drives to escape from them back to the passive, dependent, irresponsible position of child to mother. Linda's dynamics spurred her to take on and enjoy weighty responsibilities that were unnecessary; for her husband was quite happy to support her, and she could have chosen a life of relative ease and leisure as the children grew up, with the younger ones requiring decreasing attention while the older went away to college.

These two patients exemplify the kind of responsibility which we are discussing here.

Psychoanalytic therapy is very largely concerned in almost every patient with keeping him going independently and responsibly in life or returning him from a dependence upon a hospital or upon *others* who are responsible for him to *his own* independent responsibility. This concern must always be clearly recognized and the dynamics thoroughly understood and analyzed.

The relation of responsibility to adaptation must of course take into account the age of the individual and the environment to which he is expected to adapt. As mentioned above, the small infant is necessarily relatively free of responsibilities, which increase usually to a plateau during maturity; then aging diminishes the individual's waning physical powers and energies.

Acquaintance with one's own childhood emotional patterns increases one's ability to handle and outgrow those parts of them that cause troubles in one's life. In other words, this insight increases one's ability to take responsibility for himself. "Know thyself"—this is a sound and important goal. The means for achieving it, at least in part, should be provided by *education* offered to all students at the upper high school and college levels. This can be done by providing professionals who are qualified to discern the childhood patterns in each student in a few interviews. It should be an essential of a liberal education.

To summarize, responsibility is a fundamental force or capacity for development and for psychopathology. It is seen throughout the animal kingdom, particularly in mammals. The newborn are almost completely helpless; a long course of development leads to the ability to take responsibility for self, mate, young, and society. Responsibility has received little specific study in the psychoanalytic literature, where it is dealt with chiefly in regard to the problem of free will and psychic determinism, and psychoforensic problems of responsibility for one's actions. The basic psychodynamics of responsibility stem mostly from its conflict with the contrary forces of regression. A person who yields to regression and withdraws from responsibility usually feels inferior, and his hurt narcissism mobilizes the fight-flight reaction with hostility, anxiety, and further withdrawal. A person who does not relinquish responsibility but has an underlying protest against carrying it also sustains an arousal, by the protest, of his fight-flight reaction, with the usual consequences of anxiety, anger, and tendencies to regress. There is a specificity to responsibility. One person can take responsibility easily and enjoyably for home and children, but not for work. Another person is the opposite. It is vitally important for analytic theory and therapy to be explicitly aware of responsibility and its dynamics in the childhood pattern of every patient and to analyze it thoroughly.

The capacity for responsibility for self and others seems to derive from all three parts of the personality—id, ego, and superego. Ethological studies show that responsibility in the *id* is expressed by man and all forms of mammals as parental love and care and in forms of work to obtain food and shelter. In addition, a direct appeal to the *ego* to understand and carry responsibility is important therapeutically. The care and attention given a child by his parents throughout his development are models of parental responsibility; thus it becomes an intrinsic part of the child's *superego*. Responsibility is also connected with narcissism, strengthening the ego's self-respect and pride. To reject responsibility can be a negative, hostile defiance of the parent and the superego. The capacity for enjoying responsibility seems part of the libidinal development to object interest. In this country, the idealogy of responsibility stems historically from the pioneer ethic, in which, of necessity, the individual who did not work did not eat.

References

Benedek, T. (1950): Climaterium: a developmental phase, *Psychoanal. Quart.* 19:1–27.

————— (1959): Parenthood as a developmental phase, *J. Am. Psychoanal. Assn.* 7(3): 389–417.

Brenner, C. (1971): The psychoanalytic concept of aggression, *Intl. J. Psychoanal.* 52(2):139.

Carthy, J. D., and Ebling, F. J., eds. (1964): *The Natural History of Aggression.* London and New York: Academic Press.

Chagnon, N. (1968): Yanomamo social organization and warfare, in *The Anthropology of Armed Conflict and Aggression,* ed. M. Fried, M. Harris, and R. Murphy. New York: Natural History Press, pp. 128–129.

Erikson, E. (1965): Psychoanalysis and ongoing history: problems of identity, hatred and nonviolence, *Am. J. Psychiatry,* pp. 241–250.

Freud, S. (1914): On narcissism: an introduction, *S.E.* 14:73–102.

————— (1916): Some thoughts on development and regression, *S.E.* 16:339.

————— (1940a): An outline of psychoanalysis, Part I, *S.E.* 23:144.

————— (1940b): Ibid., Part III, Chap. IX.

Hartmann, H., Kris, E., and Lowenstein, R. M. (1949): Notes on the theory of aggression, in *Psychoanal. Study of the Child.* New York: International Universities Press, III/IV, pp. 9–36.

Mark, V., and Ervin, F. (1970): *Violence and The Brain.* New York: Harper & Row.

Matthews, L. (1964): Overt fighting in mammals, in *The Natural History of Aggression,* ed. J. D. Carthy and F. J. Ebling. London and New York: Academic Press, pp. 23–32.

Parens, H., and Saul, L. (1971): *Dependence in Man.* New York: International Universities Press.

Rochlin, G. (1973): *Man's Aggression, The Defense of the Self.* Boston: Gambit.

Saul, L. (1971): *Emotional Maturity*, Third Edition. Philadelphia: Lippincott.

———— (1976): *The Psychodynamics of Hostility.* New York: Jason Aronson, Inc.

Storr, A. (1968): *Human Aggression.* New York: Atheneum.

19
RAISING CHILDREN AND
A PROGNOSIS

To be happy at home is the ultimate result of all ambition, the end to which every enterprise and labor bends, and of which every desire prompts the prosecution.

Samuel Johnson

The kind of clinical observations used in this book provides an understanding of the adult which we trace back to its roots in early childhood. In this process we search for causes for the problems we endeavor to resolve. Can we, by observing the child from 0–6, predict what problems he will have when he becomes an adult? To do this with precision and reasonable confidence (scientifically speaking) would require intimate, detailed knowledge of the emotional interplay of the child with those close to him and responsible for him during those earliest years. To obtain such observations would be in itself a formidable task. Predictions would have to be written down and checked with the observations of the adult 20 or 30 years later. Enormously difficult as such a study would be, it has been already undertaken. (Escalona 1963, 1968) But until full results are in from a number of different researchers on this critical question, can we deduce anything from the observations made in this book? I think so.

We have observed symptoms and problems in the adult and traced them to disorders in human relationships occurring in earliest childhood. Reviewing the clinical examples, we can deduce that the child's treatment in childhood determined his current problems as an adult. Therefore, we can make a list of "don'ts" for parents. But can we reduce even these to a few essentials? This author's conclusions are:

The fundamentals of childrearing are simple, if not always easy. Basically, the key is *good feeling* between child and parent and others in the child's orbit. Proper childrearing is not a matter of techniques, is not strictness or permissiveness or even the question of "spank or don't spank" . . . the essence is to keep an interchange of good feelings no matter what. How can one do this? Again, by having good feelings toward one's child. It comes into this world helpless; it will react to its parents and those responsible for it in accordance with how those individuals feel and behave toward it. If the child feels their love, their respect for its personality and identification with it, their attempts to understand its needs and feelings, then the child will respond with just such feelings itself, and will identify with those close to it, becoming like them. Quite simply, the goal is to have good feelings going both ways: parent to child and child to parent.

We can also conclude that a child which is born into a home where it is wanted, loved, respected, and (so far as possible) understood, and which is secure in this love from birth to age three, already has a certain core of emotional security and health, some strength to withstand less ideal circumstances from three to six. If he has these mutual good feelings throughout his full 0-6 until even seven or eight, then he will have a more secure core of strength and adaptability. If such a favorable situation exists through adolescence, then he can be expected to get through life without severe emotional problems unless very unusual pressures upon him occur—such as capture and torture by psychotic criminals or by an enemy in wartime.

This same method of prognosis for the child's adult life also holds generally for the prognosis of analytic treatment. We have already indicated that individuals with no good relationships from 0-6 usually do not come for treatment or cannot be held in treatment for long; they have no really good relationship as a basis for the transference. If there is only a single fairly good relationship from 0-6 (e.g., Terry Weston p. 81), then it is apt to be difficult for the patient to continue, and the analysis itself is likely to be long and strenuous. The better a child's interchange of good loving feelings from 0-6, the better the prognosis for a rapid and effective therapy (As, for example, in the case of Martha Mason, p. 234).

References

Escalona, S. (1963): Patterns of infantile experience and the developmental process, *Psychoanalytic Study of the Child* 18:197-244.

———— (1968): *The Roots of Individuality: Normal Patterns of Development in Infancy.* Chicago: Aldine.

SECTION IV: SOME RELATIVELY UNEXPLORED AREAS

Order and simplification are the first steps toward the mastery of a subject—the actual enemy is the unknown.

Thomas Mann,
The Magic Mountain

The effects of childhood patterns on everyone's life as a source of strengths and also of distortions, conflicts, and problems in his or her personality raise interesting questions.

A number of these questions have received relatively little study compared with their importance. Discussion of some of these here may help to establish their place in theory and to increase the effectiveness of therapy and prevention. The following chapters are suggestive rather than final.

20
BUILT-IN CONFLICTS?

The preceding chapters and cases provide evidence that the treatment of a child from 0–6 by those persons within its emotional constellation produces a permanent emotional pattern. If this treatment has included threats, frustrations, abuses of omission and commission, then the child's fight-flight reactions are activated largely toward these individuals, whether parents, siblings, or other relatives. Conversely, if the child is treated with love and respect, it responds with these same feelings and attitudes toward others, and the fight-flight response is kept minimal, even in the face of all the "dos" and "don'ts" necessary for socialization—necessary because the adult will live in a society, a human culture, and not as an animal in nature. If the human relations are good, the fight-flight and hostility and withdrawal are minimal, and the child will be relatively free from neurosis, psychosis, perversions, addictions, and criminality.

Is a good childhood emotional pattern only an ideal which can never be fully achieved? If so, is it because of the ignorance or the emotional disorders of the parents, or are there intrinsic factors in the child? If the latter, what can the intrinsic factors be? Except for organic defects and the extremes of psychosis, it is hard for this author to accept the idea that ordinary neurotic emotional disorders are in the genes, and thus far there is no convincing evidence of this. Yet some much-loved children *do* show considerable variation in the strength of their fight-flight response, which raises the possibility that it could be in part and perhaps indirectly a hereditary factor. One example is the "hyper-kinetic child" who (and observation of their 0–6 is always limited) has been reared as well as possible, but improves in his behavior over the critical years only with the use of drugs.

Thus we cannot ignore the question: are there some conflicts that are unavoidable, that is, "built-into" the mind of suffering humanity despite near-perfect childrearing and ideal childhood patterns of feelings toward others? If these conflicts are recognized, is there some hope of ameliorating them?

The idea of conflict in neurosis was central for Freud from the beginning. Initially, he saw the main conflict as between the repressed and the repressing forces; what was repressed he saw chiefly as sexual impulses. As attention turned after Freud's *The Ego and The Id* (1923) to the repressing forces (the first major study being Anna Freud's *Ego and the Mechanisms of Defence*, 1937), emphasis fell upon the ego's defenses. There is, however, another common conflict which can be viewed (at least in part) as between instincts themselves rather than between instinct and ego or superego (Alexander, 1961, pp. 90–111). A simple example is the overcompensatory conflict. Here perhaps both the ego and the counter-instincts combine against the repressed. An example with which every analyst is familiar was first described by Freud in connection with homosexuality, namely, the boy who becomes overly close to his mother and overly identified with her, and is thus made too dependent and feminine. As an adult, such a person often overemphasizes his independence and masculinity, as though the ego has summoned up extra strengths and virility to deny and repress the femininity. Therefore, it may be an oversimplification to call this an "instinctual conflict," because the ego also plays a determining part in it (Alexander, 1961).

Freud discovered and introduced the concept of childhood trauma, especially sexual trauma, causing neurosis in later life. After he found that a patient only fantasied a trauma of a sexual seduction that never really occurred, Freud turned to the idea of the child's immature ego struggling with instincts that it was forced to repress because they were too powerful for it to handle. This is still trauma, but what causes lifelong problems is almost always *long sustained* injurious treatment rather than a single transient shocking experience. After *The Ego and The Id*, a conflict between id impulses and repressing forces of ego and superego (repression by the ego at the behest of the superego, as Freud put it) became known as a "structural" conflict. But it is well to give attention also to conflicts between instincts or "instinctual conflicts," both for analytic theory and because all conflict generates some fight-flight reaction evidenced as hostility and aggressive impulses, or as regressive impulses; these in turn create problems in psychopathology and in all human affairs.

The oedipus would seem to be a built-in, intrinsic conflict; it is the inevitable outcome of the sexual impulses and the biological difference in sex of the parents. The woman then becomes for the male the prize, the object, with other males as rivals. As Freud pointed out, the little girl is not equipped biologically to ever really possess the mother. This biological difference is important because of imprinting, i.e., because the sexual feelings tend to attach to the imprinted object, the original object of the strongest feelings, thus making complications in the libidinal development of women (Freud, 1933). But with good childrearing, that is, good relations with the child, the oedipus complex is resolved without appreciable difficulty.

Probably sibling rivalry can be grouped with the oedipus as an inevitable, externally stimulated conflict. Of course, as we repeatedly emphasize, the intensity of the individual emotional forces involved in these conflicts and hence the outcome is strongly influenced by the individual treatment of each child and its resultant childhood emotional pattern.

Some additional conflicts which seem inevitable are:

1. The forces of development and maturity versus the opposing forces of regression (Saul, 1971).
2. Narcissism versus object interest—one's interest in oneself and one's own welfare versus one's interest in others (Freud, 1916).
3. The conflict between love and sex. Love and sex should supplement each other, and we all like to see sex in a setting of love; but they are often opposed, and sometimes a person is more free sexually with an individual he *does not* love where the sex becomes more of a physical force, and if there is love and respect for the love object, the sex may be inhibited (Freud, 1912).
4. The conflict between tendencies toward monogamy and toward promiscuity. Here the sex drive leads one to involvements with the opposite sex regardless, but that does not eliminate what seems to be a monogamous mating force in humans like the long-term mating in many animals (Carrighar, 1965), a trend to settle down, to be joined as one man and woman to provide the stability needed by the children for their proper emotional development.

These four conflicts are predominately instinctual, rather than structural ones formed by training and social standards.

Emotional conflicts seem to develop the intellect, through the ego's struggle to solve them. Every conflict also seems to produce some friction and frustration and therefore some hostility, just as in the physical world all processes result in some heat. One or another of the four conflicts we have mentioned is apt to be prominent in every patient.

It seems important for theory, for the reduction of human hostility, and for therapy to watch for these apparently built-in conflicts: between developmental and maturational forces and the forces of regression; between narcissism (self-interest) and interest in others; between love and sex; and between impulses toward monogamy and those toward promiscuity. With proper childrearing, however, any built-in conflicts would probably produce minimal unhappiness and tension, in contrast to the dire effects of improper treatment of children.

Clinical practice furnishes abundant examples of all the conflicts we have mentioned, as does day-to-day experience in living and literature. Conflicts between love and sex and those between marriage and promiscuity are rather similar. The person with whom one has sex can be very different from the individual one loves, marries, and wants as parent for one's children. This is clearly seen when a person disappointed in love tries to forget himself by plunging into sex, or, conversely, when one tires of sex and is happy to settle down into love and marriage. This has been given poetic expression in Ernest Dowson's well known poem "Cynara":

> Surely the kisses of her bought red mouth were sweet;
> But I was desolate and sick of an old passion;
> When I awoke and found the dawn was grey.
> I have been faithful to thee Cynara, in my fashion . . .

Some patients defend themselves against their impulses to promiscuity; others defend against their monogamous tendencies.

The conflict between narcissism and object interest as related to love is portrayed by Wagner in his well-known operas based on the legend of the Niebelungen. Alberich, a deformed repulsive dwarf, is interested in the Rhine Maidens and striving to love and be loved by them. They reject him heartlessly, and with this rejection he turns completely from interest in women to desires for money (the gold) and for power as symbolized by the ring. This theme was also delineated by Freud in connection with Richard III (Freud, 1916), whose speech in Shakespeare's play says that because he was deformed and could not have love he will turn to power:

And therefore, since I cannot prove a lover . . .
I am determined to prove a villain,
And hate the idle pleasures of these days.

One might say, in terms of libido theory, that he defends himself against love which has brought him only rejection and the pain of narcissistic hurt, by flight back to an "anal" level.

A certain similarity exists between these three forms of built-in conflict because they deal largely with the *direction* of the libido.

The conflict between the forces of maturation and regression, however, is in a somewhat different category; any stress is apt to trigger a tendency to regression. In other words, if one is hurt sufficiently in life or if the struggle becomes too much for the ego to handle, then the person tends to withdraw psychologically and go back to earlier patterns. This usually includes a withdrawal from responsibility (see Chap. 18).

While struggling with the difficulties of life, both internal and external, a person may be helped by some form of "counseling"; but once he has given up and retreated psychologically from life, he usually requires thorough analytic work to get him securely into a mature functioning with sufficient security to cope and adapt and carry his responsibilities.

It used to be thought that certain criminals—those who committed murder and other crimes of violence—were the product of defects in society. Gradually however we have had to face the fact that these hostile crimes of violence are not confined to those who suffer in society, but can occur in anyone, and the basic cause lies in the psychopathology of the individual (Saul, 1976). They are psychopathic, emotionally disturbed individuals. True, society may play a role; but it is not the simple direct factor it was once thought to be. In other words, a ghetto or slum may result in poor rearing of children, but poor rearing can occur at all levels of society.

Childhood from 0–6 (Freud, 1940) is where the psychopaths are made, regardless of socioeconomic status and other neuroses. The cause in childhood of a generation of violence-prone psychopaths means that prevention is possible at least in theory, even though "cure" and "rehabilitation" usually are not. Every attempt at treatment and cure should be made; but once the psychopathic or criminal personality is formed, the prospects of changing it are relatively slight

(Saul, 1965). Prevention by proper childrearing remains the best hope, despite its difficulties. This means that after thorough therapeutic trial is made, we may still have to face the unwelcome conclusion that nothing can be done at present except to separate these violence-prone individuals from society for the protection of the innocent. Much as we resist such a conclusion, it may well be that only force and quarantine can prevail against the violent acting-outers.

In light of these considerations of the sources of violence in structural and instinctual conflicts *within the personality*, we must face the fact that our whole system of protecting society based on criminal punishment may be naive as well as ineffectual, at least for this type of offender. For the sources of hostility and violence are psychological, rooted deep in the relationship of the child to its parents. This problem cannot be solved only by such simple steps as the repeal of capital punishment, or by building more playgrounds, or passing another law, however immediately desirable such steps may be. Our most valuable discoveries of science, such as atomic energy, might well be utilized some day by men of hostility for their own hostile purposes. If we do not find some solution for these violence-prone persons, they may destroy our race.

Perhaps man has developed or evolved from the animals too rapidly for his own survival; he has drawn too far away from the primitive instinctual mechanisms by which the so-called lower animals rear their young—with love and proper care—so that the price of this great intellectual development may be our present prevalence of serious emotional problems, stemming from these disorders in the instinctual mechanisms, particularly those of childrearing. Whether or not there are built-in conflicts, we certainly see many children who develop into adults that are brilliant intellectually, yet hate their parents for mistreatment at their hands, and therefore are criminals at heart—hostile and dangerous to their own species. In the end, they may eliminate our species because they have transferred their child-hood hatred of their parents to all humans.

Ironically, although conflicts may have developed man's intellect, this high intelligence and this cultural existence seem to have brought about serious emotional problems instead of maturity. And yet the intellect could be man's only hope of salvation, for through it he can reach those instincts of self-preservation necessary to control the most dire threats to man's whole existence—such as pollution, nuclear weapons, and overpopulation. This requires basic knowledge of all the sources of human hostility—reactions to current external difficulties, childhood emotional patterns, and possible built-in conflicts.

To summarize then, conflicts exist between instinct and ego or superego, between the forces of training, normality, and the requirements of social living. These are structural conflicts. Or the conflict can be between opposing instincts themselves. The distinction is not always sharp.

Certain human emotional conflicts seem universal. Two of these— the oedipal and the sibling—are interpersonal. There are others that are intrinsic, built-in, such as between (1) developmental-maturational forces and the regressive ones; (2) narcissism and object interest; (3) love and sex; (4) monogamy and promiscuity. These four are predominately instinctual conflicts, not structural. But they do not cause such severe disorders as abusive treatment of children may effect.

Conflicts involve frustration, stress, and anxiety, which in turn stimulate the fight-flight reaction; the latter generates regressive tendencies and hostility, which is mankind's central problem. It may be that the ego's struggles with these conflicts has helped develop the intellect, which in turn may be the cause of other emotional problems but also an instrument of cure and prevention.

References

Alexander, F. (1961): The relation of structural and instinctual conflicts, in *The Scope of Psychoanalysis*. New York: Basic Books.

Carrighar, S. (1965): *Wild Heritage*. Boston: Houghton Mifflin.

Freud, A. (1937): *The Ego and The Mechanisms of Defence*. London: Hogarth Press.

Freud, S. (1912): On the universal tendency to debasement in the sphere of love, *S.E.* 11, p. 177.

———— (1916): Introductory Lectures on Psychoanalysis, Part III, *S.E.* 16, p. 214.

———— (1923): The ego and the id, *S.E.* 19.

———— (1933): New introductory lectures on psychoanalysis, *S.E.* 22, p. 112.

———— (1940): An outline of psychoanalysis, Part II, *S.E.* 23.

Saul, L. (1965): "Hostility" and "Criminal Acting Out and Psychopathology," chapters in *Crime, Law and Corrections*, ed. R. Slovenko. Springfield, Ill.: Charles C. Thomas.

———— (1971): *Emotional Maturity*, Third Edition. Philadelphia: Lippincott, pp. 23–78.

———— (1976): *The Psychodynamics of Hostility*. New York: Jason Aronson, Inc.

21
WILLPOWER, RESPONSIBILITY, AND THERAPY

As we know and have tried to demonstrate, childhood patterns that are disordered and too strong cause emotional disorders of all sorts. This they do by affecting the person's accustomed thinking, feeling, and behavior. In suitable cases, analytic treatment can reduce these disordered childhood patterns to help free the ego from their automatic dictates. But this is usually a lengthy process, and occasionally a person is in a critical situation in which we strive to keep his ego intact to tide him over. Insofar as we are successful in this endeavor, we can see that in the struggle between the powerful automaticity of the childhood pattern and the rational control of the ego we cannot only reduce the power of the unconscious pattern, but we can also strengthen or at least help the ego temporarily in dealing with it so that the individual does not seriously damage himself or his ongoing life.

I

The ego is generally described as having three major areas of function: (1) perception or awareness of the external and internal world; (2) integration of these perceptions with memory, reason, feelings, etc.; and (3) executive direction of behavior.

Psychoanalytic therapy utilizes insight to increase self-perception, and, through reducing emotional distortions, encourages more accurate perceptions of one's own motivations and reactions, and therefore of the outside world. This insight allows for fuller integration within the ego of these perceptions with the other ego functions. Much has been written about these first two areas of ego function and how they can be dealt with psychotherapeutically. However, the third ego function, the executive direction of behavior, has received less attention. We have been led to conclude that under certain circumstances when a patient's basic dynamics have been uncovered and are well understood, the analyst can mobilize or implement the executive functions of the ego by using direct suggestion, encouragement of various activities or solutions, and helping the patient to develop a stronger sense of the power of his own will.

When one examines historically how psychoanalysis evolved, it becomes clear why direct suggestion and willpower have been not only ignored, but condemned.

Originally, psychoanalysis grew out of hypnosis, which depended on the hypnotist's power of suggestion and will. Freud soon discovered the immense power of the unconscious and the instincts, and how little of what motivates behavior is consciously perceived. These findings led him away from the use of suggestion or will in favor of exploring unconscious material and instincts and their vicissitudes, as well as the effects of these on the whole emotional life, including the conscious ego. Also, the Victorian era in which psychoanalysis evolved used the strength of authority to combat bad, evil, or sinful thoughts, actions, and feelings. This forced individuals to repress their unacceptable inpulses and feelings. Freud explored through free associations and dreams, and found these repressed, unacceptable impulses living in the patient's unconscious. He concentrated his therapeutic efforts on removing these repressions and making the unconscious conscious.

A turning point in Freud's career and his de-emphasizing of "will" occurred in the early Dora case (Freud, 1905) when, after a promising beginning, she abruptly terminated treatment. This led Freud to formulate the very important concept of transference. He explained her abrupt termination as being due to her transferring her feelings toward Herr K. onto him. "She took revenge on me as she wanted to on him." He also pointed out the limitations of the therapist's influence on the patient as well as the limits of the patient's own willpower in the following statement, "In spite of every theoretical interest and of every endeavor to be of assistance as a physician, I keep the fact in mind that there must be some limits set to the extent to which psychological influence may be used, and I respect as one of these limits the patient's own will and understanding." As Farber (1966) points out, Freud then decided to study the motivation of will and did not consider the psychology of will itself.

In examining the behavior of patients who lived by Victorian morality and willpower, Freud discovered the real causes for their actions to be unconscious wishes and instincts rather than the rationalized self-serving and self-deceiving reasons which had become their "willpower." May (1969) concludes that "in describing how 'wish' and 'drive' move us rather than 'will'," Freud formulated a new image of man that shook to the very foundations Western man's emotional, moral, and intellectual self-image. But along with this inevitably went an unavoidable undermining of will and decision and an undercutting of the individual's sense of responsibility. The image that emerged was of man as determined—not driving any more but driven. Man is "lived by the unconscious," as Freud agreeing with the words of Groddeck put it. As Freud wrote, "the deeply rooted belief in psychic freedom and choice . . . is quite unscientific and must give ground before the claims of a determinism that governs mental life" (1938).

Alan Wheelis (1956) writes:

Among the sophisticated the use of the term "willpower" has become perhaps the most unambiguous badge of naivete. It has become unfashionable to try, by one's unaided efforts, to force one's way out of a condition of neurotic misery; for the stronger the will the more likely it is to be labeled a "counter-phobic maneuver." The unconscious is heir to the prestige of will. As one's fate formerly was determined by will, now it is determined by the repressed mental life. Knowledgeable moderns put their backs to the . . . couch . . . and in so doing may fail to put their shoulders to the wheel. As will has been devalued, so has courage; for courage can exist only in the service of will, and can hardly be valued higher than that which it serves. In our understanding of human nature we have gained determinism, lost determination.

May (1969) sees this

as modern man's most pervasive tendency to see himself as passive, the willy-nilly product of psychological forces . . . . The modern individual so often has the conviction that even if he did exert his "will" . . . or whatever illusion passes for it . . . his actions wouldn't do any good anyway. It is this inner experience of impotence, this contradiction in will, which constitutes our critical problem.

Arieti (1972) notes that

in the early psychoanalytic era, in which one of the main concerns was to fight Victorianism, will came to be seen as the agent of repression, not as the agent of liberation . . . . The result was that almost all of the twentieth-century psychology, psychiatry, and psychoanalysis joined arms to fight the concept of will. Papers or chapters on will were soon eliminated from scientific meetings or textbooks, or received very little attention. Any study of will or volition—when differentiated from motivation—fell into disrepute and was considered unscientific, to be relegated to the novelist, the theologian and perhaps to the philosopher.

Arieti further points out how Freud contradicted himself on the question of will: "Although Freud saw the unconscious wish as the main determinant for human behavior, he also wrote 'where id was, ego must be.' Freud did not see psychoanalysis as liberating the id to unleash primitive unconscious wishes but as liberating the ego from 'the unwanted, unconsciously determined oppression exerted by the id.'" Arieti believes that "psychoanalysis has the function not of restricting, but of enlarging the sphere of influence of the will."

There is a paradox which psychoanalysts face if they believe that the psyche is ruled only by strict determinism. What good can psychoanalysis do as treatment if human behavior is determined solely by unconscious factors and instincts? Knight (1954) answers this question as follows: "Whatever human actions or decisions seem to indicate the operation of free will, or a freedom of choice, can be shown, on closer inspection and analysis, to be based on unconscious determinism. The causal factors were there and operative, but were simply not in the conscious awareness of the individual." Knight goes on to say that psychotherapy "operates deterministically to achieve for the patient a subjective sense of freedom." Knight is implying that this subjective sense of inner freedom found in the psychologically mature person is an illusion.

Arieti (1972) believes that

the illusion to which Knight and others refer is not freedom, but "complete freedom." We never have complete freedom and it is illusory to think so. The issue is not between determinism and free choice, but between relative determinism and relative free choice

.... It is one of the aims of man to increase his capacity for choice and to decrease determinism in every possible way, to move away from physical necessity and toward free will . . . I believe that the greatness of psychoanalysis resides mainly in having recognized the restrictions to free will imposed by repression and in having developed methods to remove these restrictions.

II

With the tremendous growth of insight and knowledge of psycho-dynamics, our clinical experience shows that we can, *in carefully selected patients under certain circumstances*, restore the therapeutic elements of suggestion and will, thereby mobilizing the ego's executive function in addition to the utilization of insight, perception, and integration, while not diminishing these latter functions but rather strengthening their therapeutic effectiveness.

The sagacious use of suggestion, of an appeal to the patient's willpower and the application of the therapist's willpower, when the dynamics are thoroughly understood and the analyst knows clearly what he is doing, provides a lever to ease the patient out of a regression and to strengthen his determination to function in spite of incapacitating anxiety, depression, or inhibition until these factors are further diminished by analysis. Most patients do best when on their feet, functioning, and not withdrawn, waiting passively for analysis to bring their millenium.

It is, of course, absolutely essential that the analyst not use his influence to persuade his patient of anything that represents the analyst's own values, rather than the patient's, or try to influence the patient toward any change which is not unmistakably therapeutic as seen from a thorough understanding of the patient's psychodynamics.

It is also essential that the analyst know precisely the state of the transference and the counter-transference situation. Included in this appraisal should be as close an estimate as is possible of how the analyst's use of suggestion might alter the transference situation itself.

Some patients who were lacking in direction by parents are naturally deficient in strong identification with them to guide their adult behavior. These patients are apt to want identification with and guidance by the analyst, and this may be therapeutic *if* the analyst is wise, strong, and good, and if he has excellent human relations. But other patients have been overly controlled, even dominated, and this control has inhibited their own capacities for decision and responsibilities. Such patients often unconsciously try to manipulate the analyst into a directing counter-transference. This is harmful because such a patient should be outgrowing his submissiveness and learning to make his own decisions and to direct his own life successfully and independently. As Freud (1910) wrote: "In most human beings the need for support from an authority of some sort is so compelling that their world begins to totter if that authority is threatened."

III

Whatever differences in opinion still exist as to the dynamics of cure in psychoanalysis, there seems to be general agreement that psychoanalysis operates through the ego. It is with the ego that the analyst works when he makes the unconscious conscious with his interpretations, usually relating childhood patterns of reaction to current life and to the transference, i.e., repressed realities of a long-gone childhood to the patient's present realities. A part of the ego is a force popularly termed "willpower." Whatever makes it and how free a person is to exert it are, as we have seen, unresolved problems. But phenomenologically it can be observed and appealed to.

By working with their egos, most analytic patients can be helped in psychoanalysis. There are, however, a few patients who appear to be good candidates for successful psychoanalysis but who fail to make progress or may even lose ground during therapy. This failure takes place usually because of the strength of regressive forces released within them. The patients we refer to show an unsuspected weakness in their egos which requires strengthening. We have found that there are certain attitudes and interpretations which the analyst can use *within the psychoanalytic framework* to assist these patients in mobilizing this latent strength.

All of the therapy of each of the authors and all we have to say in this chapter is strictly analytic, meaning based upon understanding the unconscious motivations and reactions of the patient, i.e., his psychodynamics as seen in the pscyhological realities of his childhood, current life, and transference. It is in line with Freud's statement as expressed in *Outline of Psychoanalysis* (1940) and the paper "Identity and a Point of Technique" (Saul and Warner, 1967). Experience has shown that the healthy functioning of the ego and therefore a patient's independence, self-confidence, and sense of responsibility can be increased. The point of this chapter is to clarify how that can be accomplished within the analytic setting. To quote Freud:

Moreover, the relation of transference carries with it two further advantages. If the patient puts the analyst in the place of his father (or mother), he is also giving him the power which his superego exercises over his ego, since his parents were, as we know, the origin of his superego. The new superego now has an opportunity for a sort of after-education of the neurotic; it can correct blunders for which his parental education was to blame. But at this point a warning must be given against misusing this influence. However much the analyst may be tempted to act as teacher, model and ideal to other people and to make men in his own image, he should not forget that that is not his task in the analytic relationship, and indeed that he will be disloyal to his task if he allows himself to be led on by his inclinations. He will only be repeating one of the mistakes of the parents, when they crushed their child's independence, and he will only be replacing one kind of dependence by another. In all his attempts at improving and educating the patient the analyst must respect his individuality. The amount of influence which he may legitimately employ will be determined by the degree of inhibition in development present in the patient. Many neurotics have remained so infantile that in analysis too they can only be treated as children.

In mobilizing the patient's ego strengths, the analyst does not offer himself as a model but does offer temporarily some of his own ego's strength, determination, and perseverance. (If he does not have these qualities amply, he should not be an analyst.)

Roughly four types of analytic patients can be distinguished for whom ego strengthening is indicated:

1. Those to whom Freud refers in the above quotation as "so infantile" that they need ego strengthening to mature sufficiently to cope with their lives; they are partially fixated at an infantile level.
2. Patients who *regress partially* during psychoanalysis and cannot progress without analytic intervention to help strengthen their egos.
3. Those patients with a strong tendency toward regression whose egos need immediate strengthening in analysis to prevent an immobilizing regression.

4. Those patients for whom a stressful reality situation so under-mines their confidence that they fall, or are in danger of falling, into a severe regression and need to be helped out of this as an emergency to avoid permanent trouble, such as flunking out of school or getting fired from a job.

Before giving case illustrations of our experience with ego strengthening, we will present two prerequisites to be met before using this technique. The first prerequisite is that the patient shall have been in analysis for a sufficient period of time so that his psychodynamics and the transference are clearly understood, and the positive transference is strong enough for the analyst to have an influence based upon truth and reality. Thus we are not talking about patients who are seen briefly in consultation for specific advice or help in making a decision. In some of these consultative cases it is possible to clarify rapidly the issues involved and help the patient to make his own decision. If this is done and works out satisfactorily, it often can be credited to insight plus spontaneous positive trans-ference toward the analyst, sometimes called a "transference cure." Of course it is risky, and not a true permanent analytic result.

A second prerequisite is that the patient be so mired in a regression that an impasse has been reached in the analysis. After thoroughly analyzing both the transference and the resistance without clinical progress, we may try to work out a method to strengthen the ego, mostly by appealing to the patient's sense of reality and willpower. Although interpretations of the psychodynamics in childhood, current life, and transference have resulted thus far in these patients having mainly only an intellectual insight, these "intellectual" con-cepts will become important for the subsequent analysis and improve-ment.

We can describe our orientation as assisting the patient to become committed to and then to achieve *his own* goals. First we help him to conceptualize his own goals, which at times are hazy. Usually the patient's drive to maturity and his ego ideal reveal his own values and goals. If we feel the goal is within his grasp, we discuss this with him, thereby signaling support of his efforts to reach it. If we feel the goal is mostly the product of the patient's neurosis, we make the ap-propriate interpretations. If we see the goal is a product of the more normal healthy part of the ego, we discuss this. We often encourage the patient to persevere to a healthy goal despite his tendencies to give up if we see no reason for him not to pursue this goal. Furthermore, it means that whatever doubts or obstacles he may have, whatever his neurotic problem, we feel these difficulties can be overcome.

Taking care not to impose our own values or goals on the patient, we recognize the intrinsic merit of his own realistic goals. If he has several conflicting goals, we help him to clarify those which are the more realistically obtainable. This is done by openly discussing the emotional and practical consequences of each goal. This is a type of cognitive therapy, working with the ego, but also with analytic insights into previously unconscious motivations and dynamics, which provides the patient with a sample of the process by which one can arrive at a rational decision.

We adhere to the basic rule that major decisions should not be made during analysis, at least until all the conscious and unconscious factors are thoroughly understood. But we also recognize that analysis without some outside commitment can lead to excessive introspection, regression, and interminable discussion without ever resolving anything. Rarely can an analysis proceed in a vacuum, with the patient entirely withdrawn from life and responsibility. To strengthen it, an ego must deal with real problems. On the other hand, premature commitment to a goal without thoroughly understanding all the factors and issues involved can lead to additional neurotic problems, failure, and further regression.

To help the patient to commit himself to his own goal we sometimes picture to him how we see him, to correct his own depreciated self-image. (Saul and Warner, 1967) In this "mirroring" technique we openly and honestly describe to the patient the normal, healthy parts of his personality and how by using these parts he should be able to achieve his goal. It is often startling to the patient to have his healthy side clearly outlined, and it encourages him to make use of it. It can be presented in an acceptable ego-syntonic way, pointing out his psychological realities, to encourage him to use the healthy parts of his personality to achieve his own goals. Sometimes when this healthy ego is pictured to him, he is willing and able to take a "leap of faith" based on his trust and respect for the analyst and go ahead and use his ego to cope with his life. We often use analogies or biological vignettes to clarify these realistic "ego portraits." We might say that his ego is now like a fine racing car, with intact, well-functioning parts, only needing a driver to put it in gear and set its direction.

We are trying to assist the patient in redirecting some of his psychic energy from a preoccupation with intrapsychic conflicts into dealing more with the external world. The ego has become exhausted from trying to resolve internal conflicts which so far have yielded no resolution. The ego can become functional again by coping with real problems in the outside world, many of which can be solved. This involves cathecting outside objects with libido (directing interest, attention, and emotional charge to them) in place of dealing exclusively with narcissistically (self-interested) cathected internalized objects. "He that findeth his life shall lose it, and he that loseth his life for my sake shall find it" (Matthew 10:39)—this is a way of expressing "object interest," and we do not hesitate to quote it when appropriate.

The analyst's personality as well as his ability and experience, of course, plays an important part in all therapy, and especially in carrying a patient through a critical period, during which time the patient's ego may temporarily have to use the analyst's strength as in childhood it used the parents'.

IV. Case Illustrations

These ego-strengthening techniques are illustrated by the following vignettes for each of the four categories previously mentioned.

The first type is one which Freud (1940) describes as "so infantile that in analysis too they can only be treated as children." In these cases the analyst has, eventually, to provide maximum structure and support and even be authoritative at times, always recognizing that he will have to analyze the patient out of the dependent submissive transference. Freud's (1918) analysis of the Wolf Man provides an example of such a technique. Initially, the Wolf Man seemed to be producing valuable and interesting material for analysis, but he then sank into a prolonged regression with dependent receptive feelings toward Freud. To mobilize the Wolf Man's ego strength, Freud arbitrarily imposed a fixed deadline for completing the analysis. The Wolf Man responded by putting a higher value on the time still available in his analysis and digging in and working harder to understand the material he then produced. In his subsequent visits with Freud and Ruth Mack Brunswick (Gardner, 1971) the Wolf Man showed more clearly his regressive and dependent clinging. Freud subsidized him financially and he developed the illusion that he was virtually a favored son in Freud's own family. Ruth Mack Brunswick later used a harsh confrontation to impress the Wolf Man with the ego-alien (unacceptable) reality that he was not a member of Freud's inner sanctum. As Blum (1974) has pointed out, the Wolf Man now is regarded as showing a rather classical borderline personality, having childlike features interspersed with some psychotic delusions.

*   *   *   *   *

A young female college student provides a current illustration of ego-strengthening in a woman partially fixated at an infantile level. Amanda left college after her first two weeks because she felt it was beyond her ability to cope with the academic and social life. She then tried taking a menial job in her college town. After three weeks she quit this job and reluctantly returned home, feeling that she had no alternative. She took a job teaching nursery school but felt overwhelmed after a month and quit. She became progressively more depressed and seriously suicidal and had to be hospitalized. Eight months of a total-push hospital program prepared her to live outside the hospital. Her past history shows why her personality had not matured to the point of coping with these life situations, and why she felt such a failure and developed no confidence. She was the youngest of four children and by far the most angelic as a baby. She was adored by her parents, siblings, and relatives. In a way, that seemed to be a form of overprotection which overcompensated for some rejection of the added burden of a fourth child. She was grossly overindulged, and her passive-receptive-dependent trends were overly cultivated by having everything done for her. For example, she was carried so much that she did not learn to walk until she was four years old. She would eat only soft foods because she did not like the effort involved in chewing meat. She was intimidated by her oldest sister and brother, and would hide rather than argue or fight with them; this increased the passive retreat to mother. She was a good student until high school, but did not relate well to other children. In high school she avoided studies and got by on her charm and reputation for brightness.

Soon after returning home from college she regressed so far as to be unable to take care of herself, reacted to this with depression and suicidal attempts, and was hospitalized for treatment, which consisted of psychodynamically based psychotherapy (Saul, 1972), chemotherapy, and efforts to involve her in scheduled activities. The basic neurotic problem centered on her passive-dependent needs, which had been so overly indulged in childhood, and also her massive infantile rage, which was aroused by any expectations of independence or responsibility. Accompanying this rage was the flight reaction seen in avoidance of activity and responsibility and, with the rage, the development of escape and failure patterns, such as deliberately failing in order to excuse withdrawal from any responsible effort. Her hospital activities were arranged for graduated success. Also the analyst encouraged her to lessen her self-criticism and her underlying need to be so outstanding by pointing out the reality of her youth, health, strength, and brightness. There were, of course, many failures along the line, and her basic ability and potential for achievement had to be constantly pointed out to her. Her view of the analyst as a critical task-master had to be interpreted as a projection of her own harsh superego. He had to walk a tightrope, being supportive but not indulgent and encouraging her to commit herself to a reasonably independent life of her own, but not to expect too much. The analyst had to balance encouragement with ego-syntonic (acceptable, welcome) interpretations and nonobtrusive interest. One key was to constantly point out the disastrous effects of her periodic regressions, which led her into avoidance, withdrawal, and self-destructive ideation and behavior. She also had to be reminded that she had the basic ingredients to cope with life and that she had to develop her willpower to feel better. Actual reminders were given of what activities had given her success and how passivity or escape had exacerbated her depression. Many times she could not see beyond her current depressed state and had to borrow the analyst's view of her good potential for the future in order to keep striving for cure. The medication was of some help in getting her to a point of increased activity. After over a year of exhausting effort by the analyst and herself, she stabilized sufficiently to spend increasingly long periods out of the hospital at home, and eventually to interest a young man; this development in turn provided great impetus to further improvement.

*   *   *   *   *

An example of partial regression during analytic treatment requiring analytic intervention to help strengthen her ego was a young matron, in her mid-thirties, who was depressed and had almost daily outbursts of rage, especially at her long-suffering husband and even at her half-grown children. She was a master rationalizer, which gave a paranoid coloring to her thinking, through her invention of all sorts of excuses for her temper tantrums (e.g., that her husband looked at other women when they went out, that he "put her down" by his attitudes, etc.). The excuses were all in the vein of her being subtly rejected and persecuted.

This was a fairly routine analytic case. It quickly became evident that the basic reasons for her rage lay in earliest childhood. She was never openly mistreated, but she had no memories at all of her mother, although she had many memories of other persons in her life even before age three. At that age, her father died suddenly and her mother, who now had to work, was even less available and interested. After some months of analysis, Mary could see that during childhood she had repressed and also consciously suppressed her anger at her mother for this neglect; even now, 35 years later, her mother still had no idea how furious Mary was at her.

Mary, now in her thirties, continued feeling as she had at age three and one-half—unloved and unimportant. Her desires for love and recognition continued with the intensity they had in childhood; so did the sense of their being frustrated, and so did the rage because of this. She had no close friends. She had left her home town where she had a few friends, but found none in her new home. She always yearned for her home town and made frequent trips back, but never established close relationships either there or in her present marital home, for she could not tolerate closeness to people. In the first place, she had never been close to either parent and had no childhood pattern for being close. Secondly, she felt that she dared not let herself feel close because by so doing she would only suffer a repetition of the relation to her mother—neglect and lack of interest—and the pain of this would be more than she could stand. In brief, her needs for love and closeness were inseparable from her feelings of frustration and rage.

After about a year of analysis, she understood this but had not solved it; her rage in the transference and against her husband was so unmanageable that there was threat of depression or paranoia or both. She complained bitterly of her loneliness and lack of love and recognition. Of course, this was all interpreted as fully as possible, in the childhood pattern, in her current life, and in the transference. An upturn occurred after we frankly discussed the realities:

"Nobody gets all the love and recognition and status he wants. You are not singled out for abuse. Thoreau said, 'The mass of men lead lives of quiet desperation.' Why? In part because they do not get these things. But how can they? Who is there to give all the love that everybody craves? Everyone *wants* it; how few there are who can give it.

"Mary, I'm sorry it is so difficult for you, but this is just reality. You cannot demand at thirty-five what you wanted at three. At three you should certainly have had it, but why go through life not only frustrated but ruining what love you *can* get for what is no longer possible? You are sacrificing what you *can* get in present reality for what you fantasy as a potentiality—a present reality of love from husband, children, and friends for the sake of desires of thirty years and more ago for what you should have had from your mother.

"You are like a child, not getting what it wants, and indeed what it should have, who then nurses a grudge, and goes into the garden to eat worms. Use your good sense, come out of the garden, and enjoy what you have in reality, and can have a lot more of as you outgrow these excessive childhood demands and outworn childhood patterns and rage for the real satisfactions you can attain in daily life. Dare to be close; dare to give and accept love. By trial and error you will learn what works. Remember that although to love and be loved may be the greatest, it is not the only pleasure. You are a more than adequate person, healthy and attractive, and you have interests and musical talent. Use them and enjoy them, and don't go through life in a chronic dudgeon."

Of course, this was not all one oration, but gives the gist of what was repeatedly communicated to Mary with the purpose of reassuring and helping her ego in its struggles with a problem she could see but was not able to resolve. It was also a kind of interest and help she had yearned for from her mother, but had never received. She was told her real strengths to counteract her feelings of inferiority, which stemmed from her mother's apparent failure to value her adequately.

*   *   *   *   *

Ella, who was twenty-four and of average attractiveness, provides us with an example of a person whose ego needed immediate strengthening to prevent an immobilizing regression. She complained of anxiety. She was an only child of parents nearly forty when she was born. She was alone in receiving the full emotional focus of her parents, who encouraged her dependence upon them by overprotectiveness. Her mother was a strong personality and very efficient; anything Ella tried to do, such as helping in the kitchen, her mother tended to take over and do with such efficiency and dispatch as to discourage any competition. Thus Ella was bound to them as an only child, and by exaggerated dependence, and by their blocking her efforts at initiative and responsibility. The anxiety came from her mostly unconscious rage at her parents for dominating and holding her. The rage caused intense guilt and was directed against herself; thus, she was bound to her parents by masochism also. In brief, her problem was "self-defeating masochistic dependence" upon her parents.

Ella was soon conscious of strong wishes to have a home and a life of her own, but stubbornly resisted every step toward this. She was invited to visit one of her few friends in a distant city. Although she said she was eager to go, as the time approached, she advanced all sorts of reasons against doing so: it would cost too much; what would they do together there? Her friend had a boyfriend and Ella (although quite pretty) seemed unable to attract and get on with boys; she did not want to accept money from her parents for the trip; what if the anxiety got unbearable?—and so on.

I said, "I think these are mostly rationalizations for not going; the real reason is what we know so well now: your overattachment to your parents and your fear of venturing out of the nest. You cannot be made secure on the couch. You can learn why you are so anxious, but eventually you must decide to step out and endure the anxiety. If you were four years old, it would be justified; a four-year-old cannot travel alone and handle unexpected situations. But while you seem to feel like a four-year-old, you are twenty-four, strong, healthy, attractive, intelligent. There is no reason for you not to handle this on your own. Do not fear the anxiety; it is uncomfortable but in no way dangerous. Nothing bad can happen, only the discomfort. But you must stand and face it, until with practice you get used to handling life on your own. Your muscles do not get strong by analyzing. You cannot wait until you are strong enough to saw wood. Rather, it is the opposite: it is by sawing wood that you get strong muscles. It is by experience in handling life on your own that you will get emotionally stronger. If you really feel up against it, phone me, but if you determine to bear the anxiety you will not have to."

Ella made the trip to visit her friend, and reported, "You were right! I had some anxiety but I had a good time, saw all the sights and wished that I could have stayed longer." It is not always so easy, of course. Some patients panic and flee back to the nest.

But the whole pattern of nature is for the young to be cared for while helpless but to mature into leading independent lives. When the bird can fly, it leaves the nest, and we do not hesitate to discuss this with a patient. Of course, if Ella thoroughly enjoyed living at home, it would not be for the analyst to bring this up. But she was so miserable at home that she was desperate and at times somewhat suicidal. It seemed clear that it was the biologically healthy part of her, the drives to independence and to maturity, which she strove so unsuccessfully to fulfill, that brought her for help. She complained that other girls got married and had careers, but she could not get away from home. Incidentally, she had gone away to college but had been so unhappy and anxious that she returned home at the end of the first year.

If Ella feared a weekend trip to visit a friend, you can imagine what resistances she raised against taking a job when the opportunity arose. I spoke to her in the same vein as about the trip, relying mostly upon interpretations but emphasizing the realistic fact that there was nothing wrong with the instrument: she had looks, youth, health, strength, and intelligence, and could do anything anyone else could. Of course she could manage the job. She would never get strong and independent except by stepping out and taking the responsibility, however much of a struggle it might be initially.

"You so much want a life of your own," I said, "but you resist working to achieve it. But working to achieve, making the responsible effort, will not hurt you; quite the opposite, it will make you stronger and more mature. As Freud said, 'Necessity is a hard master but under him we become potent.'" This was an appeal to her ego not to wait for the analysis to give her independence and maturity while she spent most of her days in bed at home, but to face reality and use her willpower, and behave as a responsible, productive, independent (RPI) adult even if she felt like a passive, receptive, dependent (PRD) four-year-old child (Saul, 1971). "If you do not have a virtue," I quoted, "assume it—and you will grow into it."

Needless to add, the analyst must estimate the patient's emotional stability and capacity and never try to move the patient beyond his or her emotional means. After two years of unremitting effort by analyst and patient, Ella actually obtained and held a job and moved out of her home into an apartment with another girl.

* * * * *

An example of a severe regression requiring emergency help in strengthening the ego was John, a handsome, brilliant college student who had made straight A's in high school and was an outstanding athlete as well. No therapist, but only his own motivations pushed him so far beyond his emotional means at the end of his first year in college that he broke down into a schizophrenic psychosis, the narcissistic (egoistic, prestige, and admiration-seeking) elements being clear from the beginning in his delusions of being Christ come to save the world. He had been much adored at home and was in intense narcissistic competition with an older brother and a younger sister. Roughly, his central conflict was between his excessive narcissistic demands upon himself (largely from his parents' great expectations of him) and the passive-receptive-dependent (PRD) needs (Saul, 1971), exaggerated by parents who could and did provide everything, so that John grew up with nothing to think about but achieving glory for himself. His collapse was nearly complete and required a year of hospitalization in an institution near his college. During this stay, his dependence on the hospital and withdrawal from his independent life as a student were both, unfortunately, encouraged by the hospital therapist, so that his self-cofidence was injured even further. He had been dating a beautiful, talented, brilliant coed. But he was told at the hospital that he should break off with her "because he had nothing to offer a girl."

When he was first seen, his good self-image—in fact, his elementary self-confidence and self-respect—already shaken by the psychosis, were shattered. And this condition played into his now reactive depression and his withdrawal from all effort. But he was now able to analyze, and all that could be understood about him was freely discussed with him and interpreted, extreme care being taken to keep scrupulously close to reality.

It was evident that the therapeutic goal was to bring him back to a reasonable level of functioning, somewhere near that when his breakdown occurred, but on a more sound, mature, realistic, emotional base. He should continue his education to get the tools for an independent, reasonably secure future career, rather than try to defeat his brother in competition or to show off to his parents, as in childhood. At this time he was making no effort, because in his thinking he saw himself as absolutely nothing and was sure that he would never be anything, while simultaneously he felt driven to heights of glory.

He was told in definite terms, "That is not reality, that is your depression speaking, and your reaction against your excessive narcis-sistic need for glory, your rage at this defeat, this blow to your self-esteem, a rage turned against yourself. The truth is that you are as good as ever, which was superb. You have the same athlete's body, the same brilliant scholar's mind, only you are out of adjustment. You are like a fine motor car, let's say a new Cadillac, which is unused as yet but will not run; not because anything is missing or broken, but only because its carburetor is out of adjustment."

John gradually improved enough to take a single course, and a little later supplemented this college work with a part-time job. Nonetheless, he had a powerful urge to withdraw. Of course it was important that he not again regress so far as to require hospitalization, and this required very careful evaluation of the balance of emotional forces within him. There was no question but that he suffered terribly, but he was told, "This is the time to use your willpower. I am very sorry that it is so painful a time for you, but you cannot give in to your wishes to escape by returning to the hospital. If you did you would suffer much more. Keep your fighting spirit, stiff upper lip, and all that. Take the bit in your teeth and do the job no matter what the pain, and probably you will become stronger."

John did use his willpower and did the studies and the job. Later he was able to take several courses and make progress toward his degree. Every appeal was made to him to use his willpower, and no matter how terrible he felt, to get the job done. All relevant quota-tions that we thought of in making interpretations were used. No sooner had he signed up for the additional courses than he phoned in desperation, in a panic and depression. But every effort was made to get him to stand his ground. "We know very well now how you react to every forward progressive step toward responsibility and independent life; you kick like a steer against it. But it is your salvation; it is the way out of mental illness to maturity and peace of mind." At various other times he was told, "Forget yourself; take your mind off yourself; how good or inferior you are doesn't matter. Your job is simply to get that piece of parchment, that degree. Forget everything else and just do that. Live from day to day—if need be, from hour to hour. There is nothing wrong with the instrument, you have the youth, strength, brains—only *use* them to do the job. 'Whatsoever cometh to your hands to do, do it with your might'; 'Who shall lose himself shall find himself.'"

"Beethoven did not become Beethoven until age thirty, some years after he became deaf. Like you he was acutely suicidal, but he decided not only to live but to continue as a musician. You know the rest; he changed from a virtuoso to a composer, a late bloomer, who was thirty before he wrote his First Symphony."

"Yes," said John, "but I am not Beethoven."

"Neither was he until he surmounted his deafness. The same with Thomas Mann, who says both in general and for himself (in *Death in Venice*) that 'almost everything great has come into being despite and in defiance of affliction and pain, poverty, destitution, bodily weakness, vice, passion and a thousand other obstructions.' You will come out of this in the end a better man. 'He who conquers himself is greater than he who taketh a city.' You can do it. Just get that degree. Analysis is showing you the problem, but the cure does not take place automatically, by magic, on the couch—it occurs only in living, in meeting the challenges of life. You do not mature out of your traumatic childhood patterns by analyzing alone, but by experience in life."

Of course, some of the quotations used with John were used deliberately, because they appealed to his healthy, proper self-regard and not to the traumatic exaggeration of his childhood narcissism. He was in fact superior both as an athlete and in his intellect. Undoubtedly he could achieve if his energies were freed from this internal spinning of wheels, if the wheels were only meshed into gear by object interest. It was a long, long hard road, exhausting for the analyst as well as the patient; but with the analytic understanding and the ego support he became increasingly able to forget himself and to direct his energies to the tasks at hand. He gradually stabilized and became calmer and more secure, no longer feeling compelled to show everyone how great he was, but satisfied to do a good job and base his independence, his security, and the love of his coed on positive qualities and not on intense competition and showing off.

It may be indicated to discuss appropriate attitudes, always in terms of the patient's own dynamics. For example, with John, what would be some alternatives to his pathologically hostile, guilty competitiveness? I discussed an attitude of "live and let live."

"The next person is like you," I said, keeping close to psychological realities. "He or she is also striving for some security and peace and satisfaction in life, and for a place in the sun. You can understand it and identify with it in an attitude of 'live and let live.'" Done this way, it is not imposing values on the patient, but is giving his ego a wider choice and indicating a way out of the fixed childhood unworkable dynamics which had even caused a psychotic breakdown. John and the analyst persevered, and John got the degree. Success breeds success. Now he has some self-confidence restored, is working and applying for a better position.

Incidentally, drugs were used to help get John into an analyzable state and keep him there. In our experience a young man who has been through so severe a breakdown, once stabilized, may break again some years later; but if he does, relatively little treatment at that time is apt to be sufficient to keep him going again, or restore him to his accustomed way of life.

*   *   *   *   *

An illustration of mobilizing ego strengths during middle age in an inhibited, repressed woman was Edith, a fifty-seven-year-old, proper and dignified married woman whose apparent poise covered a depression and insecurity of long standing. She appeared to have many natural advantages—an attentive husband with a successful career as a consulting engineer, and two happily married children. She had married at nineteen as her family could not afford to send her to college, and because her insecurity pushed her into accepting the first reasonable offer of marriage. She had one brother who was seven years older. Unfortunately for her, he was a selfish, hostile individual who took delight in tormenting his younger sister. Her mother had died when she was eight years old, and Edith recalls that she was prim and proper but far from affectionate. Correct appearance and social graces were emphasized along with diligent work and academic achievement. Edith responded dutifully to this formula for success. However, she was not praised for her achievements; they were merely noted or acknowledged because she was expected to meet her obligations. Her father initially did provide some slight warmth in this austere family group, as did a maiden aunt who was a frequent visitor. There was also a nurse for Edith's first three years who was devoted and showed physical affection to her. Edith's father became depressed and withdrawn after his wife's death. Edith's maiden aunt moved in with them, and tried to add some cheer to the gloomy, serious household. However, she too emphasized social graces and propriety and discouraged individuality and creativity.

Edith wrote poetry in a secret journal, but was careful never to show it either to her father or to her aunt, as they both criticized poetry as a luxury for the frivolous—meant only for dilettantes. Edith always had one or two very close girl friends whose life styles were considerably less constricted then hers and toward whom she silently felt great envy. Her father's law practice dwindled because of his depression and withdrawal, and Edith had to work after school in a local drugstore to supply her own clothes and spending money. She was an excellent student, and was accepted at two top-flight women's colleges but could not go because her father refused to let her apply for scholarship help. She was shy and awkward around men, and dated very little in high school. Small wonder, then, that she married Fritz at nineteen. He was ten years older, already a successful engineer and socially prominent, much to her aunt's and father's relief. Fritz explained to her that they would have to travel a lot in his consulting work, and that it was important that his new bride make a good impression on his clients. Edith like the idea of travel, and was well trained to impress people. She soon learned however that her marriage was not to provide her with the happiness she hoped for. There was plenty of security, often to the point of boredom, but Fritz turned out to be rigid, austere, and penurious. He even hoarded words and tried to use them minimally and still express himself precisely. His sexual technique was equally constricted, which was very disheartening to virginal Edith. She learned to endure these deficiencies, especially when two sons were born before their fourth anniversary. Edith poured her energy into her children and thoroughly enjoyed them. It was not until the sons were teenagers that Edith had her first life crisis.

She was a regular churchgoer, and was very much attracted to her minister. He seemed to have all the warmth, charm, and intellect that both her husband and her father lacked. She found herself spending more and more time at church in an obvious effort to be with the minister. He reciprocated her interest and feelings, and soon they were caught up in a nonsexual love affair which lasted five years. Both agreed that it would be ruinous if they allowed their sexual feelings any expression, but in all other ways they were full of mutual love and respect, and felt completely compatible. Neither of the spouses suspected anything more than that they were good friends striving diligently "to do God's work." Edith bloomed and felt alive as she never had before. She even started writing poetry again, which she shared with the minister. The relationship was abruptly terminated when Fritz had to move his family to South America because of his work. Edith felt that all was lost, but hoped that letters and infrequent returns to the United States could keep the relationship alive. This plan did not work out, as both felt constrained in writing for fear that their letters might be intercepted, and the minister gradually phased her out and appeared to have switched his affections to another more available woman.

Edith was slowly crushed by these circumstances and became depressed. Her children were away at college, and Fritz was becoming even less communicative and more fixed in his ways, and gave her less. She was starved sexually and emotionally. She sought psychiatric help and saw a Jungian analyst for three years. This helped her somewhat, as it kept her depression from generating constant suicidal thoughts. It also opened her eyes to symbolism, mysticism, and dream interpretation. However, the next 15 years were bleak ones for her, and she had to work hard to keep her head above water, mainly as a hospital volunteer and as a secretary for her husband, including the handling of a voluminous correspondence concerned with his extensive stamp collection. Her heart obviously was not in this work, and she loathed the constant close contact with Fritz. Her suicidal thoughts returned, and she sought analytic help. She wanted no medication because she had a long history of drug sensitivity, and she also feared having any medication in the house lest she take an overdose.

The first year of the analysis was spent in trying to help her out of the disabling depression and feeling of helplessness and to provide her with some reason to live. It was clear that she had had some emotional nurturing in early life that gave her some inner sense of being worthwhile and helped her to survive the austerity and deprivations of her subsequent existence. It was also clear that her anger toward her deprivers was turned in on herself to a dangerous degree. She could recognize this intellectually but felt helpless to change it. It was then suggested to her that she was not so helpless and that she could separate her life more from her husband's, as she had often longed to do, stop being his secretary, and build a life of her own. At first she demurred, feeling that it would be disloyal to Fritz and that he needed her. Finally she "gave it a try," but soon complained that she then had to contend with her guilt to him and did not have enough to do. To fill the vacant time in her life, it was suggested that she return to her former interests such as poetry. Again, she felt guilty because of the childhood attitudes she had learned about the "frivolous nature" of poetry. She was not able to overcome these feelings and to write any poetry, but with encouragement she did rekindle her interest in art and photography. At first she devalued her drawings and photos. She was finally asked to bring her work into her analytic sessions, and together we studied the content. This proved useful both in understanding her unconscious and also in giving her an increasing sense of value. She was told in all candor that she was a bright and talented person whose creative powers had been suppressed throughout her life by the austere depriving family members and then by her own self-depreciation.

She became increasingly creative and productive and with more encouragement worked out an audiovisual art appreication course for high school students. Her approach was psychological; she used her own feelings and life experiences to illustrate the impact of great art. This course was an instant success, and led to a request that she write and illustrate a book on the subject. She became anxious and could not believe her success. She developed fears of impending doom, insomnia, and palpitations of the heart. Her dreams indicated her fears of punishment from her original family members because of her success. Her husband reinforced this anxiety by showing obvious envy and anger over her new life and success. However, he did agree to see another analyst to help him to adjust to the changes which her new life required of him. She was told that she had every right to be successful, that she had suffered enough and had worked hard and obviously had real talent. She had difficulty in believing this, and so it had to be repeated again and again. She often would imagine that the analyst was angry at her because of her own guilt about her success. However, with continued interpretations of the irrationality of her guilt and with reassurance and encouragement, she went on to write a successful book. She tentatively brought up other creative projects, and was given strong support to continue with her creative self-expression.

As she valued herself more, her relationship with her husband improved because she dealt with him more equally, openly, and realistically, and no longer served as his doormat. After three years of analysis, she finally began valuing herself and her creations. More important, she developed a genuine feeling for the strength of her own will and how she could choose and then pursue her own goals without inner criticism or fear of criticism by others. Her only regret was that she had not released her inner creative power earlier in her life. She also expended a good deal of her newly unblocked creative energy in helping others find themselves creatively and begin to be productive. Her middle-aged status never became a deterrent to her new zest for living and creating.

For the adult man or woman, three major tasks seem fundamental for achieving a satisfactory mature life. First is the task of self-preservation, of finding one's work, one's means of subsistence; fortunate is the person who finds financial security through work he truly enjoys. The second task (not necessarily second in time, however) is that of finding a mate. This choice is crucial, for only those children born into a secure, happy marriage will avoid later emotional disorders of all kinds. The third task and often last to be accomplished is "finding oneself"—recognizing one's identity and feeling secure in it. This task is strongly affected by choice of work and mate, and may take 50 years to achieve. All three fundamental tasks are strongly influenced by the childhood dynamics and are therefore interrelated. One's identify is closely involved with one's work, including that of housewife and mother.

V. Discussion

Freud (1919) may have been anticipating direct suggestion for strengthening the ego when he wrote:

> It is very probably, too, that the large-scale application of our therapy will compel us to alloy the pure gold of analysis freely with the copper of direct suggestion . . . but whatever form this psychotherapy for the people may take, whatever the elements out of which it is compounded, its most effective and most important ingredients will assuredly remain those borrowed from strict and untendentious psychoanalysis.

The encouragement, suggestion, and appeals to the patient's determination and willpower that we have been discussing are not a dilution or substitute for sound, basic analysis but, properly used, a part of it. If in any sense analogous, they would be like the chromium alloy which toughens steel to make it more effective.

All psychotherapists now feel the pressure to treat more people more efficiently and effectively, and there is a growing interest in the literature on how to do so by a more direct influence on the ego. Alexander and his early Chicago followers were pioneers in trying to decrease the frequency of interviews without sacrificing the quality of treatment (Alexander and French, 1946). Face-to-face psychotherapy is now increasingly common, with the patient and analyst both taking a more active role and sharing the responsibility in the "therapeutic alliance." Such techniques as direct confrontation, emotional flooding, and behavior therapy directed at specific symptoms are currently being used and studied with greater frequency (Frank, 1973).

New studies in the field of ego psychology (Laughlin, 1970; Hartmann, 1964) have helped to open the door to a deeper understanding of how the ego may be better understood and consequently influenced more efficaciously. An example of this process is found in Menaker's recent paper (1968) on "Interpretation and Ego Function." She points out that the ego should not be viewed "as a closed system seeking stabilization through the reduction of tension within its confines, but as an open system striving expansively toward optimal realization of its potentialities, for then one's view of the nature and function of communication between individuals changes and a new perspective on the therapeutic interaction appears." She cites

the operation of choice in the patient's motivation toward therapy as a means of achieving a higher level of ego-integration, optimal expressiveness and self-realization, thereby striving to achieve a self-conception more consistent with his ethical goals and his conception of, and need for, love and relatedness. It is important to bear in mind that not only *conflict* can motivate a patient toward therapy, but also *ego-ideal* aspiration. When the therapist has an awareness of this fact, even though it remains unexpressed or even unconscious on the part of the patient, his interpretations are geared toward the support of such strivings and aspirations. He approaches the therapeutic task with a belief in the patient's capacity to transcend himself. Such belief is as crucial for the patient's betterment as the young mother's belief in her infant's capacity to grow is for his actual development. The transmission of this belief—this basic trust in the life process—be it by implication or explicit statement, is a crucial, curative aspect of interpretation.

It might be more accurate to say that the analyst supports the strivings insofar as they are realistic, healthy, and mature and believes in the patient's capacity to mature out of his constricting, warping childhood patterns.

We submit that by using direct suggestion in certain cases in connection with thorough analytic understanding, not only can time be saved but latent capabilities can be brought out more rapidly so that the patient becomes not only less neurotic but also more productive, active, independent, secure, and sometimes even creative, to his own greater satisfaction with himself and enjoyment of living. With reference to the special technique of direct suggestion, a few comments seem in order. First, the question of whether to use it or not depends on the most thorough and accurate clinical assessment of the dynamics and of the actual and potential strength of the patient's ego. In some cases, as with borderline patients, the therapist is satisfied to help the patient to the point that his ego can deal with everyday problems realistically or even marginally, but at least in life and not as a hospitalized patient. Some such patients lack the potential to go much beyond this point. But at least they can be helped to avoid constantly relapsing into severe regressions.

In those cases, however, where the psychodynamics are clear and the analyst believes the ego can be strengthened, he must then decide on the timing and actual technique to achieve this strengthening. Often the timing can be early in the analysis, such as in the first few months. The direct suggestion must start off in an ego-syntonic fashion, acceptable and congenial to the patient's feelings. The analyst should have ample appropriate material to support everything he says, so that he can portray to the patient a picture of his functioning at a much more effective level in spite of what are temporarily handicapping symptoms. These symptoms and emotional attitudes which interfere with effective functioning have to be put in perspective so that the patient can clearly see that his psychopathology is only a small part of his total personality (see Chap. 14). It also has to be brought out that, with some basic realistic change in his self-perception and better understanding of his psychodynamics, the logjam that renders him ineffective or regressive can be broken up and his personality released to flow smoothly again. Analogies are often effective in bringing out these crucial points, such as how, on moving one log a few feet, the smooth flow of logs down a river can be re-started. Also, other mechanical analogies are useful, such as the patient's personality being like a finely tuned racing car with only a carburetor which needs adjusting to return it to good working order, and the analogy of a balance arm or seesaw, in which a slight shift of weight from one side to the other tilts the entire arm. Since many of these patients are easily wounded in their self-esteem, it is well to use analogies which depict them in a complimentary way, but always strictly realistically, with no stretching of the truth. These analogies can inspire them to work harder to achieve their ego ideals, to stregthen their egos; later in the working-through phase of the analysis, attempts can be made to lessen their narcissistic needs and excessive sensitivity to external appearances.

In "Identity and a Point of Technique," Saul and Warner (1967) emphasize the importance of pointing out the mature part of the patient's personality and of contrasting it to the childhood part that causes the problems. In certain cases in which the dynamics are well understood, possible solutions can be openly discussed with the patient, and then direct suggestion and encouragement made to carry these out.

Freud (1940) seemed to be viewing the executive behavior of the ego and its potential for action when he summarized its principal characteristics as follows:

> In consequence of the pre-established connection between sense perception and muscular action, the ego has voluntary movement at its command. It has the task of self-preservation. As regards external events, it performs the task by becoming aware of stimuli by storing up experiences about them (in the memory), by avoiding excessively strong stimuli (through flight), by dealing with moderate stimuli (through adaptation), and finally by learning to bring about expedient changes in the external world to its own advantage (through activity).

It would seem to us that many human beings have the potential to utilize their ego functions in this way, and those who are able to make effective use of this opportunity by their own volition can be said to have "willpower." As therapists, it is not only our task to help the patient develop ego where id was, but also to help him strengthen the everyday functioning of the ego in any way feasible.

Jerome Frank (1973), discussing the impact of the American culture on psychoanalysis, suggests what has led to the use of such a special technique as direct suggestion as follows:

Americans are action-oriented and are impatient for results. This may be connected with the shift in evocative therapies from leisurely exploration of the historical origins of the patient's symptoms to exploration of the forces perpetuating them in his current life. By focusing on these forces, American psychotherapists think it may be possible to correct the symptoms more promptly . . .

and we may add, to catalyze the outgrowing of the pathological childhood patterns.

Summary

In certain special situations in psychoanalytic treatment there is a need to mobilize ego strength, namely for: (1) those patients who are "so infantile" that they need ego strengthening to mature sufficiently to cope with their lives; (2) patients who *regress partially* and cannot progress without analytic intervention to help strengthen their egos; (3) those patients with a strong tendency toward regression whose egos need immediate strengthening in analysis to *prevent* an immobilizing regression; (4) those patients for whom a stressful reality situation so undermines their confidence that they fall into a severe regression and need to be helped out of it as an emergency to avoid permanent trouble, such as flunking out of school or getting fired from their jobs.

All attempts to mobilize ego strengths require an especially thorough understanding of the psychodynamics and especially of the transference and counter-transference. In addition, the patient's ego must be assessed as having the potential for more effective functioning. Usually the patient has been unable to realize this potential because of the various degrees of regression, and the analyst has already made exhaustive analytic interpretation of the unconscious material, including the transference and resistance. He may then shift to a more direct approach, pointing out the patient's ego strengths and giving him an accurate picture of how he can use these strengths toward his own goals. The aim is to help the patient use his own willpower and ego functions to gradually work on and finally resolve some of his neurotic problems. Accurately and honestly mirroring the patient's ego potentials, encouraging him to use his ego, and providing examples of how others have used their own willpower in comparable situations are usually helpful. The analyst must not impose his own values or goals onto the patient, but must work with the goals, problems, and strengths that the patient has.

Some analytic cases are presented to illustrate different ways of helping the patient to mobilize and utilize his own ego strength.

We are not suggesting any new "technique," but only that there is something which can be recognized as willpower that can be appealed to and mobilized for therapeutic effect; and the appeal is made primarily by the usual procedure of pointing out reality of insight into the patient's dynamics with encouragement to the patient in coping with it, both the external stresses and internal ones.

References

Alexander, F., and French, T. (1946): *Psychoanalytic Therapy*. New York: Ronald Press.

Arieti, S. (1972): *The Will to be Human*. New York: Quadrangle Books.

Blum, H. (1974): The borderline childhood of the Wolf Man, *J. Am. Psychoanal. Assn.* 22 (4): 721-741.

Farber, L. (1966): *The Ways of the Will*. New York: Basic Books.

Frank, J. (1973): *Persuasion and Healing*. Baltimore & London: Johns Hopkins University Press.

Freud, S. (1905): Fragment of an analysis of a case of hysteria, *S.E.* 7: 7-121.

_____ (1910): Leonardo da Vinci and a memory of his childhood, *S.E.* 11: 59-137.

_____ (1918): From the history of an infantile neurosis, *S.E.* 17: 3-122.

_____ (1919): Lines of advance in psychoanalytic therapy, *S.E.* 17: 167-168.

_____ (1938): *General Introduction to Psychoanalysis*. Garden City, New York: Garden City Publishing Co., p. 95.

_____ (1940): An outline of psychoanalysis, *S.E.* 23.

Gardner, M. (1971): *The Wolf Man*. New York: Basic Books.

Hartmann, H. (1964): *Essays on Ego Psychology*. New York: International Universities Press.

Knight, R. (1954): Determinism, "freedom" and psychotherapy, in *Psychoanalytic Psychiatry and Psychology*, ed. R. Knight and C. Friedman. New York: International Universities Press.

Laughlin, H. (1970): *The Ego and Its Defenses*. New York: Appleton-Century-Crofts.

May, R. (1969): *Love and Will*. New York: W. W. Norton.

Menaker, E. (1968): Interpretation and ego function, in *Use of Interpretation in Treatment*, ed. E. Hammer. New York: Grune and Stratton.

Saul, L. (1971): *Emotional Maturity*. Third Edition. Philadelphia: Lippincott.

_____ (1972): *Psychodynamically Based Psychotherapy*. New York: Science House.

Saul, L., and Warner, S. (1967): Identity and a point of technique, *Psychoanal. Quart.* 36:532-545.

Wheelis, A. (1956): Will and psychoanalysis, *J. Am. Psychoanal. Assn.* 4(2): 256, April.

22

A NOTE ON CAUSALITY AND DETERMINISM IN PSYCHODYNAMICS

I believe that the greatness of psychoanalysis resides mainly in having recognized the restrictions to free will imposed by repression and in having developed methods to remove these restrictions.

Sylvano Arieti, The Will to be Human,
New York: Quadrangle Books, 1972

No statistics are available that we know of, but currently there seems to be a reaction against Freud and the idea of psychic causality and determinism. Freud stated this view so clearly that it is worth quoting the passage from the 1920 edition of his *Introduction to Psychoanalysis:*

By thus bringing into prominence the unconscious in psychic life, we have raised the most evil spirits of criticism against psychoanalysis. Do not be surprised at this, and do not believe that the opposition is directed only against the difficulties offered by the conception of the unconscious or against the relative inaccessibility of the experiences which represent it. I believe it comes from another source. Humanity, in the course of time, has had to endure from the hands of science two great outrages against its naive self-love. The first was when humanity discovered that our earth was not the center of the universe, but only a tiny speck in a world-system hardly conceivable in its magnitude. This is associated in our minds with the name "Copernicus," although Alexandrian science had taught much the same thing. The second occurred when biological research robbed man of his apparent superiority under special creation, and rebuked him with his descent from the animal kingdon, and his ineradicable animal nature. This re-valuation, under the influence of Charles Darwin, Wallace and their predecessors, was not accomplished without the most violent opposition of their contemporaries. But the third and most irritating insult is flung at the human mania of greatness by present-day psychological research, which wants to prove to the "I" that it is not even master in its own home, but is dependent upon the most scanty information concerning all that goes on unconsciously in its psychic life. We psychoanalysts were neither the first, nor the only ones to announce this admonition to look within ourselves. It appears that we are fated to represent it most insistently and to confirm it by means of empirical data which are of importance to every single person. This is the reason for the widespread revolt against our science, the omission of all considerations of academic urbanity, and emancipation of the opposition from all restraints of impartial logic.

An alternative point of view considers the statistical, as opposed to a causal, origin of mental processes involving quantum theory and the well-known Heisenberg Principle (Heisenberg, 1930). Since this principle is currently referred to occasionally in some excellent contributions to the psychoanalytic literature (Arieti, 1975 a, b; Hood, 1975; Lewy, 1961; Chessick, 1974), it seems worthwhile to attempt a brief review of its content. The discussion attempted here is somewhat oversimplified for clarity, but is similar to presentations given in a number of elementary texts in modern physics. Obviously, this book is not concerned with the neuro-physiological basis in the brain of the mental and emotional life. This chapter is only meant to show that the concept of uncertainties in the observations of subatomic particles cannot be used by itself to deny causality and determinism in the mental and emotional life as observed in psychodynamics.

The Heisenberg Principle is a fundamental part of quantum mechanics, which serves so successfully in explaining phenomena involving the motions and interactions of molecules with their surroundings. (see, for example, the introductory pages of Dirac's *Quantum Mechanics*, 1958.) In the submicroscopic domain of quantum mechanics there are constraints on the observation of certain pairs of physical attributes associated with the path of submicroscopic particles, or quanta, through space and time. For example, the precise *direction* and *speed* of an individual atomic particle can be determined only at the expense of comparable precision in determining its *position*, and vice versa. This state of affairs is one aspect of the Heisenberg Principle of Indeterminacy, also known as Heisenberg's Uncertainty Principle, which is expressed in various ways by equations called the Heisenberg Uncertainty Relations. (For a detailed discussion see Heisenberg's *The Physical Principles of Quantum Theory*, 1930; Jammer's *The Philosophy of Quantum Mechanics: The Interpretations of Quantum Mechanics in Historical Perspective*, 1974, and references contained therein.)

In trying to understand the possible role which this principle plays in psychodynamics, it is perhaps slightly preferable to use the alternative term "indeterminacy" rather than "uncertainty"; for the principle deals with the limitations of making experimental determinations, and, as stated above, one expression of the principle is that it is possible to determine accurately at a point in time *either* the position of an atomic particle *or* its momentum but not both, and, further, that the degree of accuracy of determination of position is in reciprocal relationship to the degree of accuracy of the determination of the momentum, i.e., the more accurately position is determined, the less accurately the momentum can be determined, and vice versa.

The crucial point is that this degree of uncertainty, at least the minimum uncertainty, can be determined *quantitatively*. The uncertainty in position of the particle multiplied by the uncertainty in its momentum (momentum is mass multiplied by velocity) always equals or exceeds a constant figure called Planck's constant, with a value of the order* of 10^{-27}. This constant is a fact of nature, just as, for example, there is a gravitational constant that expresses the magnitude of the attraction between two masses.

Here are some examples of how the principle operates; they are given as rough approximations, in order to convey the relevant physics in a simplified way. We can write the Heisenberg Principle in mathematical form as:

$$\Delta X \times \Delta mv \simeq h/2\pi = 0.16 \times h$$

*See footnote on exponents, p. 315.

where the symbols we have used are defined as follows:

ΔX = uncertainty of position X (in centimeters from some reference point)

m = mass (in grams)

v = velocity (in centimeters per second)

Δmv = uncertainty of momentum, or mass times velocity

h = Planck's constant $(6.7 \times 10^{-27}$ erg-seconds)

The sign $\simeq$ is defined as "roughly equals."

Now imagine a billiard shot, using atomic particles instead of billiard balls.

In general, (uncertainty of position) times (uncertainty of momentum, $m \times v$) roughly equals $0.16 \times h$:

$$\Delta X \times \Delta mv \simeq 0.16 \times h$$

which can be written equivalently as:

$$\Delta X \times m \times \Delta v \simeq 10^{-27} \text{ erg-seconds}$$

i.e., the figure for uncertainty of position (ΔX) times mass (m) times uncertainty of velocity (Δv) must come out to about $0.16 \times h$, or 10^{-27}.

Example 1:

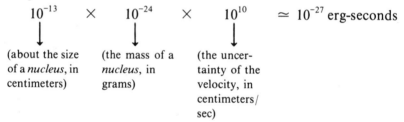

In Example 1, we have arbitrarily assumed that we know the position of a *nucleus* "precisely," i.e., to an accuracy equal to its own size, and the price we must pay to make the equation balance (i.e., come out to $0.16\ h \simeq 10^{-27}$) is an uncertainty in momentum, here represented as an uncertainty in the velocity, of a whopping 10^{10} centimeters/second (i.e., $10^{-13} \times 10^{-24} = 10^{-37}$. To make this equation come out 10^{-27}, Δv must be 10^{10}).

Example 2:

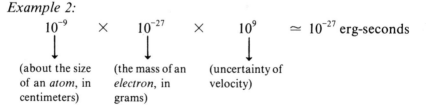

In Example 2, we consider an *electron* in an atom and ask only to confine our uncertainty in position to the extent of the whole (relatively large) atom. But the mass of the electron is small (10^{-27}) compared to the nucleus in Example 1, and we thus wind up with having to accept almost as large an uncertainty in velocity as we got in Example 1: i.e., since $10^{-9} \times 10^{-27} = 10^{-36}$, to make this equation come out to the constant 10^{-27}, Δv must be 10^9.*

Now consider a situation involving two ordinary-size billiard balls. Postulate a reasonable requirement for a "perfect" shot, which implies, let's say, that DX (the uncertainty in position) $\simeq 0.01$ (one-one hundredth) centimeter. Suppose the mass (m) of the billiard ball to be 100 grams. Substituting their values in the above equation:

$$\underset{\text{1/100 cm}}{\Delta X} \quad \times \quad \underset{\text{100 gm}}{m} \quad \times \Delta v \simeq 10^{-27} \text{ erg-second}$$

or:

$$10^{-2} \times 10^2 \times \Delta v \simeq 10^{-27} \text{ erg-second}$$

and thus, since:

$$10^{-2} \times 10^2 = 1$$

we have:

$$\Delta v \simeq 10^{-27} \text{ centimeter/second}$$

If the velocity of your shot in reality is, reasonably, about 100 centimeters per second, i.e., 10^2, the uncertainty in velocity due to the Heisenberg effect is thus about one part in 10^{29},** which is perhaps 25 factors of 10 more accurate than is needed to sink the ball in the end pocket!

The important consideration illustrated here is that the Heisenberg Indeterminacy Principle is obviously operative in the tiny realm of atoms and electrons (see previous examples 1 and 2), but is simply not relevant to something as large as an "effective" billiard shot. Nor in this sense could we expect it to be relevant to the function of the

---

*Reminding the reader of exponential notation: $10 \times 10 = 10^2 = 100$; $10 \times 10 \times 10 = 10^3 = 1000$; $10^6 = 1,000,000$. That is, the small figure, called the 'exponent,' indicates the number of times that the 'base' (10) is multiplied, and thus the number of decimal places to the *left* of the decimal point that must be used when writing the number. With the minus sign, it tells the number of places to the *right* of the decimal point, e.g., $10^{-2} = 1/10 \times 10 = .01$ or $1/100$; $10^{-3} = 1/10 \times 10 \times 10 = .001$ or $1/1000$; $10^{-6} = .000001$ or $1/1,000,000$; $10^{-37} =$ the number 1, 37 places to the right of the decimal point. To bring this back to 27 places, we must move the decimal 10 places to the right.

**10^{-27} (27 places to the right of the decimal point), divided by 10^2 (2 places to the left or 100) = 29 places to the right.

mind, which involves perhaps 10^{23} molecules, with total macroscopic dimensions that are enormous compared to the atomic domain. Even the electricity of the action potential of a single nerve impulse of a single fiber or a single brain cell involves such quantities of electrons as to be too large for the Indeterminacy Principle to be of any significance.

One can extend the concept of the principle by *analogy* to a host of tantalizing philosophical problems dealing, for example, with processes of memory, and so on; but if such a pursuit is to be taken seriously, there must be a supportable theory in which this analogous principle is set. This implies some physical significance to a constant that is analogous to *h*. There is, of course, the possibility that some cooperative and coherent behavior exists involving single electrons within the brain, which may indeed be elucidated and governed by quantum mechanics and thus implicitly by Heisenberg's Uncertainty Principle. But here, as Bohm points out in his *Quantum Theory* (1951), we are on "exceedingly speculative grounds," and this question remains unresolved.

If an analyst cannot find the cause for something he observes in a patient's feeling, thinking, or behavior, it is not because electrons cannot be used to observe precisely other electrons; nor can it be deduced from this principle that there is some failure of causality in the working of the brain or mind. If there is, this would have to be established on some other basis than that of intrinsic limitations in the methods of observing subatomic particles. When we fail to understand something in our patient, the place to look first, of course, is in our own limitations of psychodynamic understanding and method, while we still watch for other factors.

When we, as analysts, consider these uncertainties and indeterminisms, even in the relatively precise observation of physics, we must indeed be modest and humble before the extremely crude observations we can make of the workings of the unconscious, especially considering its limitless individual variations from person to person, and the countless variables in every person's childhood influences and patterns. It is conceivable that some of the dogmatism that has crept into psychoanalysis since its beginnings reflects an overcompensation for the difficulties and extreme uncertainties in the analyst's observations and interpretations of its primary data—a process which this book tries to make at least a trifle more precise.

References

Arieti, S. (1975a): Psychiatric controversy: man's ethical dimension, *Am. J. Psychiatry*, pp. 39–42, January.

———— (1975b): Letter to the editor, *Am. J. Psychiatry*, 132: 978–979, September.

Bohm, D. (1951): *Quantum Theory*. Englewood Cliffs, New Jersey: Prentice-Hall.

Chessick, R. (1974): *Technique and Practice of Intensive Psychotherapy*. New York: Jason Aronson, Inc.

Dirac, P. A. M. (1958): *Quantum Mechanics*. Oxford, England: Oxford University Press.

Freud, S. (1920): *A General Introduction to Psychoanalysis*. Garden City, New York: Garden City Publ. Co.

Heisenberg, W. (1930): *The Physical Principles of the Quantum Theory*. New York: Dover Publications, Inc.

Hood, J. (1975): Free will and psychiatry (letter to the editor), *Am. J. Psychiatry* 132: 978, September.

Jammer, M. (1974): *The Philosophy of Quantum Mechanics: The Interpretations of Quantum Mechanics in Historical Perspective*. New York: Wiley & Sons.

Lewy, E. (1961): Responsibility, free will and ego psychology, *Intl. J. Psycho-Analysis*, 42: 260–270.

EPILOGUE
CHILDHOOD PATTERNS AND THE
PLIGHT OF HUMANITY

Reflect that man creates the evil he endures.

Charles W. Peale

Cruelty and violence, both individual and organized, are part of the bondage of *homo sapiens*—the only known species throughout which individuals torture, injure, and kill each other, both individually and *en masse*, and which may now annihilate itself and many other species with a bang by the bomb, or with some unimaginable slow torture by pollution and destruction of the ionosphere, or by overpopulation. But all of its individuals are not alike. Some persons are repelled and disgusted by cruelty and killing; organizations have developed to oppose violence and seek harmony and love. This is the message of most of the world's religions, although it is not always lived up to. What makes this different in individual humans—the contrast between those who need only the slightest excuse, if any, to trigger cruelty, violence, and murder and those others who deplore and despise such behavior? Why this disparity between such anti-human feelings and behavior and the prohuman motivations of mercy, compassion, and love? This is an all-important question. An understanding of childhood patterns holds at least part of the answer.

There is no longer any doubt that every human during his or her earliest, most formative years, out of his inherited qualities interacting with his environmental factors, develops a *pattern* of motivations and reactions toward others that constitutes an essential part of his permanent personality and character, i.e., of his accustomed feelings, thinking, reactions, and behavior. How much pressure of hostility exists in a person and how ready that individual is to act out his hostility are features of his childhood pattern. Insofar as this childhood pattern is shaped by how the child is raised, especially from

"I wonder what it is in childhood that causes one guy to grow up a burglar and another guy a con man."

Drawing by D. Fradon; © 1966
The New Yorker Magazine, Inc.

0–6, the rearing of children is the critical factor in determining mankind's propensity to act out hostility toward his own kind.

Another book by the author (*The Psychodynamics of Hostility*, 1976) is devoted to the relationships of the childhood patterns to human hostility in many of its forms and directions.

INDEX